**See what B2B
leaders are sa,**

MW01616415

In this insightful and practical look at B2B Ecommerce, Brian Beck combines the urgency of getting involved now with Ecommerce with practical how-to advice. Brian lays out plenty of useful details on how manufacturers and distributors should incorporate digital strategies in areas ranging from technology infrastructure and traditional sales forces to customer experience and marketing.

—**PAUL DEMERY**, Editor, *Digital Commerce 360 B2B*

Beck's work is like a Harvard Masterclass for B2B Ecommerce. From miniscule to gigantic and everything in-between, all companies would be wise to follow Beck's words of wisdom, he identifies the landmines so you don't have to find them the painful way. You could spend hundreds of thousands on consulting services from supposed gurus and not get 10% of the insights revealed here. Beck is a jedi for the B2B Ecommerce age. Ignore his insights at your own peril.

—**BRIAN SMITH**, Director of Operations,
Farmer Boy AG

Until Brian's book, no one has truly delved into the challenges of B2B Ecommerce strategy creation and long-term development. He has captured the most salient lessons from his 20+ years of experience driving Ecommerce to compile the quintessential B2B strategic playbook for any leader in the space. For those who are ready to be the disruptors in their industry and rightfully view their digital journey as an evolution, this is the book for you.

—**MARK CRIST**, Global Director of Ecommerce,
Jacob Holm and Sons AG

Finally, **a comprehensive guide** for all B2B leaders looking to capitalize on this next wave of digital Ecommerce transformation.

—**AMIT GUPTA**, VP Digital Solutions & Ecommerce,
Pall Corporation, a division of Danaher Corp.

Brian Beck's book is timely and provides a good foundation of case studies for readers to carefully consider as they put their own growth strategies together. Given the rapid ascent of Ecommerce as a true game-changing paradigm shift, "Billions" provides a framework for re-thinking sales strategies as well as the increasingly important role of marketing in sell through. Brian's experience in the B2B and B2C space with companies in multiple industries makes him uniquely qualified to provide his view on this important topic.

—**SHARON M. VESSELS**, Vice President, Marketing
& Ecommerce, NORMA Americas

Few executives have a broader and more insightful perspective on the evolving e-commerce landscape than Brian. If you want a blueprint on how to position your organization for B2B success, you will not be disappointed. It's thorough, seriously researched and well worth reading.

—**JOHN TOMICH**, CEO & Co-founder, Credit Key

I wish this book had existed before we launched Chamfr, our online medical components marketplace. Reading this book would have saved us time and money! Brian's content and advice is simply spot on in so many ways. This is a must read for anyone even remotely interested in B2B Ecommerce and digital transformation.

—**JULIE SCHULTE**, CEO, Chamfr

Hands down the best resource available today to help you get started on your B2B Ecommerce journey. If your business has been struggling with the why, how, and what of Ecommerce . . . this is the place to start. From start to finish you will be continually learning and generating ideas to advance your sales. Brian has taken all the complex concepts associated with B2B and broken them down into actionable insights. If you are a leader in manufacturing or distribution, don't go another day without this great resource!

—**KRISTINA HARRINGTON**, President and
CEO, GenAlpha Technologies

What a great resource for b2b commerce! Brian proves he is a true expert in commerce, and the examples he shares are well worthy of your time! It is very clearly B2B's time to shine. Read this book.

—**Jason Nyhus**, Senior Vice President, Digital River

This is the definitive reference guide to doing B2B eCommerce the right way. As an industry veteran, I can easily say this book is one of the best resources for any business regardless of their digital maturity. I look at this book almost as a survival guide. It covers topics ranging from the justification and business case, to the people to the organization, to the business dynamics, and even successfully selecting and implementing technology. My advice: read this book cover to cover, then keep it on your desk—because every B2B digital leader will encounter every aspect covered in this book over time. It will surely serve as the best reference guide for how to navigate these situations. The real world examples and case studies really breathe life into everything Brian shares in this book.

—**John Bruno**, VP Product Management,
Elastic Path and Former Senior Analyst for
B2B Ecommerce, Forrester Research

BILLION DOLLAR

DOLLAR

B2B ECOMMERCE

SEIZE THE OPPORTUNITY

BRIAN BECK

Monrovia Media

Edited by Daniel Waldman
Book design by DesignForBooks.com

Printed in the United States of America

Contents

Case Studies

by Chapter

Foreword

BY ANDY HOAR, FOUNDER OF THE B2B
NEXT CONFERENCE AND CEO OF PARADIGM B2B

What if Circuit City had gone digital-first in 2007 instead of doubling down on an archaic offline-centric buying model? What if Borders had diversified beyond physical media in 2010 and aligned with the new shopping and buying preferences that its customers were demonstrating?

Yes . . . these are unknowable hypotheticals. But they're highly-instructive questions for today's B2B companies. In the face of seismic change, it's quite tempting to do nothing on the grounds that doing something unfamiliar may produce a less favorable outcome. But if B2C has taught us anything, it's that inaction is often the riskier bet in this new era of omnipresent commerce.

In my 8 years covering the space, including 6 years at Forrester Research where I ran the B2B Ecommerce practice, I witnessed a sea change in the approach that practitioners took to accommodating digital-centric customer behavior. Initially many adopted a "slow-follow" approach hoping that customers might reject the "consumerization" of B2B and return to the warm embrace of the traditional analog-centric approach. But those B2B companies quickly learned that "digital-first" was not merely rhetoric. It was real and here to stay.

For example, B2B distributor Grainger realized in 2017 that its premium pricing strategy was out of step with buyers enjoying unprecedented transparency and insisting on more competitive pricing. In response, Grainger decided to radically overhaul its core pricing approach and critical parts of its long-standing value proposition.

Similarly, B2B wholesaler Essendant discovered in 2013 (when it was then named United Stationers) that its underlying business had been fundamentally disrupted by Amazon and other pure play distributors. However, unlike Grainger, Essendant waited too long to initiate much-needed strategic changes. In the interim, the company experienced severe "brain drain," customer defections, partner realignments and more. As a result, Essendant started a slide from which it still hasn't recovered.

As Brian points out in this book, B2B sellers must now radically rethink their core value propositions and recalibrate their go-to-market strategies. With B2B buyer behavior now largely digitally-driven, B2B sellers must fundamentally reinvent their customer engagement strategies and tactics.

As a peer I often shared the conference stage with, Brian was one of the early innovators in the space and witnessed the transformation from the inside. His observations clearly led him to create this well-timed and appropriately detailed book with solidly-researched case studies that demonstrate how companies can accelerate B2B Ecommerce without compromising customer satisfaction and loyalty. In addition, Brian's book details both why and how to both confront and capitalize on a surging Amazon and ever-rising customer expectations.

Digital professionals from companies of all sizes, degrees of maturity, and funding levels will take away powerful lessons learned and hard-earned best practices by reading this book. I recommend it to all practitioners, consultants, and industry insiders looking to gain advantage in a complex and rapidly-changing B2B space.

Andy Hoar

Acknowledgements

This book is the outcome of three-years of work and a boatload of persistence. When I started this endeavor in 2017, I had about thirty articles I had previously written about B2B Ecommerce and digital transformation. I said to myself, "How hard can it be to assemble a book out of all this good material?" Well, I now see why people don't write books every day. After more than one hundred interviews, seemingly endless research, hundreds (actually, probably thousands) of hours of writing, dozens of revisions, and the constant pestering of my editor (my steadfast ally, Daniel Waldman), we are here.

But this book needed to be written.

I believe B2B Ecommerce is on the cusp of exploding. It is the last great frontier of digital commerce. I lived the first round of Ecommerce growth as a VP of Ecommerce and CEO of B2C (business-to-consumer) Ecommerce companies. Retailers took on the risks by venturing into the then unknown and unproven world of Ecommerce and demonstrated that online buying wasn't just a passing fad. Some of the world's most valuable companies have resulted (has anyone ever heard of Amazon?)

Now it is B2B's turn.

I truly hope this book helps you take advantage of the incredible opportunity in front of you. I wrote this material from the heart, and sometimes I am quite direct. But I did this intentionally, for those acting now will reap great rewards. And the biggest obstacle to B2B growth is simply the organizational fortitude to take action. I am calling you to action.

I want to thank so many people. To those B2B CEOs, business owners, and leaders who were the first movers and became the examples presented in this book, thank you. You are the trailblazers that others can learn from.

To the all of the individuals I have had the opportunity to lead, be led by, or observe their leadership, thank you. I want to express particular thanks to Kevin Hill, my business partner at Enceiba, whom I first met at Harbor Freight Tools a decade ago. Together we created an enormous Ecommerce business for that firm in an incredibly short period of time. Now we are taking over the world at Enceiba helping companies build world-class Amazon businesses.

To the strategy consultants, my colleagues and friends who have worked with me on dozens of Ecommerce advisory projects over the past five years—Steve Jones, Jay Holan, John Kinsella, Marty Schmid, Cynthia Pillsbury, and others—thank you for your time, dedication, and hard work as we helped our clients become digitally transformed organizations. I highly respect each of you, have enjoyed learning from and working with you, and am tremendously grateful to each of you.

I also want to give very special thanks to my "partner in crime" in this book—my editor, Daniel Waldman. You have been an awesome partner throughout this process. I literally could not have done this without your help. Daniel, thank you for your skill, persistence, talent, and patience on this journey. You make a great Jewish mom. And I am thrilled to now also call you a friend.

To my clients, I owe you a very large debt of gratitude. We worked hard to break new digital ground together, and for this I am forever grateful. You are the fiber that made this book possible. I want to express special thanks to Dave Grimm at illumina, Matt Wingham at Cardinal Health, Brad Mountz at Mountz, Dan Gdowski at Big Ass Solutions, and the teams at Charlotte Pipe, NDS Pro, Norma Group, AC Pro, Sunridge Farms, Frontier Co-Op, Brasseler, and countless others that I've worked with over the years.

I also want to extend thanks to Andy Hoar, for being a consistent light for our industry, providing provoking thought leadership, and working as a trusted ally in inspiring change and evolution for B2B. I am also grateful to the team at Digital Commerce 360—Paul Demery, Mark Brohan, and others—for being the unbiased voice of the industry, recording and marking the miles as we travelled together on this Ecommerce journey. I can still recall our first interviews on the B2C side almost twenty years ago, when retail Ecommerce was still young. What a trip it has been!

To my parents, Richard and Katie Beck, thank you for teaching me persistence, instilling in me an incredible work ethic, providing for my education, pushing me when I didn't want to be pushed, being there for me as life threw curveballs my way, and grounding me with a solid foundation of faith and values. And thank you for reminding me of these things even when I didn't want to hear it. Without these ingredients, I would not have been able to follow this career path, live a happy life, or write this book. I Love you and am eternally grateful to you both.

And to my family—my amazing wife Leia and awesome son Grant—you two are my all. I can't express in words how much your constant support and love meant to me as I worked to get through writing this book. You gave up early mornings and late evenings and weekend time so I could finish this, and I am so grateful. Thank you, thank you! I Love you both more than words can express. You are the reason for this book, and it is dedicated to you.

Finally—I want to thank God most of all, because without God I wouldn't be able to do any of this. It all comes from Him.

Q&A

What's the biggest challenge B2B companies are facing when it comes to Ecommerce?

One thing: inaction. Many B2B companies are uncertain on what to do and how to do it. The fact that business results are "just good enough" can lead to complacency, which delays Ecommerce and digital initiatives. As a result, many firms are missing their opportunity. In just a few years, companies that continue to ignore the digital-centricity of their buyers are likely to face steep challenges from competitors who took action. This is the fundamental reason I wrote this book—to help companies take action and seize the opportunity in front of them.

What's something that most B2B companies get wrong about Ecommerce?

Too often, companies think Ecommerce is just about building a transactional web site. It's not. It's about evolving the entire business—culturally, structurally, and operationally—to be digital-first. This means demolishing traditional organizational silos, empowering the entire company to think digitally, and aligning all selling channels. Ecommerce isn't the end of the sales team; it's the beginning of a more efficient and effective organization, sales team included.

Why should a company act now when it comes to planning and deploying an Ecommerce operation?

Developing an Ecommerce operation takes a significant amount of time and resources. B2B companies who don't act now will likely face steep struggles in the near future, as competition intensifies and customer expectations continue to climb. Some may even go out of business. My advice: Don't be one of these companies. Act now.

Is it ever too late for a B2B company to add an Ecommerce operation?

Unfortunately, yes. I believe the time will come where some companies will fall so far behind that catching up will not be possible. Take heed of the B2C retail sector, and don't follow the examples of Sears, Circuit City, Borders, The Limited, and others.

What's the most important thing a CEO reading your book should take away?

Over my 20+ year career, I've worked with many CEOs at manufacturers, distributors, and brands. The one thing I always stress is that change needs to start at the top. They must provide leadership in the face of uncertainty and internal resistance to change. Developing and implementing an effective Ecommerce operation is a resource intensive undertaking that, when executed effectively, will yield significant results in terms of revenue and profit, customer satisfaction, competitive advantage, and enterprise value. But it has to start at the top.

The Time is Now

1

This Story Has Been Told Before

The year was 1998. Sears, Roebuck and Company, one of the oldest and largest retailers in the United States, had just released its prior year earnings. Profits were strong, and the company's retail revenues had increased by a healthy eight percent.[1] The merchant opened 87 new stores in the prior year and was ranked as the second largest retailer in the nation, based on gross revenue. In the company's annual report, the executive chairman reported, "We are confident that the changes we are making throughout our organization will further strengthen our competitiveness . . . customers often do not recognize that we meet or beat our competitors for price and overall value on a consistent basis." Sears believed they knew how to meet their customers' needs, seemingly better than their customers knew themselves.

The year was 2017. After a six-year, $10 billion losing streak with no turnaround in sight, Sears warned investors in March of that year that "substantial doubt exists related to the company's ability to continue as a going concern." The company's very viability was in question. Sears was down to 894 U.S. store locations, from its peak of 3,500 locations in 2005, and had slashed its workforce by more than 50

---

1 http://media.corporate-ir.net/media_files/NYS/S/reports/ar98/company/annrep98/aco2.htm

percent.[2,3] By 2014, Sears' total debt had surpassed its market capitalization, which stood at four percent of its former value. Many stock analysts and industry pundits were reporting the firm would soon file for bankruptcy. Looking for ways to save cash, management was shrinking inventory levels. In some stores, employees hung bedsheets to hide store departments that stood completely empty of products. By the time you read this book, Sears may no longer exist. Retail analyst Cathy Hotka called the Sears Holdings' situation "the world's longest liquidation sale."[4]

On October 15, 2018 Sears filed for Chapter 11 bankruptcy. Its CEO stepped down and the 125-year-old retailer began planning to close more than 140 stores.[5] An unprecedented fall from grace.

What happened?

The answer lies with both too little, too late, and a solid dose of hubris. During this 20-year period, Sears focused on maximizing shareholder returns and turned away from focusing on its customers, their wants and needs. Along with a serious case of organizational inertia, management's overconfidence caused the company to fall behind—far behind.[6] Apparently this Internet thing, among other factors, had become a place where customers were researching and buying products. Management recognized this trend way back in the 90s and made some investments in Ecommerce, but it wasn't

---

2 https://www.investopedia.com/news/downfall-of-sears/
3 https://www.washingtonpost.com/business/capitalbusiness/the-big-missteps-that-brought-an-american-retail-icon-to-the-edge-of-collapse/2017/06/01/19f4bee4-35a3-11e7-b4ee-434b6d506b37_story.html?noredirect=on&utm_term=.281098e4a210
4 https://www.forbes.com/sites/paularosenblum/2017/05/10/sears-ceo-our-companys-troubles-are-everyones-fault-but-mine/#4e8db19976b1
5 https://www.cnbc.com/2018/10/15/sears-files-for-bankruptcy.html
6 http://www.businessinsider.fr/us/sears-obsession-with-wall-street-2016-3

enough.[7] In addition, the company's slow-moving culture proved difficult to change.[8] The investments did little to shift the company's overall direction, break it free from organizational inertia, or create the change need to compete in the digital age.

Over that same 20-year period, Amazon, Sears' rival and a major reason for the company's fall from retail prominence, looked at things differently. The CEO of Amazon, Jeff Bezos, designed his company to put the customer first. In a quote from 2010, Mr. Bezos highlighted his belief about the changing state of retail. He noted:

> *The balance of power is shifting toward consumers and away from companies . . . The right way to respond to this if you are a company is to put the vast majority of your energy, attention, and dollars into building a great product or service and put a smaller amount into shouting about it, marketing it.*[9]

Since the late 1990s, the retail economy has shifted, and consumers are now in charge. Mr. Bezos is listening. His publicly stated goal is for Amazon to be, "The earth's most customer-centric company."[10]

And Mr. Bezos and Amazon are winning as a result. From the period of 2006 to 2016, Amazon's market capitalization

---

7   https://www.washingtonpost.com/business/capitalbusiness/the-big-missteps-that-brought-an-american-retail-icon-to-the-edge-of-collapse/2017/06/01/19f4bee4-35a3-11e7-b4ee-434b6d506b37_story.html?noredirect=on&utm_term=.281098e4a210

8   https://www.huffingtonpost.com/entry/worst-companies-to-work-for_us_575b26b0e4b0e39a28ada793

9   https://www.inc.com/jessica-stillman/7-jeff-bezos-quotes-that-will-make-you-rethink-success.html

10   https://www.amazon.jobs/working/working-amazon

increased by 1,934 percent while Sears' value fell by 96 percent. Amazon's total sales were a mere 17 percent of Sears' revenue in 2005. Sears' sales went on to fall by 14 percent over the following five years, while Amazon's nearly quadrupled. In 2011, the online retailer's revenue surpassed Sears, then completely lapped it in 2013. In 2016, Amazon earned $136 billion in sales to Sears' comparatively meager $22 billion.

These are fundamental changes in buyer preferences and behaviors, and Sears isn't the only company to fail to effectively respond to them. In fact, much of the retail industry—particularly traditional department stores and many in the "big box" retail category—have been unable to keep up with shifting buyer preferences and compete with Amazon and other Ecommerce companies. Reviewing the market caps of the top 10 retailers in the country during the period from 2006 vs. 2016 is quite revealing, as shown in the following graphic.[11]

Company	Market Value 2006 ($B)	Market Value 2016 ($B)	% Change
Sears	$27.8	$1.1	-96%
JCPenney	$18.1	$2.6	-86%
Nordstrom	$12.4	$8.3	-33%
Kohl's	$24.2	$8.8	-64%
Macy's	$24.2	$11.0	-55%
Best Buy	$28.4	$13.2	-54%
Target	$51.3	$40.6	-21%
Walmart	$214.0	$212.4	-1%
Amazon	**$17.5**	**$355.9**	**+1,934%**

11 http://www.visualcapitalist.com/extraordinary-size-amazon-one-chart/

The rise of Ecommerce is a primary challenge to the market dominance that traditional retail firms enjoyed for so long. Big box and department store sales have plummeted during this period, as consumers increasingly conduct their shopping online. Visual Capitalist, a market research firm, estimates that the 2020 revenues of the traditional retailers highlighted in the below graphic will be equal to just 57 percent of their totals in 2006. Meanwhile, Amazon grew its revenue an astounding 31 percent from 2016 to 2017, and is expected to reach almost $400 billion in total revenue by 2020.

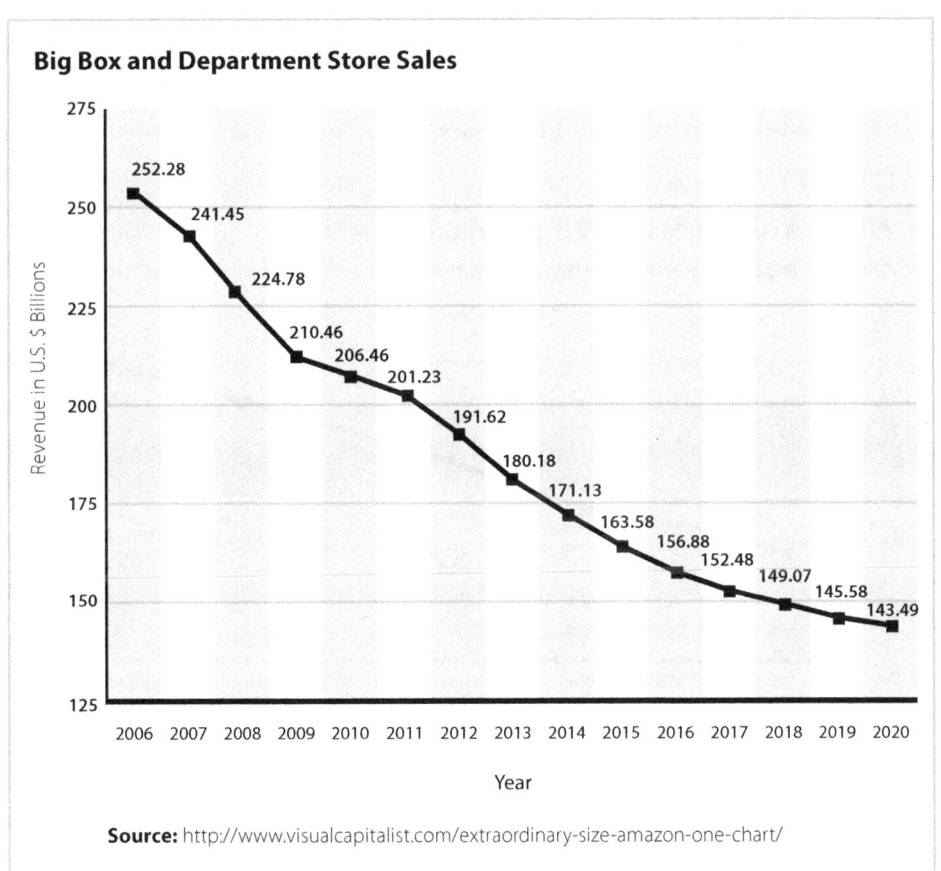

Big Box and Department Store Sales

Source: http://www.visualcapitalist.com/extraordinary-size-amazon-one-chart/

Some forgiveness may be in order here. There was no precedent at the time for the massive and rapid change in buyer preferences that impacted Sears, JC Penny, Lord & Taylor, Kmart, Toys 'R' Us, Macy's, and dozens of other large retailers. The shopping mall, once a symbol of the vibrancy of American commerce, is now a dated and deteriorating retail model. There is a dramatic discrepancy between retail square footage in the United States and current consumer buying preferences. Analysts predict that 25 percent or more of all malls in the U.S. will be closed by 2022.[12] Retailers—and the entire system that was developed over decades to support them—have been forced to react to these changes. While merchants could see and feel these trends as they arrived, they had no way of knowing the massive scale of impact they would have on their businesses.

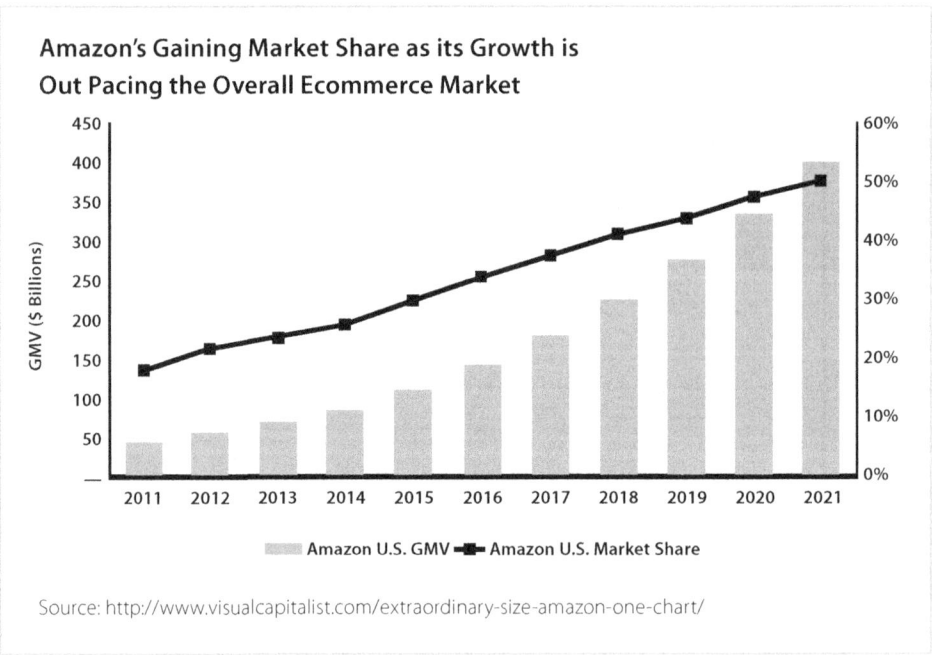

Amazon's Gaining Market Share as its Growth is Out Pacing the Overall Ecommerce Market

Source: http://www.visualcapitalist.com/extraordinary-size-amazon-one-chart/

---

12 http://fortune.com/2017/05/31/malls-retail-stores-closing/

The same cannot be said for B2B companies, including manufacturers, brands, and distributors across all traditional industries. Many B2B companies have not yet had to contend with these changes outright, but they need to study and learn from their B2C counterparts. Disruption is upon our industry and ignorance is not an excuse for inaction. Be warned—change is here. Right now. Unless you want to be Sears in 10 years, you need to take action immediately.

Lessons for B2B

B2BecNews—a sister publication of Internet Retailer and owned by Vertical Web Media, the preeminent industry publisher of content on Business to Consumer (B2C) and Business to Business (B2B) Ecommerce—released a study in 2018 indicating that only 40 percent of manufacturers have an Ecommerce web site.[13] However, the industry is catching on. That same study found that 70 percent of companies that did not have an Ecommerce web site planned to launch a site by 2019. The window for action is closing.

The time is now.

B2B leaders across the globe must sit up and pay attention or suffer the fate of companies like Sears. Those who are taking action today are capturing a competitive advantage and driving enterprise value right now. This is across all kinds of industry sectors. Consider these companies:

- Illumina: A multi-billion dollar biotechnology manufacturer that has grown Ecommerce to a substantial double-digit portion of sales in less than

---

13 https://www.digitalcommerce360.com/2018/01/12/what-manufacturers-doing-ecommerce/

two years, with a considerable part coming from incremental units purchased online, increasing their share of existing customers' wallets.

- Kelly Paper: A large, privately-held paper distribution company driving three percent higher gross margins from orders placed online, which are over 50 percent of total sales.

- Mountz: A $20 million tool manufacturer finding an entirely new market for its products by using digital marketing to reach new customers its sales force did not have time to get to, adding millions in top-line revenue.

- Henry Schein: A multi-billion dollar dental equipment distributor leveraging Ecommerce to auto-generate subscription renewals with customers, improving renewal rates, making its sales team more effective, and freeing sales associates' time to engage in more strategic activities with customers.

- Evergreen Enterprises: A mid-market manufacturer and brand of home products that added millions in revenue by seizing control of their marketplace presence on Amazon and is now investing in further growing the channel.

- Augusta Sportswear: A mid-market manufacturer of sports team apparel driving more than 50 percent of sales, and all of its growth, from Ecommerce.

These are just a few examples; more are entering the market every day. B2B buyer behavior has shifted fundamentally, just as it did in B2C. And while B2B Ecommerce, as of this writing, remains at least a decade behind B2C

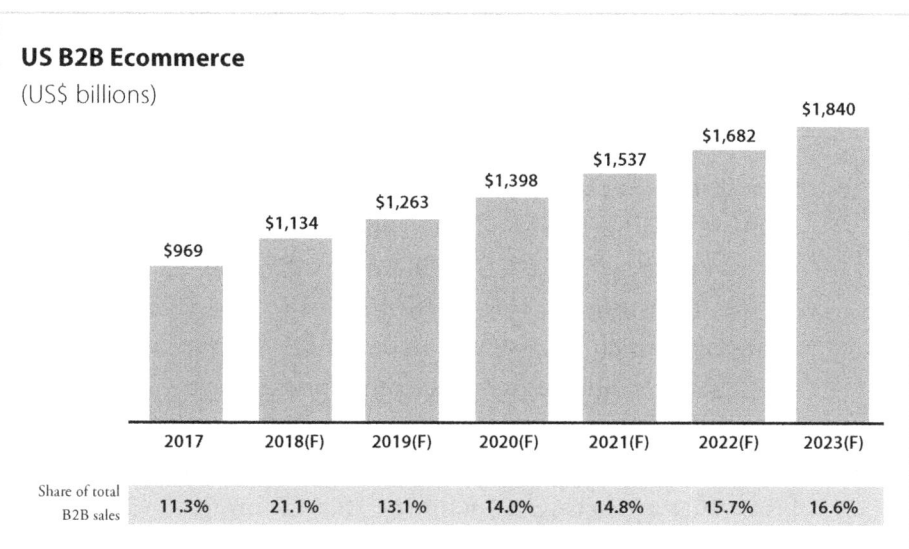

US B2B Ecommerce
(US$ billions)

	2017	2018(F)	2019(F)	2020(F)	2021(F)	2022(F)	2023(F)
	$969	$1,134	$1,263	$1,398	$1,537	$1,682	$1,840
Share of total B2B sales	11.3%	21.1%	13.1%	14.0%	14.8%	15.7%	16.6%

F = Forecast
Source: Forester Analytics: B2B eCommerce Forecast, 2018 to 2023 (US)

B2B Dwarfs Retail
(in billions of U.S. dollars)

Retail e-commerce, U.S. — $453 Billion

B2B e-commerce, U.S. (estimate) — $600 Billion / $1 Trillion

Ecommerce in terms of availability of products for sale on the web, the fact of the matter is that B2B Ecommerce is twice the size of B2C in terms of absolute revenue. In 2017, U.S. B2B Ecommerce was estimated to amount to over $900 billion in sales vs. B2C's $453 billion.[14] 2018 volumes were estimated to have crossed $1 trillion, and are projected by Forrester to reach over $1.8 trillion by 2023.

A milestone was reached in 2018, when electronic commerce, including Ecommerce, EDI (Electronic Data Interchange), and other electronic procurement methods exceeded offline commerce channels in B2B for the first time in history, accounting for 50.7% of all B2B transactions.[15] Firms that are acting are winning this Ecommerce revenue.

The sell side is what is holding back the sector from even more explosive growth. Forrester Research found in a 2017 study that 38 percent of business buyers make more than half of their work purchases online, and more than 55 percent of buyers will do the same by 2020.[16] Why aren't more B2B buyers buying online currently? The answer is staggeringly simple: the companies they want to buy from aren't selling online! B2B sellers are being dragged into Ecommerce by their customers. This will continue to evolve as younger, digital native buyers come into the workforce. As I noted above, those sellers that are actually listening are reaping the benefits.

The time is now.

---

14   https://www.digitalcommerce360.com/2017/06/05/u-s-b2b-e-commerce-course-hit-1-18-trillion-2021/

15   https://www.digitalcommerce360.com/industry-resource/key-findings-from-the-2019-u-s-b2b-ecommerce-market-report/

16   https://www.forrester.com/B2B+eCommerce+Will+Reach+12+Trillion+131+Of+US+B2B+Sales+By+2021/-/E-PRE10026

My Goal in Writing this Book

My goal in this book is to provide you—the B2B executive, manager, business owner, or entrepreneur—with a solid foundation of Ecommerce knowledge, and to give you the tools to lay out and execute an Ecommerce roadmap for your organization. I have been in the Ecommerce field for over 20 years, working the first 17 as an operations executive, and since then as an advisor, consultant, and board member for both B2B and B2C Ecommerce organizations. I've been the owner of the P&L and have managed every aspect of building highly successful Ecommerce operations—from startups with little revenue to large firms with hundreds of millions in online revenue. I have managed first-hand all of the functions of Ecommerce, including: web merchandising, digital marketing, user experience, technology selection and implementation, customer support, fulfillment, and other operating areas. I have built companies from concept to Inc. 500 and Internet Retailer Top 500 prominence. And, in recent years, I have translated this knowledge and experience into advisory services to help B2B companies of many sizes—from tens of millions to many billions in total revenue—engage in digital transformation. It is very exciting and engaging work, and I love what I do.

I don't tell you about my experience to brag; I'm telling you about it because I've made every mistake discussed in this book and have learned a ton along the way. My goal is to share this hard-earned knowledge with you, to help you understand what makes for a successful Ecommerce operation, and to allow you to avoid common mistakes along the way. In reflecting back on my two decades in this field, what I find most amazing is the consistency of challenges, misconceptions, and opportunities in Ecommerce across all types of organizations and in wildly diverse industries, including:

- The consistent desire for today's customers to research and purchase products online (yes, this includes old line industries where traditional buying methods have existed for decades—YOUR customer is changing).

- A mix of fear, legacy thinking, and business performance that is "good enough" in traditional channels preventing action by many product sellers (who wants to sign up to be the B2B version of Sears? Anyone?).

- The need for leadership to break the chains of traditional business practices, demolish silos and inaction, create alignment, and begin digital transformation.

- Management concerns about channel conflict (external and internal sales channel alignment).

- Management concerns about brand protection in a digital world.

- Worries that Ecommerce will eliminate personal relationships and that the sales force and other traditional selling channels will hate it and fight it to the death.

These factors can create inaction, even as B2B buyers clamor for the ability to purchase online. I am encouraged every day, though, as more companies reach out to seize control of their digital destiny.

When I started this effort in 2017, I was amazed to find no book on B2B Ecommerce existed in the market. So I decided to write one. With the precedent of B2C retail turmoil in plain site, my hope is that you will use this book to get in front of trends and create opportunity for your organization.

The time is now to take action.

What You Will Learn

I created this book in what I hope you will find to be a logical manner. My intent is to allow you to first understand the foundational requirements of Ecommerce and the importance of leadership. I then go into detail around specific tactics you will need to successfully execute the creation and launch of an Ecommerce operation. I will give you the ability to see the forest from the trees and create a strategy, and then provide you with details to guide your execution in each critical area necessary to build a thriving Ecommerce operation.

Here is a preview of what you will learn:

- Leadership and Alignment—In Chapter 2, I discuss the need for leadership as an essential catalyst to drive change. Without leadership and getting the right, *experienced* people on the bus with you, B2B Ecommerce does not happen effectively. Period. Sorry, your long-time IT techie person or your 23-year-old nephew won't get it done for you just because they know how to use social media or write software code.

- Revenue Drivers and Return on Investment (ROI)— All solid business decisions start first with an understanding of customer needs, and then of the expected benefits and costs associated with a new endeavor. In Chapter 3, I highlight how to put the customer first in this process, the drivers of financial return (revenue and profit enablers), and the common costs (both capital expenditures and ongoing expenses) that need to be considered.

- Organizational Evolution—In Chapter 4, I highlight
  the key roles and functions that need to be added to
  the organization in order to create a well-functioning
  Ecommerce operation. Tremendous amounts can
  be learned from the B2C world in this area, and
  entirely new concepts and roles to B2B—such as
  web merchandising—are introduced. Accountability
  structures and key performance indicators are also
  shared.

- Aligning Selling Channels—Most B2B organizations
  have long-established selling channels, such as a
  direct sales force, independent sales reps, distributor
  relationships, call centers, and other channels. These
  channels are often centered squarely on personal
  relationships between representatives at buyers and
  sellers (both executive and line level). In Chapter 5, I
  discuss how Ecommerce, when properly aligned with
  traditional sales channels, can actually make the entire
  sales function more effective.

- Managing Channel Conflict—With Ecommerce
  comes new levels of pricing transparency and potential
  shifts in where sales are transacted. This often threatens
  legacy sales channels. But this should not prevent you
  from acting. In Chapter 6, I reveal the tactics that
  B2B sellers are using to effectively manage channel
  conflict, capturing opportunity while also maintaining
  traditional channels and recognizing their true value to
  the end customer.

- Developing an Amazon Strategy—No book on
  Ecommerce is complete without an in-depth look at
  Amazon. Amazon was responsible for 49 percent of

all US Ecommerce in 2018.[17] Given this company's extraordinarily prominent role in this industry, and their very considerable investments in the B2B sector (called "Amazon Business"), I dedicate Chapter 7, aptly named "The Amazon Chapter," to reviewing what they are doing and the opportunity (and challenges) it may create for you. As a player in the modern digital economy, you must have an Amazon strategy, whether you sell on the marketplace or not.

- Leveraging Digital Marketing—With an effective Ecommerce web site, opportunities are available to your marketing team to capture new customers and sales via digital marketing. In Chapter 8, I define and cover how you can use digital marketing channels such as paid search, search engine optimization (SEO), email marketing, and other modern marketing methods to build traffic to your Ecommerce web site, reinforce your relationships, and acquire new customers.

- Building an Ecommerce Technology Foundation— Your Ecommerce platform and related systems are the ground game in your online selling playbook. Getting the right platform in place is absolutely critical to your long term success. Taking the time to do this right the first time is very important (I've learned the VERY hard way that shortcutting this process is a bad idea). In Chapter 9, I give you a step-by-step plan to documenting requirements and conducting a platform selection process.

---

17 https://www.cnbc.com/2018/01/03/amazon-grabbed-4-percent-of-all-us-retail-sales-in-2017-new-study.html

- Creating a Successful Online User Experience—
  Too often, B2B companies do not realize the
  absolute criticality of a well-functioning online user
  experience and web site design that follows established
  conventions. Well-intentioned executives often launch
  an Ecommerce web site without considering the
  user experience, presenting to the customer with a
  hard-to-use interface that does not follow B2C best
  practices. They then wonder why they aren't seeing
  massive sales gains. Today's B2B online buyers are also
  online consumers in their personal lives, and these
  experiences inform their expectations in B2B buying.
  In Chapter 10, I review how B2B companies can
  "steal smartly" from B2C, while also accommodating
  common B2B workflows to make buyers jobs easier. I
  present several case studies of companies that learned
  the value of following online user experience best
  practices.

- Being a Digital Organization—It is not enough to
  just put an Ecommerce web site online. A full digital
  transformation touches all parts of the organization. In
  Chapter 11, I describe the characteristics of a digital-
  first organization and share how Ecommerce impacts
  and shifts processes across the entire company.

- Our Digital Future—One of the things I love the
  most about Ecommerce is that it constantly evolves.
  With the advent of things like Artificial Intelligence,
  Internet of Things, and Virtual Reality, merchants
  are learning to tie the physical and virtual world
  together in new ways. For sellers, this means enhanced
  personalization and even deeper relationships with
  buyers, all facilitated by digital means. These are the
  topics of Chapter 12.

I have used case studies throughout this book to bring concepts to life. You will find examples from companies as large at Cardinal Health, with over $130 billion in total revenue, to Mountz, with less than $100 million. While the industries and company sizes vary, the stories and lessons are remarkably similar. Buyers are shifting research and purchase behavior online, and by following best practices and making the buyers' jobs easier via Ecommerce, these companies are winning.

Your time is now! Let's dive in!

The Leadership Imperative

2

Just get us a web site, and we'll be Amazon.

I f it were only that easy. In fact, nothing could be further from the truth. When we look at the history of how today's biggest Internet-based businesses evolved, we see a lot of organic, bottom-up approaches. Sergey Brin and Larry Page, the founders of Google, were computer science grad students working on a project. eBay was built in Pierre Omidyar's living room. Facebook was built in a college dorm room. Amazon was started by a dreamer named Jeff Bezos working out of his garage and using money provided by his parents. These stories are fun to read, but they do very little to actually inform us about how a highly evolved, complex, and multi-faceted organization with decades of selling history, long-established business relationships, and entrenched functional silos can undertake a serious, meaningful, and effective digital transformation.

In fact, these examples above do just the opposite: They mislead us into thinking digital transformation *should* be organic and bottom-up. In today's reality, however, successful digital transformation requires commitment from an organization's top-level management. Google didn't really take off as a business until Eric Schmidt took over as CEO; eBay only grew when Meg Whitman was brought onboard; Facebook only started making money when Sheryl Sandburg joined. And these companies began as "digital natives," born purely of and through the Internet and without legacy organizational structures, leadership "fiefdoms," and traditional approaches to selling and communicating. Free of this history, these companies personify the definition of digital and somewhat unfairly set the bar for other industries.

Confronting the Brutal Reality of Your Organization

In the B2B world, many manufacturers, brands, and distributors are struck with organizational inertia. "If it ain't broke, don't fix it" is a common mindset—even if not expressed—of divisional and executive leadership. Whether they realize it or not, companies are tied down and limited by their processes and traditional ways of doing business, and in some ways are victims of their own historical success. Traditional selling channels—the direct sales force (outside and inside), distribution and resale partners, telesales, catalog, and other methods—have driven many companies to tremendous revenue and profit levels in their categories. These legacy selling channels will continue to be an important part of the buyer-seller relationship in B2B industries.

However, the world has changed.

While these companies are living in collective inertia, *customers' expectations have dramatically shifted*. Today's B2B customers expect to have a buyer-focused experience, informed by the retail purchases they make in their own personal lives as consumers. And the fact of the matter is that this purchasing experience has either shifted directly to, or is heavily influenced by, digital platforms. As younger professionals come into the workforce, "digital native" is no longer a name for a category of buyers; it is every single individual that B2B organizations interact with.

Good leaders combine data with excellent intuition and situational awareness to make smart decisions. If you are a leader in a B2B organization, here are a few facts you need to know about digital behavior of business buyers as of this writing:

- **69 percent** of buyers say they want omnichannel and multichannel services.[18]

- **67 percent** of B2B purchases are influenced by digital channels.[19]

- **61 percent** of all B2B purchases start with online research.[20]

- **62 percent** of B2B buyers say they use only digital content to research and narrow down a vendor list.[21]

- **58 percent** of B2B industrial manufacturer purchasers start the buying journey with an online product search.[22]

---

18 https://www.accenture.com/t20180522T025432Z__w__/us-en/_acnmedia/PDF-78/Accenture-Verge-B2B-Digital-Commerce.pdf
19 https://www.thinkwithgoogle.com/advertising-channelsb2b-buyers-online-and-offline/
20 https://www.accenture.com/t20180522T025432Z__w__/us-en/_acnmedia/PDF-78/Accenture-Verge-B2B-Digital-Commerce.pdf
21 https://go.forrester.com/blogs/the-ways-and-means-of-b2b-buyer-journey-maps-were-going-deep-at-forresters-b2b-forum/
22 https://www.thinkwithgoogle.com/advertising-channels/b2b-buyers-online-and-offline/

- B2B buyers who engaged digitally with a business before making a purchase are **2x–8x more likely to purchase again from that business.**[23]

If you are selling products to businesses, these trends are impacting you whether you realize it or not. What should you do about it? In this world of shifting customer expectations and digital centricity, it actually starts with a simple concept: **leadership**.

In my work with B2B firms, I often cite the seminal business book *Good to Great* by Jim Collins. This excellent work documents tactics that some of the most successful companies in history have used to exceed their peers in terms of growing enterprise value. One of my favorite parts of this book is Collins' constant cry to leaders to "confront the brutal reality" of their situation and act. The facts above highlight a brutal reality that many executives continue to ignore at their own peril. Why? Change is not easy, and particularly difficult when a business continues to perform at somewhat acceptable levels through traditional sales channels. It is even harder to confront change when the change agent (in this case, the digital and Ecommerce expectations of business buyers) is completely unfamiliar to the executive-in-charge. The result is inaction driven by a combination of fear and not knowing where to start. The "brutal reality" is that ignoring digital transformation is not sustainable, and that customers are forcing change. But here's the good news: Companies that are listening are being massively rewarded. Why shouldn't your company be one of them?

Executives who believe that there is not enough return on investment ("ROI") data on B2B Ecommerce available

---

[23] https://www.thinkwithgoogle.com/advertising-channels/b2b-buyers-online-and-offline/

are mistaken. The truth is that the business case for B2B Ecommerce has been made; B2C has proven processes and methods, with proven margins, the majority of which can be applied to B2B. As we will discuss later in this book, the business case for digital transformation is clear and crosses multiple aspects of business performance—from incremental revenue and identifying new customer segments to improved competitive positioning and large efficiency gains. B2B executives should not be asking, "Should we commit to a digital transformation?" They should be asking, "How do we make this change happen?"

It bears repeating that digital transformation isn't only about opening an Ecommerce store. It is not about hiring an intern to manage your web site. True transformation comes from looking at the organization, both its processes and people, and figuring out how to evolve the entire operation towards a sustainable future. It means making digital a central part of every aspect in how the organization functions, with the focus being on making it easier, better, and faster to serve the customer. Successful change is incremental, more evolutionary than revolutionary. However, the process can be uncomfortable for the organization. Intestinal fortitude is required! Leaders will have their skills and talents tested.

The Foundational Elements of Organizational Evolution

There are four key foundational elements of organizational evolution necessary to prepare for and execute a successful digital transformation. These are:

- Redefining leadership, starting from the very top.

- Getting the right people on the bus (and the wrong people off it!).

- Establishing cross functional alignment and accountability frameworks.

- Hiring real Ecommerce experience, and giving that leader actual executive authority.

I will cover each of these topics sequentially.

Redefining leadership, starting from the very top

Digital transformation simply won't occur without this single ingredient: senior leadership driving change. This needs to come from the very pinnacle of the organization. The CEO, and even above him or her, the Board of Directors (or owners of the firm), need to not only buy into the goal of becoming a digital-first organization, but also need to embrace this change and find ways to incentivize and empower the entire organization to evolve.

This usually starts with something that is uncomfortable for many highly successful senior B2B executives and board members: a recognition that change is necessary, coupled with a genuine willingness to learn and listen, look outside the organization for help, and to operate and invest in an area where they typically have little or no experience. This runs counter to the way many B2B organizations have operated for decades, where leadership is defined by deep product knowledge, extremely long-term customer relationships, long employee tenures, and very conservative decision making. A common refrain is, "We know what our customers need better than our customers do."

By necessity, the new leadership approach takes a page from the entrepreneur's playbook, requiring a stomach for dealing with uncertainty and entering uncharted territory, as well as forcing organizational change. This is territory that many B2B companies and executives have not entered for

100 years or more, when many of these venerable companies were first founded. It is new terrain, and this can be very uncomfortable for leaders to deal with head on, and thus, easier to ignore than confront. This is a brave new world, and leadership in this market means recognizing that a leader doesn't need to have all of the answers. Leaders must change by gathering information, gaining comfort with operating new and unfamiliar channels, and surrounding themselves with the right kinds of people to help them thrive.

CASE STUDY

**Petra Industries: Creating the Distributor
of the Future through Bold Leadership**

*"The number one thing you need is the right people
from moment one."*
—Bill Stewart, CEO Petra Industries

The year was 2001 and the CEO of Petra Industries knew he needed to take action. The company was a successful, 20-year-old mid-market distributor of electronics representing over 550 manufacturers and selling products to large retailers and other resellers. The business was profitable and growing at a modest pace. It would have been easy for management to rest on their laurels and enjoy their success.

The company's CEO, Bill Stewart, wouldn't have it.

Stewart saw the rapidly evolving consumer adoption of the web for research and buying in retail markets and foresaw this coming to his industry. "I knew my business buyers were also consumers, and they would be looking online to research and purchase products," he says.

So he took action. His first step was to recognize the need for a foundation of clean and accurate product data, and rapid Ecommerce fulfillment to support his retail partners' own Ecommerce efforts. He then added capabilities for customers to order directly via Petra's web site, accommodating their business workflows and specialized pricing.

Today, Petra considers itself a digital-first company, enjoying a considerable and growing portion of its revenue from Ecommerce.

Stewart says it wasn't easy, and staying focused was the key.

"The number one thing you need is the right people from moment one, and bringing in new talent can be the catalyst to evolving legacy thinking," he notes. "It is also critical to communicate a clear vision to the entire organization from the very top, and that started with me."

Stewart credits the company's success with confronting the reality of what was happening in related markets and taking action. **This is leadership**.

"You have to start somewhere—to get something rolling, get your people on board and keep layering on," he says. "As you do, more is revealed. The important thing is to get started."

As a distributor, Petra recognizes the company needs to add value beyond only price and selection. As Stewart puts it, "We have not been immune to trends and pressures, the market is still intense. However, having digital tools in place has helped us to maneuver and grow the business, even as disruption occurs."

As such, Petra is well positioned to continue its growth trajectory.

Get the right people on the bus (and the wrong people off it!)

Leaders cannot be successful without the right team around them. This is not a new concept, but one that needs to be re-thought in many B2B organizations. The "right team" must go beyond loyalty to the organization (which does have value), and should include a healthy dose of new digital expertise as well as a willingness to embrace change (and not just accept it).

Another key concept found in Jim Collin's book speaks to the importance of getting the right team in place. Collins calls this "getting the right people on the bus," and making sure positive contributors are along for the ride and helping to drive. Digital transformation at large, legacy organizations is impossible without a concerted team effort, and eliminating rogue agents and negative thinkers working against digital initiatives is imperative to success. The job of the leader is to get the right people in place, and—equally important— the wrong people out of the organization. This could mean making some difficult decisions about long-term employees who may be resisting change. We will discuss some of the key people to look for in the following sections and chapters, starting with the Ecommerce leader.

Establish cross-functional alignment and accountability frameworks

B2B organizations of all sizes contain departments that are impacted by digital transformation. Sales teams may view Ecommerce selling as a threat to their customer relationships and compensation structures. Marketing budgets, and traditional advertising and lead generation approaches are all challenged by new digital marketing methods. Finance must account for revenues through new selling channels.

Information Technology (IT) has new systems to integrate and maintain. Customer service is handling orders through new channels and concerned that customer self-service via the web will make their roles irrelevant. Fulfillment must ship individual orders in smaller quantities using unfamiliar shipping methods, and often at a much more rapid pace.

There is virtually no aspect of the organization that is untouched by Ecommerce. As a result, cross-functional involvement and communication related to digital efforts is critical. This is not an easy task. Structures such as steering committees, shared vision and objectives, key performance indicators (KPIs), and service level agreements (SLAs) are important to establish early in the process in order to avoid internal conflicts and to ensure effective execution. I will cover structures to enable alignment and communication in more detail in Chapter 4: The Organizational Evolution.

Hire real Ecommerce experience and give your leader actual executive authority

To enable digital transformation, B2B organizations need to hire people with relevant Ecommerce experience who can lead and drive change with the full support of the CEO and board. Without knowing *what* to look for in this leader, too often B2B organizations look *within* the company to promote (typically to the IT department). It isn't that internal leaders can't succeed; but, in my experience, they almost always lack the skills and experience to understand what is necessary to drive digital engagement and Ecommerce sales.

In a recent study of successful digital transformation leaders, global consulting firm Korn Ferry found that organizations can hire "fully formed" executives, but they also need to cultivate these leaders from within. The study of 500 executives responsible for digital transformation at their firms identified six key characteristics of high-performing digital leaders. The successful executives exhibited strength in the following areas:

- Managing ambiguity
- Adaptability
- Cultivating innovation
- Emotional intelligence
- Change agility
- Engagement and persuasion[24]

Melissa Swift, a Korn Ferry Senior Client Partner, summed these findings up nicely in a LinkedIn post, saying:

> *Great digital leaders have a "pioneer mentality," they excel at embracing ambiguity, power through an unstructured world, and—contrary to curmudgeonly "move fast and break things" stereotypes—marshal the troops using a good deal of emotional intelligence.*[25]

In short, the study found that successful digital leaders exhibit a strong collaborative ability paired with the ability to "sell" and align various parts of the organization to work together toward the goals of digital transformation. These leaders demonstrate great comfort in operating without perfect information, while "selling the dream" of what digital can be within the organization. These characteristics are often seen in entrepreneurs, and, in a sense, Ecommerce is a new

---

24 https://dsqapj1lakrkc.cloudfront.net/media/sidebar_downloads/Global-Digital-Leadership-Paper-Digital.pdf
25 https://www.linkedin.com/pulse/right-people-look-wrong-melissa-swift/

business within many traditional B2B organizations. These traits can, and should, be incorporated into what you look for in your digital leader.

In addition to these personality traits, I recommend that organizational leaders also possess functional skills and expertise in the area of Ecommerce. Leaders should have at least some experience in the following areas:

- Deep understanding of the importance of web site usability and Ecommerce features to drive engagement and online sales conversions

- Web merchandising (yes, this applies to B2B, and not just online fashion apparel retailers!)

- Expertise in digital marketing, such as email, Google advertising, marketplaces (including Amazon), display advertising, influencer marketing, social media, and other digital approaches

- An understanding of and experience with foundational technologies such as Ecommerce platforms and content management systems (CMS)

- Management of product data and other content for use in Ecommerce applications, as well as for marketing and customer support purposes

- Understanding of the organizational structure needed for success in Ecommerce, as well as the kinds of people and skill sets necessary to successfully operate an Ecommerce function

- Knowledge of fulfillment and customer support functions necessary to create a holistic Ecommerce experience for customers

- Experience managing an Ecommerce Profit and Loss (P&L) statement

Many of these skills seem like they apply solely in a B2C setting. In fact, they apply to B2B as well. It should be noted that this list does not diminish the unique nature of B2B workflows, purchase patterns, support for traditional selling channels, customer-specific pricing structures, and other B2B-specific requirements that need to be managed in a B2B Ecommerce function. Understanding the unique needs of B2B are critical to getting it right, too. However, seasoned Ecommerce pros can learn these aspects of the organization, and develop an understanding of the company's product lines, and can surround themselves with a team of people who understand B2B workflows and other business details. The Ecommerce-specific skill set is almost always the missing element in B2B organizations. And true mastery of the Ecommerce function takes many years of practical, hands-on application.

Moving outside of the traditional "promote from within" approach of many B2B organizations, companies should strongly consider bringing in someone from a B2C Ecommerce leadership role to fill a similar role in the B2B enterprise. Many retailers and consumer brands have Chief Digital Officers, Vice Presidents of Ecommerce, and similar titles. B2B firms can find success in recruiting from these ranks. And this approach can be used at all levels of the organization while building an Ecommerce function.

A good example of this is Ergodyne, a leading manufacturer of workplace safety gear. The company looked to consumer brands when hiring for digital marketing talent in 2013. They hired Theresa Kuske, who was working at the time in B2C digital commerce for the Occasions Group, a brand of printed products for consumers. Six years after her hiring,

Ergodyne maintains category-leading web site functionality, including real time inventory lookup, rapid checkout, quick-reorder tools, and a consumer-like online shopping experience, enabling a fast growing Ecommerce channel.

In another example, in 2018, American Tire Distributors (ATD), one of the largest independent suppliers of tires in the U.S., hired a well-known online retailing executive to lead its digital efforts, Ivy Chin. Prior to ATD, Chin served as Senior Vice President of Digital at the multi-channel retailer PetSmart. At ATD, she is responsible for all information technology and the company's digital strategy, and is bringing two decades of consumer Ecommerce experience to the role. Prior to PetSmart, Chin worked in executive roles at Belk Inc, a regional department store chain, and as Vice President of QVC.com, both of which have large B2C Ecommerce operations.

CASE STUDY

**Beckman Coulter: Hiring
from B2C for B2B Success**

"You aren't really looking for me"—oh yes, we are!

Beckman Coulter knows testing—of the life sciences kind. Originally founded in 1935 by Caltech professor and scientist Arnold Beckman, the company is a leader in the biomedical testing field, serving diagnostics and life sciences industries. Beckman Coulter Life Sciences sells its products to healthcare and laboratory professionals, pharmaceutical and biotechnology companies, universities, medical schools, and research institutions worldwide. Today, the company generates over $1 billion in annual sales and is a part of Danaher Corporation, a global holding company.

The company is *very far* from a typical B2C retailer. But in 2015 the firm started to embark on true digital transformation and knew it had to look outside to tackle an Ecommerce effort. It turned to the B2C market to recruit.

Enter Beth Davis, a 10+ year veteran of the B2C Ecommerce field, including significant stints at Sears and several consumer-oriented digital marketing agencies. Beth joined Beckman Coulter in 2016 as head of Ecommerce operations, bringing consumer-like Ecommerce sensibilities and approaches to the company's Ecommerce operation.

How did Beth end up at a traditional B2B firm? Sears sells women's dresses, perfume, and jewelry—a far cry from the immunochemistry systems and hematology instruments that Beckman sells.

"I talked myself out of the interview several times," says Davis. "I loved the retail side, and this company seemed very different. I didn't think I was the right fit. And I told them that. I said, 'You aren't really looking for me.'"

Ultimately, Davis realized that she could bring significant value to the organization, and decided she was up for the challenge of bringing her Ecommerce background to an entirely new industry.

Now she is enjoying the role and finding ways to make considerable impact. "It was a culture shock at the beginning, but I was able to bring all kinds of new things to Beckman. These are tactics that have been used for many years in retail Ecommerce but are brand new to B2B."

For example, Davis helped to champion the concept of rapid online account registration. Previously, Beckman had required a very long, seven-page registration process for creating a new account via the web site. Applying B2C principles of minimizing steps to obtain a "conversion," Davis streamlined the process down to just a few pages. This led to a 51 percent increase in new account creation via the web site, and a higher number of new customer leads generated via the web.

In another example, noticing that more than 50 percent of web site visitors were using on site search to find products, Davis introduced a new, more advanced site search and indexing tool from a company called Coveo. This solution is now delivering 40 percent higher pageviews from users who use onsite search on beckman.com and increasing those sessions' average time on site by 47 percent.

Impressive achievements. However, it took a while to accomplish these milestones. "When I first joined, people were asking me why we needed a web site at all. They said, 'Can't we just push customers to the call center?' I was taken aback and didn't quite know how to respond." She quickly realized her job was as much about education and organizational alignment as it was about building Ecommerce capabilities.

"To find success in B2B Ecommerce, you need to educate and listen to people, understand their concerns, assuage their anxiety, and show them how Ecommerce can benefit the organization" says Davis. "Patience is required. But the impact you can make is substantial. It is worth it." And B2B firms are wise to listen to those with real-world Ecommerce experience. Hiring the right talent from B2C can help to educate traditional B2B firms about Ecommerce and pay significant dividends.

"Now, I love it," say Davis. "I'm able to really make an impact and set the company on a course to success in Ecommerce."

And Beckman is benefiting from Davis' expertise. When Davis started in 2016, the company had a goal of shifting 10 percent of volume from its traditional ordering portal over to Ecommerce. Then they applied Ecommerce best practices and launched a B2C-like checkout process in 2018. Since the launch of this B2C shopping experience, the company's daily Ecommerce orders have increased by 33 percent. A win for Beckman on multiple levels, as a good portion of this revenue is incremental and higher margin, and a clear signal of the value of bringing B2C expertise into a traditional B2B manufacturer.

There are lessons learned here for other B2B players. Namely, hiring from B2C can be a path to driving change, infusing fresh thinking into the organization, and just simply "getting smart" on Ecommerce.

It is critical to have an open mind when reviewing the backgrounds of B2C professionals. Given the frenetic pace of retail and the rapid change in Ecommerce since its inception in the 1990s, it is not uncommon to find frequent job changes among seasoned Ecommerce executives out of the retail sector. Many have held roles for one to three years at a number of different companies. Don't let this scare you. In most cases, it is more a sign of how the Ecommerce industry has matured, which has created a highly competitive demand for talent, and less about the executives' capabilities. In fact, many of these executives are looking for a long-term home, and would enjoy the relative stability of the B2B sector.

Companies should seek seasoned leaders for these roles and provide them with real authority—and accountability—within the organization. Too often, I see "leaders" appointed to run a B2B Ecommerce operation with less than five years of total experience. Organizations seeking true digital transformation will look for individuals with at least ten years of Ecommerce-specific experience, and provide this individual with a VP, SVP, or C- level title, reporting directly to a C-level executive, often the CEO, President, or other senior level leader.

This role also must be empowered to be a change agent, and the leader must be given some time to build their own support and capital in the organization. Anything less diminishes the organization's ability to execute and drive true transformation. The person leading the digital transformation needs to have enough organizational power and influence to lead the hard, sometimes uncomfortable effort of confronting legacy silos and processes with the goal of bringing change. And, as the Korn Ferry findings cited earlier in this chapter point out, change must be driven in a collaborative way that aligns organizational stakeholders. The digital leader should "own" a P&L statement for Ecommerce, even if this is only shared internally. The P&L will ensure the organization properly tracks its efforts and can measure success over time.

CASE STUDY

Illumina: Leadership Driving Ecommerce from the Top in an Unlikely Product Category

illumina®

Digital Dave and breaking down silos

Illumina is a $3+ billion manufacturer of biotechnology research systems and consumables used in genomics research, and is considered the world leader in its category, selling its products to research labs, universities, and other healthcare and medical institutions across the globe. The company's systems sell at a broad spectrum of pricing, up to $1 million per instrument, and are traditionally sold through a direct sales force. Not a likely candidate for Ecommerce selling, as conventional wisdom would have it. However, with a culture of constant innovation and pushing boundaries, illumina sees things differently.

Observing industry trends towards using the web for transactional and support activities, illumina sought to break down the preconceptions of what Ecommerce could be. They set aside the notion that Ecommerce was only for low price point products in small volumes. They put the customer at the forefront of the online experience and made a decision to aggressively pursue digital transformation, putting capital and people in place to make it happen. They hired an executive with deep digital user experience and a consumer Ecommerce background to lead their efforts. They were not afraid to take action.

Today, illumina generates a significant portion of its revenue from Ecommerce. In its first two years selling online with a new web site, the company has well exceeded its original business plan. Web site traffic is up from 1 million site visits per year to over 6.5 million visits since the implementation of its digital program, and today the company regularly experiences multi-million dollar online checkouts. Expensive capital equipment as well as consumables (chemicals used in the company's machines) are both sold via the company's web site. Pushing boundaries and defying convention is paying off.

Dave Grimm, illumina's Senior Director of Digital Experience (or "Digital Dave," the aforementioned Ecommerce executive), says that, "A desire for a B2C like digital experience with rich use of behavioral and user data is the driving force to our successful implementation of Ecommerce, and its adoption across the organization." Further, Digital Dave notes, "To get this done, we needed to align all of our selling channels and break down silos, and we could not have done that without leadership from the senior team, as well as a clear vision on changing how we go to market."

When Illumina learned that its customers wanted to buy its products via Ecommerce, the company decisively made the shift to prioritize digital channels. The company is now reaping the benefits.

Organizational Evolution Enables Transformation

In my work with B2B firms, I have found there are essentially four progressive stages that many companies go through in aligning the organization to position themselves for transformation. These are highlighted in the following graphic and described below:

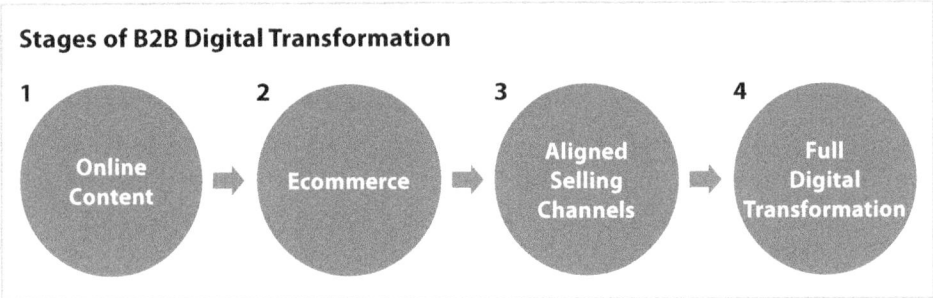

Stages of B2B Digital Transformation

1. **Online Content**: Both internally and externally-facing, your business needs a digital presence that provides the sales team and customers with the information they need to do their jobs, including product data, application/user guides, and support information. Most B2B organizations start their digital journey with online content web sites with access to this information.

2. **Ecommerce**: Often referred to as a web or commerce portal, Ecommerce is at minimum a basic shopping cart and payment gateway to enable online transactions. Today's B2B buyer expects to transact on your web site. Many companies start their foray into Ecommerce with a "portal" that enables basic online ordering functions, which is often an extension of the Enterprise Resource Planning (ERP) system. As the limitations of these portals are realized (often related to poor user experience and limited functionality), companies

will deploy more sophisticated Ecommerce platform solutions (a detailed review on how to select a platform is contained in Chapter 9).

3. **Aligned Selling Channels/Omni-Channel**: This is where things get fun and companies start to see real efficiencies. In this stage, companies fully empower the sales team with the digital tools they need for selling, including real-time product inventory information and syncing of online and offline customer behavior data. Companies are providing customers with online self-service capabilities and offer advanced mobile capabilities.

4. **Full Digital Transformation:** Digital is at the center of all customer interactions, and the organization reaps the financial and operational benefits. The ROI model is realized, with benefits flowing from incremental revenue, enhanced share of wallet from existing customers, an optimized and aligned sales team, and efficiencies being realized throughout the organization. Companies at this stage are realizing as much as 50 percent of their revenue from Ecommerce.

Ultimately, the organization itself must learn how to be comfortable with Ecommerce, even if this is accomplished piece by piece. For example, Device Technologies, a large medical equipment distributor, built an Ecommerce store for its employees to buy its own products as a first step. This storefront was internal only, but by doing this, they were able to show the entire organization that it was not only possible to sell their products online, but also demonstrated the value Ecommerce brings to their customers. (For more details on this, see the company's case study in Chapter 9.)

The road to digital transformation isn't an easy one, it's not flat, and it can take multiple years. There are bumps along the way, and there will be roadblocks. But having empowered and accountable leadership in place, with the right experience, skills and knowledge, is the first step.

Key Chapter Takeaways

- Launching an Ecommerce web site is a complex process, and therefore requires experienced leadership.

- Ecommerce requires a distinct set of skills, many of which aren't typically possessed by B2B leadership or staff.

- Therefore, it's often integral to hire from the outside to lead a digital transformation. Hiring experienced people from B2C Ecommerce is an excellent approach that can accelerate transformation for B2B firms.

- It is also essential to ensure that the organization—starting from the top—is committed to creating an Ecommerce experience that works. That means getting the right people on the bus, and the wrong people off of it.

Customer-centered ROI Drivers and Investment Considerations

3

Consider this: Forrester Research reported that B2B Ecommerce companies generated more than $1 trillion in revenue in 2018, up 17 percent from 2017. What's more, Forrester predicts that B2B Ecommerce sales will rapidly expand over the foreseeable future, with the market ballooning to $1.8 trillion by 2023.[26]

Clearly this is more than a trend; it's nothing short of a revolution that is driving dramatic Return on Investment (ROI) for companies taking advantage of these shifts in buyer behavior. Conversely, organizations that fail to recognize and act on this dramatic market shift are risking their very existence. Ecommerce is an enormous opportunity for companies that take action, particularly those that make moves prior to competitors. It can be transformational for B2B businesses. As I will cover later in this chapter, the ROI drivers for B2B companies are even stronger than for B2C retailers because there are multiple points of benefit.

Note that while the opportunity for return is substantial, organizations can become ensnared in their own organizational inertia, which arises from a somewhat irrational devotion to outdated processes that were not developed to support

---

26 https://www.digitalcommerce360.com/2018/12/17/the-1-trillion-b2b-e-commerce-market-arrives-early/

Ecommerce. In the last chapter, we covered what it takes to overcome this inertia. Assuming your leadership and organization is aligned and ready to take transformative action, the next step is to understand Ecommerce's ROI model for your business. Creating specific ROI goals will help you establish a roadmap of milestones that will guide you down the path to success.

But prior to mapping out a plan to capture ROI, there is an important first step that must be taken, and this is centered on your customer.

Step One: Putting the Customer First

Implementing a new Ecommerce operation is a significant investment in people, process evolution, and technology. There are many things for management to consider, including Ecommerce platform selection, marketing your new site to internal and external audiences, changes in process and work-flows, and sales channel alignment. Given the potential large investments, organizational disruption, and time necessary to roll out in an Ecommerce effort, the essential first step is to develop a firm understanding of your customers' expectations for a digital experience. Otherwise, you risk sinking significant capital into a web site that your customers may not use.

A change of mindset is usually required when embarking on this process. Organizations cannot rely on their traditional understanding of customers' needs. Instead, set aside preconceptions and take a fresh look at how your customers want to interact with your firm, focusing on digital channels. I have noticed a strong tendency for successful, well-established firms to say something like, "We know who our customers are and why they buy from us." However, the emergence of digital technology, coupled with an increasing population of younger digital natives in the workforce, has dramatically changed what customers expect, their purchasing behaviors, and how businesses must fulfill their customers' needs. An open mind is required to truly reap the benefits of this first step and build the foundation for longer term success.

Rediscover Your Customers

A number of methods exist to develop an understanding of who your customers *really* are and what they expect from your digital experience. I recommend employing most or all of these tactics to gain well-rounded insights. A key element in this discovery process is testing your own assumptions about your customer. Challenge yourself to ask uncomfortable questions and get out of your comfort zone. It helps to seek the assistance of a professional customer research consultant to assist you in this process, as internal teams can find it difficult to think objectively or, at minimum, ask the right questions.

There are five tools available to you to understand your customers' digital expectations. They are:

1. **Customer Surveys**: Sometimes called quantitative research, surveys can reach hundreds or thousands of your customers at once, and are a good way to capture feedback *en masse*. You will need to limit the number of questions asked (generally speaking, twelve or fewer questions results in higher survey completion rates) and ensure you don't ask leading questions. You can create and manage surveys inexpensively using online tools like Survey Monkey (www.surveymonkey.com), which can be distributed to your email list with a link to the survey. You can get results from a survey very quickly, often within a day or two. When well-executed, surveys can provide an excellent broad sense of your customers'

desires, and provide a basis for further exploration with other customer research tools.

2. **One-on-One Interviews:** An element of what is called qualitative research, one-on-one customer interviews can be conducted over the phone or in person. I recommend using a skilled, neutral interviewer, as opposed to someone from within your organization, in order to maintain objectivity. Additionally, a formal structure for collecting and analyzing feedback is useful to ensure that questions are administered uniformly and responses are analyzed without bias. Develop an interview guide with a series of questions in advance to manage conversations consistently. A typical customer interview will last 15 to 25 minutes, and usually conducting between 10 and 15 interviews will yield excellent insights into your customers' preferences and needs.

3. **Focus Groups**: Another element of qualitative research, focus groups are a discussion conducted with 8 to 12 customers simultaneously, designed to explore key themes and needs. As with interviews, it is best to prepare a discussion guide in advance and to engage a skilled and experienced facilitator to conduct the conversation. I highly recommend holding multiple focus groups across various customer types and segments, and perhaps in different geographic markets, to capture subtle differences in needs.

4. **Web Analytics and Testing**: In the digital world, data surrounding how customers use your web site can be very informative and can lend insights into their digital experience needs. Web analytics is software that captures how web site visitors interact with various components of your site, including what web pages they visit, what pages they are on when they leave

your site, how long they stay on your site, what they consider buying, and even where they came from before visiting your site. Observing these behaviors for all of your web site visitors allows you to understand what your customers are truly interested in and also reveals areas of opportunity to improve the digital experience. For example, if you observe that most of your web site visitors are leaving after viewing a certain page (what is called "high page exit ratio"), you can improve that page to be more engaging or perhaps remove it from your site. Modern web site software also allows you to test different versions of web pages and elements of a page in order to create the most engaging experience.

5. **Your Sales Team**: Finally, your sales team can provide excellent insights into your customer's digital expectations. Because they are on the front line with customers on a regular basis, the sales team will frequently be the first to hear from customers regarding their online preferences. Sales teams should be involved early in the data gathering process, but do not rely solely on sales team input. Combining multiple data points through qualitative and quantitative research will provide a well rounded perspective on customer needs.

In leveraging these tools, it is important to create questions that challenge traditional assumptions the organization may have about customer behavior. Don't be afraid to ask questions you think you already know the answer to, as the answer you heard five years ago may be very different than what you hear today. Examples could include:

- Who within the customer's organization purchases our products and what other responsibilities do they have within your organization? Who uses our products at your organization?

- How do different people in your company use the web to research products prior to making a purchase?

- Do you use a mobile device in researching or purchasing our products (or similar products from other companies)?

- What web sites do you use in researching and purchasing products for your business?

- How do you learn about new products that you use in your business?

- What role do search engines, such as Google, play in purchase decisions for your business? How about marketplaces like Amazon?

- Have you ever purchased a product from Amazon for use in your business? What type of product(s)?

- What other products do you purchase that are similar or related to what we offer? And where do you buy them?

- From what other companies similar to ours have you purchased products? How would you rate their overall customer experience? The digital experience? Describe the experience.

- How would you like to use the web for support, conducting tasks such as order status look-up, requesting service on products, account administration, checking credit limits, and other tasks you handle via phone, email, or fax today?

The questions can be different for your business, but the key is to identify changes in product research, buying, and support behaviors, and define your customers' expectations around the digital experience they are looking for from you. Ultimately, listening carefully to your customers and analyzing the answers should help you understand the role that digital plays in their work.

Results of this process can be surprising. For example, I was recently working with a very large Fortune 500 medical products distributor that conducted customer research as a part of its Ecommerce feature prioritization process. Prior to conducting a customer survey and interviews, the internal team felt that online promotions, such as discounts and free shipping on products, would not be well received by customers. After all, this is a global leader in their category and a traditional B2B seller by all measures. Their belief was that consumer-like promotions would not be effective. However, the team discovered that customers would in fact respond to online promotions, and were actually receiving them from competitors. The company was losing business to its rivals in some cases because it was not offering similar promotions. If it had not conducted the research and put the customer's voice into its prioritization process, the company would not have known this was an issue, and they would have continued to assume this type of digital experience was not relevant to their customers.

The point for you: customer research works and is critical to understanding how expectations have changed.

Segment into Customer Personas

Once research has been conducted across multiple points of data collection, the next step is to use your findings as the basis to develop customer personas. "Personas" are essentially definitions of different types of customers. Marketing software firm Hubspot offers the following succinct definition:

"A buyer persona is a semi-fictional representation of your ideal customer based on market research and real data about your existing customers. When creating your buyer persona(s), consider including customer demographics, behavior patterns, motivations, and goals. The more detailed you are, the better." [27]

Companies that actively utilize personas find that they are foundational as a way to frame and understand their customers' needs, and allow them to exceed the results of competitors' that fail to use this approach. According to a research study conducted by a group of marketing research firms led by Cintell, "71 percent of companies who exceed revenue and lead goals have documented personas." [28]

Create a profile for each of your customer personas, including the roles they play at their organization, their pain points, and what might make their jobs easier. Get as detailed as possible here so that you can ensure the next step in designing your digital experience is accurate. You may need to have as many as five to 10 personas to accurately describe your customer base. Things to consider incorporating when creating personas include:

- Demographic/psychographic information (age range, education, other attributes)

- Personality characteristics and motivators

---

27 https://blog.hubspot.com/marketing/buyer-persona-definition-under-100-sr
28 https://unleashpossibledotblogdotcom.files.wordpress.com/2016/02/final-bench-mark-study-understanding-buyers-2016-cintell-2.pdf

- Job focus

- Role in the buying process (e.g. requestor, influencer, end user, etc.)

- Organizational characteristics (e.g. company size, industry vertical, etc.)

- Goals and challenges

- Fears (e.g. making a poor product purchase decision, missing an opportunity to capture cost savings)

- Ways they use digital in the purchase process or other daily tasks

- Sources of information

- Internal influencers, and those he or she influences

A typical customer persona might look something like the following:

Marketing Michael

"Digital tools are the key to help me acquire leads and new customers."

Goals: Generate leads for the sales team, generate web site traffic and brand awareness

Challenges: Too much to do, too little time, not enough resources, channel "mess"

Job Success Measured by: Leads Generated, Web Site Traffic, Brand Awareness measures

Tools: CRM, content management system (such as Wordpress), web analytics (such as Google Analytics)

Background	Learning	Job Role	Responsibilities
Title: Marketing Director	Publications / Blogs: HubSpot, Moz	Reports to: President	Generating leads for the sales team
Organization size: 150 employees	Social Networks / Associations: healthcare industry associations (e.g. HIDA), LinkedIn	Team: Small team of three marketers, typically content marketing, digital marketing, creative / designer	Managing brand communications
Industry: Healthcare distribution	Member of Digital Doughnuts, avid Twitter user		Generating product awareness

To Michael, we must be a trusted resource of product information and support, providing digital tools to meet his ongoing goals of lead generation and customer acquisition via digital channels

(Note: This is a real, but anonymized, persona created for one of my clients.)

Create Customer Journey Maps

Once you understand who you are speaking to (your personas), the next step is to create customer journey maps. These "maps" provide a vision for how you will meet customer needs at each stage of the purchasing process. They serve as a roadmap for creating digital experiences that are relevant and useful to both the customer and to your business.

While customer journeys may vary to some degree based on the industry and complexity of your products, you can generally boil down the process into five steps: Awareness, Consideration, Acquisition, Service, and Loyalty. These steps are displayed in the following graphic.

Stages

Awareness Consideration Acquisition Service Loyalty

These are the five main stages every customer passes through during their relationship with your business. For each step, document how you expect customers to interact with your company, the needs they have, and how you can take action in these important moments. For example, in the consideration phase, will new potential customers learn about new products via your sales team, an email newsletter, by product associations on your web site, or by a combination of these channels? And what are you doing at each step to inform and influence the prospect towards your products?

Based on your work in the previous step, you will want to create a journey map for each customer persona, as not every customer has the same needs or makes purchases in the same way. For example, your customer might have individuals with different roles within the same company. This customer may have people in a procurement role, who have a different journey than the actual users of the product, who may request your products from a procurement department. To address these different needs, you will need to document how each persona interacts with your business as they travel through the sales funnel. From there, you can more easily design and develop a digital experience that responds to each segments' needs. An example of a completed journey map is highlighted in the following graphic.

Example Customer Journey Map

Stage	Awareness	Consideration	Decision	Delivery & Value	Loyalty & Advocacy
Customer Activities	Hear from colleagues, see online/offline ads & social media, read trade publications, view at trade shows	Compare and Evaluate Alternatives	Place an order	Receive order, contact customer support, enjoy product	Re-order product, share experience
Customer Goals	None yet	Identify the optimal solution	Find product on preferred buying channel, order easily & quickly	Receive order, contact support, enjoy the product	Repeat good experience, share feelings
Touch-points	Word of mouth Social media Trade shows Traditional media	Word of mouth, website, branches, social media, content / articles	Web site, Email, Marketplaces (Amazon)	Products, packaging, delivery experience	Word of mouth, social media, referrals
Business Goals	Increase awareness and interest	Increase visits / engagement on web site, lead generation	Increase online orders and conversion rate	Product and experience meets / beats expectations	Turn customers into advocates
KPIs	Number of people reached	New site visitors Content downloads	Online sales, Conversion rate	Product and seller reviews / satisfaction ratings	Re-order rate, customer satisfaction
Activities	Content marketing, marketing campaigns –online and offline, PR	Create marketing campaigns centered on thought leadership	Optimize product findability, content on marketplaces, ease of online checkout	Organize fulfillment and service functions	Ease re-ordering, survey for satisfaction, manage / improve with feedback
Team Responsible	Marketing	Marketing, CRM, Analytics	Ecommerce, Marketing, IT	Fulfillment, customer support	Marketing, customer service, Ecommerce

Customer Feedback Doesn't End with Launch

The last step in ensuring that you have a customer-centric approach is recognizing that this is not a static process. Customer needs evolve and shift over time, and your job is to keep your finger on the pulse so that you can continue to meet these needs. Customer advisory panels can provide an excellent ongoing feedback method to ensure that you continue to hear your customer's voice. A customer advisory panel should consist of at least eight to 10 participants and include different types and sizes of customers, as well as a variety of roles from each company. Don't just select your largest customers; you need diversity within the group. Meet with your panel once or twice each year and share with them your plans for improvements, new web site features, and your overall digital roadmap. Most importantly, gain their feedback on these plans to ensure you are on the right track.

One of my clients, Cardinal Health, has put this customer centric approach into practice. Cardinal Health is a $100+ billion healthcare products and services company, and a global leader in its category. The firm sells its products to more than 90 percent of hospitals in the United States. In business since 1971, the company prides itself on listening to its customers, and that was an essential first step when developing their Ecommerce web site.

"We saw customers demanding Ecommerce from us," says Matt Wingham, Cardinal Health's Director of Ecommerce for the company's medical products division. "They wanted to find products quickly and easily via online means, particularly as younger, digitally native buyers moved into procurement roles at our customers' organizations. We understood the need for Ecommerce by listening to our customers, including through our sales teams in the field and via surveys."

Today, Ecommerce accounts for a significant portion of Cardinal Health's total revenue, and the company sees it as an ongoing process. "We recognized we couldn't dictate what the market wanted, but instead needed to put the customer first," Wingham adds. "We are never done, but the important part was getting something started in Ecommerce."

Implementing a new Ecommerce operation is difficult and expensive, and businesses can make the most of their investment by taking the time to first understand their customers' needs and expectations, and then building digital experiences around them. By doing this, you are putting your customer first and setting yourself up to achieve greater Ecommerce success, just as Cardinal Health and many other B2B firms have done.

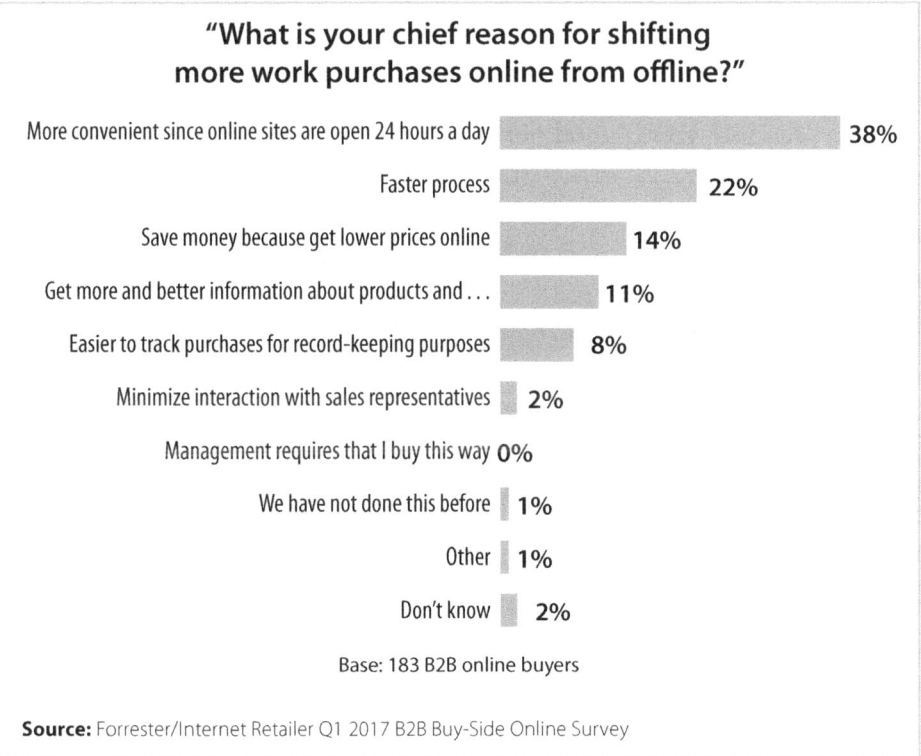

"What is your chief reason for shifting more work purchases online from offline?"

More convenient since online sites are open 24 hours a day	38%
Faster process	22%
Save money because get lower prices online	14%
Get more and better information about products and ...	11%
Easier to track purchases for record-keeping purposes	8%
Minimize interaction with sales representatives	2%
Management requires that I buy this way	0%
We have not done this before	1%
Other	1%
Don't know	2%

Base: 183 B2B online buyers

Source: Forrester/Internet Retailer Q1 2017 B2B Buy-Side Online Survey

The ROI Drivers

Once you have a clear understanding of who your customers are and what they need, it is important to define the ROI drivers in B2B Ecommerce for your company. This is foundational and translates your refreshed (or newfound) customer understanding into real numbers.

An overarching factor in thinking about ROI for B2B Ecommerce is understanding that customer adoption of digital channels is largely driven by making the buyer's job easier. This centers on transferring routine tasks to the web, allowing faster access to product data and information, and speeding up the customer's transactional processes. This becomes clear when looking at data from a 2017 Forrester Research study of B2B buyers, the findings of which are shown in the graphic on the previous page.[29] Note that the top two reasons buyers look to use online transactional channels are about convenience. Price is not a consideration until further down the list. This is good news for those B2B sellers that embrace Ecommerce. It says that making the buyer's job easier is more important than cost, and this gives you room to improve your gross margins by commanding a higher price on products sold via Ecommerce.

With this framework in mind, let's look at the individual drivers of ROI for B2B Ecommerce. We can divide ROI levers into three distinct categories:

- Increased share of wallet from current customers

- New customer acquisition and market development

- Organizational and revenue efficiencies

---

29 https://www.digitalcommerce360.com/2017/03/08/b2b-buyers-want-brand-manufacturers/

Let's explore each of these.

Increased Share of Wallet

Increased share of a customer's wallet is the most obvious and immediate ROI driver to successful implementation of B2B Ecommerce. By applying B2C Ecommerce best practices, B2B businesses can increase the lifetime value of existing customers by increasing each customer's overall spend. This may seem surprising, given the fact that many B2B organizations have a dedicated sales force that is incentivized to drive more sales from their current accounts. However, a successful Ecommerce implementation can effectively expand wallet share in unexpected ways, particularly by optimizing the online shopping process for commonly re-ordered goods and making the buyer's job easier in the process.

Increasing share of wallet through Ecommerce uses standard online cross promotion and upselling processes to introduce existing customers to products they may not know that a seller offers. Anyone who has used Amazon has seen this in the "Customers who bought this item also bought . . . " and the "Related Products" sections on each Amazon product listing page. This kind of capability is enabled by the richness of data and actionable analytics that Ecommerce can bring to your interactions with customers. This is a function that can be difficult for a sales rep to conduct in person, depending on the nature of the products being sold and the breadth of the catalog. Sure, sales representatives can carry around a beautiful, four-color brochure or catalogue with a company's top products, but this is a linear way of presenting product information and not the most efficient way to introduce items that are related, sometimes in abstract ways.

Following is an example from Amazon.com, showing how the top online retailer presents related items to specific product on the page, using its "Frequently Bought Together" functionality.

On the following page is an example of how one of my clients, HVAC distributor AC Pro, uses the same concept to present related products in an elegant and easy to understand way that allows heating and air conditioning contractors to quickly find what they need to get the job done.

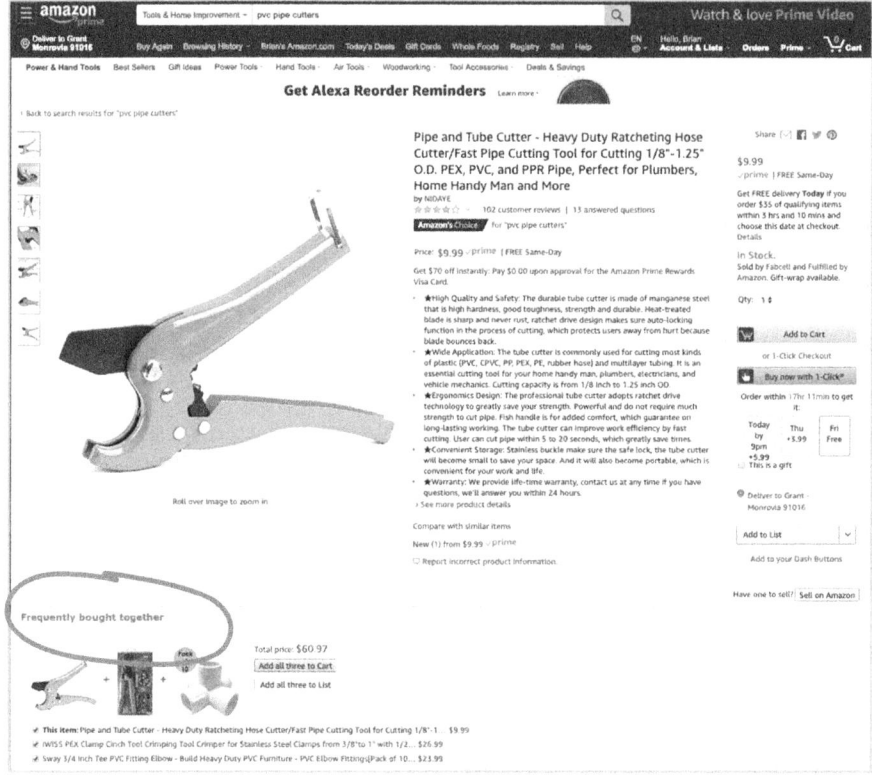

It is also important to note that the sales team has limited facetime with customers, and they may not have the opportunity in every meeting to present complementary products or to introduce new ones. In contrast, a well-executed Ecommerce web site can accomplish this task 100 percent of the time, especially when product information is detailed and properly categorized.

The whole idea here is to reduce friction for buyers and to make their jobs easier, while expanding the number of products purchased along the way. This is where B2B Ecommerce differs from its B2C counterpart. Oftentimes, B2C buyers are looking to browse product catalogs. They want to

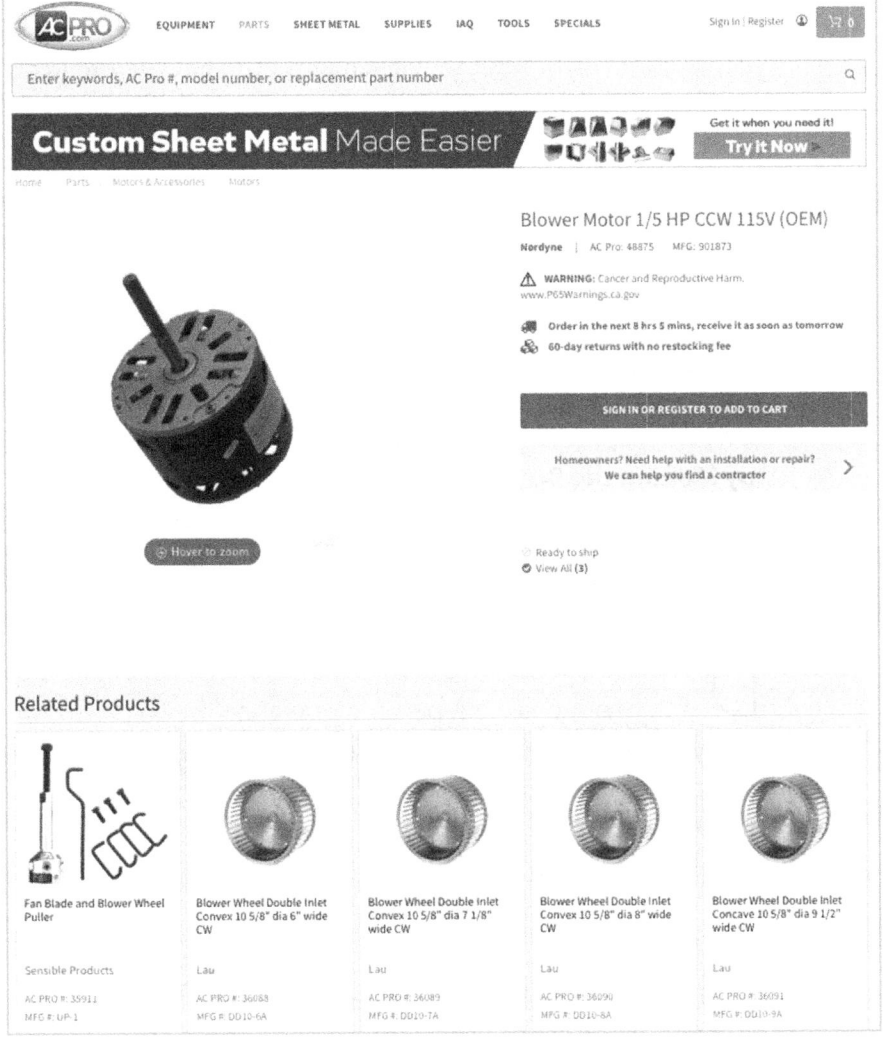

see options and are happy to click around a web site, casually looking at different categories and products. Online shopping for consumers is much more analogous to, say, shopping for clothes in a retail store. Indeed, online clothing retailers often see more page-views/session than other types of retailers.[30] Conversely, B2B buyers are looking for efficiency. They want to spend as little time as possible on an Ecommerce web site. They want to be able to easily find the products they need, purchase them as quickly as possible, and move on with their day. And if customers can conveniently add a few more items to their shopping cart that they either didn't know you carried, or didn't know they needed, then you have built loyalty, repeat business, and have ultimately grown the customer's lifetime value.

CASE STUDY

Diversified Foodservice Supply: ROI Drivers: Expanding Share of Wallet by Making the Buyer's Job Easier

Spend management tools translate to higher order values

Diversified Foodservice Supply is a US $300 million distributor of maintenance repair and operation (MRO) parts, supplies, and equipment to the foodservice industry. The company offers more than 100,000 products to independent restaurants, national chains, industrial kitchens, and resellers located across the United States.

---

30 https://www.wolfgangdigital.com/blog/e-commerce-kpi-benchmarks-study-2017/

The Company's CTO, Michael Bailey, credits B2B Ecommerce with much of the company's success within its category. He says, "We have been in Ecommerce for more than ten years, and it has been key to helping our customers meet their business needs in ways that are more difficult to accommodate manually."

For example, Diversified offers spend management tools via its web site that allow its customers to better manage their expenditures with the company, as well as their overall budgets. One functionality on Diversified's web site allows an administrative user at a customer to set the number of orders that can be placed each month. This allows customers to better aggregate and manage orders sent by a master procurement department to individual restaurant locations (which also typically have limited storage space). This reduces shipping costs and also creates efficiencies in receiving by "bulking up" orders before they are shipped, versus sending out individual, smaller shipments. The tool also ensures that orders are only placed when necessary, helping customers to optimize their inventory levels .

This web site functionality, and others like it, have translated to meaningful business results. Today, Ecommerce accounts for more than 34 percent of Diversified's total revenues, and the company's share of wallet has grown for those customers utilizing Ecommerce.

Bailey notes, "We are now seeing higher average order values from our customers who use Ecommerce, meaning we are obtaining more of their spend, mainly because we have made it easier for our customers to order and manage their spend with us."

As for what's next, the company is looking at using B2B Ecommerce to deliver more distributed buying capabilities through its web site, allowing procurement teams at large chain restaurants to authorize local restaurant managers to make purchases. This will further ease the buyer's workload, which the company expects will have additional positive revenue and profit impact.

Ecommerce also helps to build share of wallet by acting as a force multiplier to the sales team. As much as you may want to believe your sales team is acting on every lead, the fact is that they simply cannot spend time with every single customer, particularly smaller ones. To be effective, sales teams typically need to spend the majority of their energy with larger accounts that generate the highest volume. But what happens to all of the smaller customers? Should these customers' needs go unanswered? Of course not. A B2B Ecommerce site is ideal for smaller customers. The self-service nature of the web is perfect for accommodating and supporting these customers. A well-designed Ecommerce web site will help sellers capture additional wallet share from existing small customers, and even help sellers acquire new customers they could not have adequately served without Ecommerce.

For example, one of my clients is a well-established, $300 million tool producer that owns several global tool and landscaping equipment brands. The company sells its products to large retail stores like Lowes and Home Depot, as well as to smaller, independently-owned hardware stores. While it is true that these "mom and pop" retailers are becoming fewer in number, there are still thousands of these specialty retailers in the United States.[31] The company receives about 35 percent of its revenue from these smaller stores. Ignoring this customer base would be detrimental to their business growth, and providing an Ecommerce channel for these retailers has allowed the company to continue to capture sales that simply wouldn't be possible with a salesperson. Ecommerce is the key to maintaining wallet share with these smaller customers.

---

31   https://web.archive.org/web/20090509032759/
http://www.census.gov/compendia/statab/tables/09s1008.pdf

New Customer Acquisition and Market Development

When a business opens an Ecommerce web site, they expose their products and services to new potential customers, in part because of the way the Internet works. Often, these are customer segments and markets the company may not have even imagined as possible to address. As a result, Ecommerce exposes new revenue streams that simply did not exist previously. And once a company discovers a new customer group, they can plan and market to them as a unique segment using proven Ecommerce tools with the goal of growing revenue streams from these segments.

My favorite example of this is one of my clients, a company called Mountz, based in San Jose, California. The company was founded over 50 years ago, and manufactures and distributes torque tool solutions and metric fasteners for a variety of industries, including aerospace, automotive, electronics, energy, medical, and packaging.[32] Mountz's products, which include analyzers, screwdrivers, wrenches, and other precision tools, provide an extreme level of accuracy and performance that are critical to high intensity applications. Their customers, such as Boeing, Amazon Robotics, Intuitive Surgical, and Cisco, utilize Mountz's products in their own manufacturing processes. Imagine how critical it is to place the right tension on a screw that is used in a commercial aircraft, where an inaccurate measurement, even if tiny, can have serious, even catastrophic consequences.

An unexpected result occurred when Mountz allowed customers to buy their products directly from their web site. The web site started receiving visitors—and soon after orders—from bicycling enthusiasts and bike shops. This all started when these buyers found Mountz's new web site via

---

32 https://www.mountztorque.com/company/about-mountz

searches on the Google search engine. It turns out that these business owners and consumers also need the accuracy and precision of Mountz's tools for use in tuning their bicycles. Mountz offers products that are hard for these buyers to find (metric-based tooling), and the company's web site was indexed in Google for keyword searches related these items, as Mountz is an authority in this product category. In other words, once put online, it was easy for these buyers to find and purchase Mountz's products.

And now that Mountz has identified this new segment, the company is marketing directly to them using digital tools they may not have considered in the past, such as search engine marketing, email marketing, social media, marketing automation tools, a product information (PIM) system to control all product data, and even information syndication systems for platforms such as Amazon. What's more, this new segment now accounts for significant incremental revenue to the company. What salesperson in their firm could have possibly known or thought about this, when their focus has traditionally been on large enterprise customers like Boeing? Ecommerce opens new markets and drives new, incremental sales to companies like Mountz, across many industry categories.

What new markets can you potentially open with Ecommerce?

Gaining Efficiencies

The third ROI driver can also be the most substantial in terms of its impact on how an organization becomes a digital-first operation. It is the factor that often causes the most anxiety, particularly among sales teams and customer support personnel. However, as we will discuss in Chapter 5: Aligning Sales Channels, a digital-first operation makes sales and support teams more efficient, not obsolete. The perception of "competition" with traditional selling channels is not the reality in almost every case.

That said, there are *some* functions that may be performed today by humans that can be replaced or even enhanced by implementing Ecommerce, allowing organizations to reallocate resources to more strategic uses. When I look at a company's operations, I typically see tasks and functions that are repetitive, where automation or customer self-service can free up human capital that can then be reinvested in more fruitful, productive activities.

For example, many B2B businesses have what I call "bread and butter" orders. These are routine orders that don't require a lot of consultation—often re-orders or orders for commodity products. Good examples include replacement parts for equipment or consumables used by capital equipment (think ink for your printer). Consider this: Is it really productive to have a salesperson interface with a client who is only buying $50 a month worth of product, which is the same product they order every month, perhaps with some small variation? Probably not. And yet, there are many B2B companies that expect their sales teams—*even their top salespeople*—to spend time taking small orders over the phone or via email. Because . . . *hey, we give great customer service to all our customers, regardless of their size, right?* Many B2B organizations have long legacies of personal relationships as the difference makers in their business. You need to ask yourself, though, if this is really necessary in the digital age. Or better yet—how can this level of personalized service be replicated and enhanced online?

The fact of the matter is that using your sales people, or any human resource, to take these types of repeat orders via manual means (such as through paper forms or email, or even via fax machine) is a waste of time, and an inefficient use of the organization's capital. Imagine what other activities these well-compensated people could do if new orders went right to the warehouse for picking and packing? Wouldn't calling old clients to re-activate dormant accounts or pursuing new large accounts be better than processing a $50 order? Enabling Ecommerce allows you to shift these types of transactions to the web, capture these efficiencies, repurpose experienced resources, and drive real savings that add to the ROI model.

Similarly, on the support side, an Ecommerce system can vastly reduce the call load to customer service. Ecommerce systems not only allow customers to make purchases online, but they also allow them to perform mundane tasks such as changing their address, looking up their order status, reprinting invoices, researching order history, and other tasks that can be handled via customer self-service on the web site. One large client I recently worked with was able to shift almost 40 percent of their full-time staff in the call center from these labor intensive tasks over to higher-value outbound calling activities within three years of launching Ecommerce. This repurposed portion of the team is now reaching out proactively to the company's customers to offer new products and services and ensure customer satisfaction.

Gross Margin Impacts from Ecommerce

Ecommerce efficiencies don't end with operational improvements. Frequently, customers will experience a lift in gross margin from transactions completed via Ecommerce. Why is this? Simply stated: the convenience and time-savings from ordering via online channels trumps the need to get the best price. Remember that success in B2B Ecommerce is about making the buyer's job easier. If you are successful here, you can charge more for your product on the web than the customer might pay through other channels. Simply eliminating the call to the sales person eliminates the need for your sales team member to provide an obligatory discount to the customer. This is somewhat counter-intuitive, but it plays out all the time in practice.

If you are a manufacturer or brand owner, studies of B2B buyers by Forrester Research and others have shown that over 40 percent of buyers want to buy directly from manufacturers, and they are willing to pay up to 20 percent more to be able to do so.[33] That sounds crazy, but it has been demonstrated time and time again. How can this be? As a manufacturer, you own the product or brand. Quite simply, you are recognized as the authority on your product. This can produce a "halo" of trust that allows you to charge a premium. Customers recognize your expertise. They trust your brand, likely more than they trust a third-party reseller, leading to higher gross margin potential for you.

For example, I work with a company called Kelly/Spicers Paper, a division of one of the largest commercial paper manufacturers and distributors in the United States. Spicers' customers include huge newspapers like the Los Angeles Times, as well as commercial printers serving large advertisers across the western half of the U.S. In the commercial paper industry, availability of products and delivery times are paramount to meeting the production requirements of customers. Price is always a consideration, but Kelly discovered the key to meeting their customers' needs was the ability to place orders quickly and easily. To capitalize on this, the firm launched an Ecommerce site with the aim of making their buyers' jobs easier. Unexpectedly, they discovered they were able to charge a premium for online orders, even on routine replenishment orders. Customers know what they want, look up inventory and delivery information, look at the price to make sure it

---

33 https://www.digitalcommerce360.com/2017/03/08/b2b-buyers-want-brand-manufacturers/

fits their budget, and complete the order, all in less than five minutes. In other words, Kelly's buyers aren't looking for the best deal. They *are* looking for the *fastest* deal with reliable delivery times and accurate stock levels. Efficiency of ordering is more important than price, and customers don't need a discount to place the order. The result: gross margins on online sales are three percent higher than offline orders. Given that Ecommerce makes up 50 percent of the company's overall revenue, this three percent translates into millions of dollars in additional operating profit. Not a bad ROI driver!

Think about what an incremental percentage in gross margin dollars could do for your business. For most companies, this drops right to the bottom line.

CASE STUDY

Cardinal Health: Realizing ROI from Ecommerce

"We started by listening to our customers"

Cardinal Health is a global distribution leader of pharmaceuticals and medical products, with over $130 billion in annual revenue and serving more than 100,000 locations. Cardinal Health is confronted with the same challenges, changes, and opportunities inherent in today's digitized world as companies that are 1/100th its size. The difference is the need to address this evolution at massive scale. Not a simple task, but one that Cardinal is addressing head on. And because of the company's size and complexity, as well as many potential areas the company could invest in to drive growth, a strong business case was required to make investments in Ecommerce.

"Our business case started with listening to our customers," says Matt Wingham, the company's Director of Ecommerce for Medical Products and Services. "Our buyers were demanding the ability to buy online from us."

Based on conversations with their customers, Cardinal hypothesized that making their customers' jobs easier through an easy-to-use online shopping experience would result in increasing their share of wallet from existing customers. With a catalogue over 300,000 items, Ecommerce allows the company's marketers to present relevant products to customers, who may not be aware of these products.

With full control of the online assortment via Ecommerce, Cardinal Health can also present higher margin products and key Cardinal Health branded items at important moments throughout the shopping experience, such as on product detail pages or when customers are comparing clinically equivalent product alternatives. This allows the company to achieve higher profit on each sale, while also building the average order value.

A principal way Cardinal Health measures its ROI from these efforts is by looking at how the web site influences sales that are ultimately placed through its customers' traditional materials management systems. Many of Cardinal's customers use the web to research products, identify what they are looking for, then place orders through their corporate purchasing systems, usually powered via legacy Electronic Data Interface (EDI) systems.

"Much of the ROI from our Ecommerce site is driven by two things," says Wingham. "First, how the site influences purchases of our private label products, and second, how it leads to higher share of wallet from our customers versus their spend with competitors." By making products easier to find via its web site, Cardinal expects to generate up to $35 million in incremental revenue, at a higher gross margin to boot.

The key lesson: Listen to customers, build your ROI model around making their job easier, and the results will come.

ROI Is Great, but It Isn't Free

In order to achieve any of these ROI drivers, a business must implement a well-functioning system that manages inventory, processes orders, accepts various modes of payment, and delivers a great Ecommerce experience. There are training, process, and policy approaches that must be developed. This leads me to the third part of this chapter: Investment Considerations.

Investment Considerations

The old adage, "You need to spend money to make money," is nowhere more apparent than in digital transformation in B2B businesses. Another adage that might be useful here is "Evolve or die." If you are concerned about the investment costs of digital transformation, then you may not be as concerned as you should be about the alternative.

That said, businesses that want to grow and evolve still need to be strategic, not just reactive. And solid strategy comes from understanding your customers, what they want and how they buy, and then allocating resources behind the activities, technology, and infrastructure that will make ROI drivers possible. ROI doesn't materialize overnight. There is no switch you can flip and suddenly your business is growing by triple digits. Instead, achieving success takes careful planning and consideration to determine what, how, how much, and when to invest capital in a digital transformation initiative.

A useful way of framing this analysis is the "when" part of the equation. There are many up-front investment requirements, but there are also many long-term, ongoing costs. Let's take a look at the investments needed in both the short and long-term.

Upfront Investment Requirements

As I discussed in the previous chapter, digital transformation isn't only about throwing technology at a problem. There are a number of upfront investment areas required to effectively enter Ecommerce, including people, infrastructure, data preparation, and cross-functional alignment, in addition to the actual technology implementation.

People Investments

Get the right people on the bus

As we discussed in Chapter 2, success in Ecommerce is as much—or more—about organizational development as it is about launching a software platform to allow online transactions. And the core of organizational development is people. Getting the right people on the bus is an essential step to ensuring success, and should be the first area a business invests in. As I shared earlier, you need someone who is empowered in a leadership role, has a vision for and understanding of the digital landscape, and can effectively pull these pieces together to lead execution in a collaborative manner. Like any C-suite or VP level employee, they should be compensated accordingly. For a good range of what this compensation could look like, seek out models from the B2C Ecommerce world, where well-established parameters exist for leadership compensation. Don't make the mistake of putting a low-paid, inexperienced person in the leadership role. This dramatically increases your risk of failure, and will definitely extend the amount of time it will take you to realize business benefits. Be sure to check out sites like Salary.com, GlassDoor.com, and PayScale.com, and job listing sites like Indeed.com, ZipRecruiter.com, and LinkedIn.com for more information and role descriptions you can use as a starting point.

One mid-market distributor I've worked with made a smart decision when they started their Ecommerce initiative by looking to the retail sector to hire leadership. The firm knew they didn't have the skill set or expertise in house to build an Ecommerce operation, and after a fairly exhaustive search, they found a high-level executive with years of experience working in Ecommerce in the beauty retail industry. It turned out that the challenge of evolving a nearly 100-year-old business with extremely long-term relationships and traditional selling channels into a digitally-focused organization was too intriguing for this B2C veteran to pass up. Reporting to the Chief Operating Officer of the company, the new head of Ecommerce is now putting her expertise to work to improve user experience and creative for the Ecommerce site, as well as to implement an A/B testing program and merchandising fundamentals—all based on the executive's experiences in retail. While much of what is being executed is new in B2B and for the firm, these approaches have been used for years in retail Ecommerce.

In addition to hiring someone to lead your organization into the digital era, there needs to be investment in staff at all levels. This comes in the form of hiring capable managers to execute leadership's vision, and then structuring your compensation plan to incentivize success. This should carry across the organization, not just the Ecommerce function. One prime example is paying out commission to salespeople whose customers complete purchases on the Ecommerce platform, *even if the salesperson didn't close the sale*. This simple move will win over your salesforce, earning their trust while reassuring them that they are not being replaced by computers. With your move into Ecommerce, you will also be adding new functions into your organization to support online selling. Hiring the right people into those positions should also be considered an investment, and planned for in your ROI model. I will recommend an organizational structure and required roles for Ecommerce in Chapter 4.

Leverage expert third parties

Third parties can provide an excellent, experienced set of resources to help accelerate your efforts, particularly in the early stages of implementing Ecommerce. Hundreds (if not thousands) of digital marketing and technical development agencies exist in the market that can help you build and market your Ecommerce web site. You should also consider leveraging agencies to support creative efforts to design the web site and managed services providers to support the infrastructure (such as web site hosting and monitoring). While the upfront costs may seem high to use these firms, it is unlikely that you will be able to simply and quickly make internal hires who can successfully execute a digital transformation within a reasonable timeframe. Agencies bring a bevy of creative, technical, and business expertise that can accelerate a digital transformation. Not only can they build your new Ecommerce web site, but they can also help you in strategizing how to optimize it, how to roll it out to your customers and internal stakeholders, and how to develop new workflows that take advantage of the digital tools available to your team.

When initially getting into Ecommerce, I almost always recommend hiring an agency to assist with the web site user experience and design, technical development and integration, and post-launch managed services and digital marketing. Legacy B2B internal IT and marketing teams very rarely have the skill sets to effectively build and deploy sophisticated Ecommerce solutions. It is essential to select an agency that fits your company culture, has a deep level of experience in your industry or at least related industries, and has a proven track record.

But don't just take the agency's word for it. Find out who their clients are and talk to them directly. I recommend putting together a request for proposal (RFP) that outlines your business and technical requirements for the web site, so that agencies who want to earn your business can know in advance whether their expertise matches your needs. You might consider having an experienced Ecommerce consultant assist you with development of your RFP. I have assisted dozens of companies in this manner, and following a careful process increases your chances of selecting a solid partner that you can work with for years to come. Over my 20 years in Ecommerce, I have worked on both the client side and the agency side, and I can say firsthand that not all agencies are built equally, but that finding the right agency can be a make-or-break relationship that can either fuel your growth or set you back.

Don't forget about customer support

A third area of investment in people is customer support, either in the form of an internal team or an outsourced call center. As we have discussed, some functions of customer support may migrate to the web site via customer self-service, including account management, order tracking, and addressing some commonly asked questions about products. However, most B2B categories have a long history of deep customer relationships, and these must continue to be nurtured. When a customer has a problem with the web site or an order, having someone for them to talk to by phone, email, or online chat can make the difference between winning repeat business and losing it all together. Adapt policies for presentation on the web site, including mapping out online ordering and return policies. Ecommerce sellers who provide troubleshooting advice or general information that help customers quickly resolve issues have a clear advantage over those who do not.

Infrastructure and Technology Investments

Aside from investment in people and resources (either internal or external), B2B companies embarking into the world of Ecommerce must also consider infrastructure costs in the ROI model, including software and hardware investments. The first major area of infrastructure investment, unsurprisingly, is an Ecommerce platform. This includes software licenses, user experience design, creative, development, integration, data migration, and hosting for a new web site. We will cover selecting the right Ecommerce technologies in detail in Chapter 9. For now, you should consider your web site build and launch costs one of the largest "costs of entry," ranging from the tens of thousands of dollars at the absolute lowest end to over $10 million for the largest, most complex enterprise implementations. The range of costs will vary dramatically based on the complexity of your business, current technical systems environment, overall objectives, functional requirements, integration needs, and the level of design and user experience customization. Note, too, that costs have dropped considerably for B2B Ecommerce platforms in recent years. If you are in anything but the simplest of situations, you should consider hiring an expert consultant to help you through the requirements definition and systems selection process. I have done this for dozens of companies over my career, and taking this step with someone who has been through it before greatly reduces risk and accelerates the realization of benefits once you go live.

Another important consideration is system performance and speed. By way of comparison, if you were to enter a car into the Indy 500, you would want to invest in its engine, brakes, steering, and chassis systems, and not just the driver. The same is true of your web site, where performance factors are largely tied to the software solution itself, how it is hosted, and the managed services supporting the site (essentially, managed services are performance tuning and monitoring of your hosting solution). Creating budget for a high-performing, fast-loading web site is *essential* to your success on a variety of levels.

Internet users have demonstrated that they will consistently abandon web sites they deem to be "too slow." What is too slow? Consider this: studies have shown that the human attention span since the year 2000 has shrunk to as little as eight seconds. Incredibly, according to a study by Microsoft Corporation, our ability to focus is now lower than a goldfish's attention span, which the study found to be nine seconds.[34] And the human attention span is expected to continue to shrink. The point is this: presenting a fast loading web site can ensure that your visitors don't navigate away before it even loads. Hosting and managed services are critical ongoing costs that need to be a part of your plan.

You have less time than ever to connect with your online buyer.

You also must consider order processing software. Many B2B firms have Enterprise Resource Planning (ERP) systems or an existing Order Management System (OMS) that can be

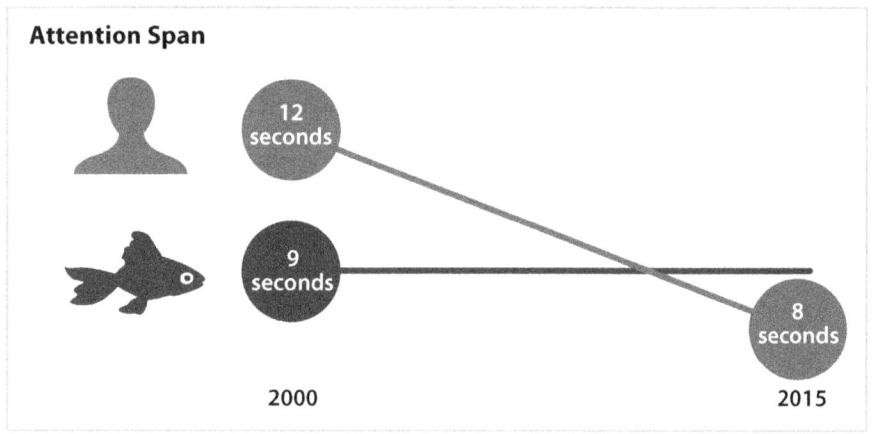

Attention Span

12 seconds

9 seconds

8 seconds

2000

2015

---

34   http://www.iflscience.com/brain/do-you-have-lower-attention-span-goldfish/

integrated with an Ecommerce platform. In the event you do not have a system like this in place, you will need to add it to your requirements for your Ecommerce solution, or perhaps consider another third party software package for processing and managing orders. Either way, Ecommerce orders must be managed, and be fully accessible by your customer support team. The order management system needs to perform at the same rapid speed as your web site. Customers have little tolerance for sitting around all day waiting for their order to be processed. Regular email updates with order status should be provided, and this requires integration with your email platform. Remember: The name of the game is to make buyers' lives easier, and a slow web site and order processing experience do not contribute to this goal.

Investments in Data and the Product Catalog

Another key area of investment has to do with a company's product catalog. In order to achieve a high-performing Ecommerce site, one that boosts share of wallet by offering relevant, complementary products, it is essential to build on a foundation of pristine and well-organized product data. I can't stress this enough, as it is frequently overlooked by managers seeking to launch an Ecommerce operation. High-quality product data includes basic specifications about each product—size, weight, price, color, application, etc.—but it also includes detailed, keyword-rich product descriptions, well-organized categorization, and clean, professional images. Video is also being increasingly utilized on the web as a compelling way to display product attributes, convey brand stories, and provide product application and training information. All of these elements are foundational ingredients to a robust, high-performance Ecommerce web site. Sadly, I see too many businesses not paying enough attention to their data, and taking shortcuts to "just get something live." This is not a recipe for success.

Consider the following product page example from Ergodyne, a manufacturer and Ecommerce leader in the safety products and work gear category, demonstrating rich

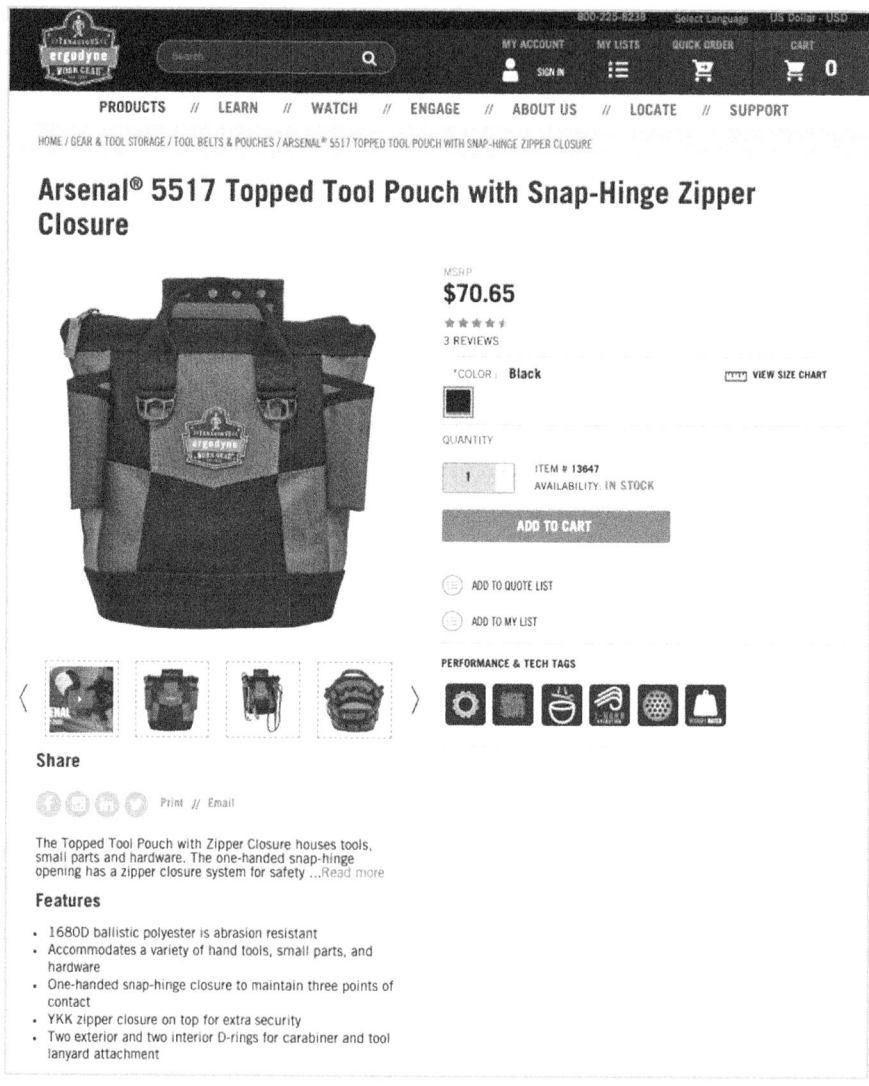

product data, images and video, and helpful buying tools
such as a size chart.

B2B Ecommerce sellers need to ensure that their sites
clearly provide rich product information in a way that is
reflective of the quotes and contracts that are being executed
by the sales force. At minimum, web sites must convey
enough information for a customer to make a purchase decision. As you get started, you should be critically evaluating the state of your product data, and make a strong effort
to cleanse the data to ensure that the content is standardized and consistent. Importantly, this also includes pricing
information. Customers must be presented with the pricing
they expect to receive when buying through other channels,
including the sales force. This pricing data is often contained
in contracts between the buyer and seller, and the Ecommerce
system must be integrated to present pricing accurately to
buyers when shopping online. Launching a site with inaccurate pricing and product information is a surefire way to
earn the distrust of your customers, and will quickly kill any
potential benefits you might otherwise receive from Ecommerce adoption. In other words, don't even bother launching
an Ecommerce site until you have consistency in this area.

In addition to product display on category listing and
product detail pages, an additional area where solid product data and categorization is critical is with on-site search
functionality. This is the area of your web site where users
can enter a keyword into a search box and receive a list of
relevant products and content based on the search query.
Given high expectations set by companies like Google and
Amazon, people don't have much patience for misleading or
irrelevant search results on your web site (remember, we are
now less focused than goldfish). Site visitors that use your on-
site search function are demonstrating a clear intent to learn
something very specific or to make a purchase. The easier it

is for them to find what they are looking for, the more efficiently they are able to do their jobs (which, as I will continue to drive home, is the key to B2B Ecommerce success).

Following is an example of effective on-site search from Ergodyne. The company presents a list of potential products of interest as the customer types their search query into the

search box (the example is "gloves"). The effectiveness of this search solution is based on the data that the company prepared as the web site was being developed, and is a key part of their success with Ecommerce.

The effectiveness of a successful on-site search experience is clearly displayed in the numbers. I typically see well-tuned site search driving conversion rates that are four to five times higher than average conversion rates. And search is based on data. Make sure that keywords are configured correctly to enable an effective search process, and take a hard look at your underlying site search technology to ensure it provides useful and accurate functionality. Many of the default search tools built into Ecommerce platforms are sub-par, but depending on the platform you are using, you may be able to install third-party software that amps up this capability. Either way, this is another compelling reason to invest in your data as a critical component to achieving ROI.

There are a number of site search tools that can greatly enhance the search function on your web site. It's important to find one that does a good job of managing your site's data and presenting search results in a merchandised way. The better this aspect of your site works, the more likely people searching your site will turn into buyers. For a list of tools, see the Resources section at the back of the book.

CASE STUDY

Bradley Corporation, Building a Data Strike Team

Creating the foundation with a "C Three" Approach

If you have a washroom, Bradley Corporation's products are likely in it. The 100-year-old Wisconsin-based company is a global leader in commercial washroom products for the restaurant, industrial, and educational markets, selling through multiple channels, including traditional MRO (maintenance-repair-operations) distributors and other channels. In 2013, the company moved into aggressively supporting Ecommerce and has reaped considerable benefits since. It started with a focused effort on product data.

"We were getting requests from our distribution partners like Grainger, McMaster Carr, and others, and [we didn't have] an easy way to provide them with this data," says Connie Beuche, the company's Enterprise Product Data Manager. Bradley knew they needed to adjust their approach if they were going to support resellers, as well as their own internal Ecommerce efforts.

"We pulled together a dedicated team of people focused on assembling and normalizing data for use on our own web site and to provide product data to our reseller partners," Beuche notes. "We even named our team the 'C Three Team.' for 'Cleanse, Compile, and Co-locate,'" she says with a bit of well-earned pride. "Team members were pulled completely off of their prior day jobs so they could exclusively focus on getting data ready for our Ecommerce efforts."

With over 11,000 products, this was no easy task. Beuche reports the effort consumed over a year for the three dedicated team members. To get the job done, Bradley used a PIM (product information management) solution from Informatica to organize its efforts and create efficiencies.

"Having a structured system to enter and ensure consistency in the data structure was really important," says Beuche. "Without this solution, it could have taken twice as long, and we would have had many more data errors."

This data has provided a solid basis for Bradley's Ecommerce success across all online selling channels. Today, virtually all of the company's customers utilize its Ecommerce site for ordering. And the company's resellers that are using data fed from its PIM system are growing at significantly higher rates than other sales channels. It has been a clear win not only for

Bradley's own Ecommerce effort, but also for its resale partners, and the firm's C Three Team is at the center of their success. Investing in a dedicated team was at the core of capturing ROI from Ecommerce.

Investments in Fulfillment

You can't just take an online order and then forget about it. The order has to get to the customer! And direct to customer orders via Ecommerce, which are frequently shipped in small quantities, often require a different set of fulfillment capabilities than shipping in bulk to traditional resale or distribution channels. As a result, another area that frequently requires investment for B2B companies is fulfillment. This includes the stocking, picking, packing, and shipping functions of Ecommerce, and may require you to set up new shipping and/or processing line (or lines), pick/pack processes, shipping software, and carrier relationships with small-package shipping companies such as FedEx, UPS, and DHL.

The good news is that if you don't already have a warehouse, or your warehouse is not set up in a way that makes this type of fulfillment streamlined, third-party logistics companies can provide these services on an outsourced basis. This can be a cost effective path versus investing in equipping your current warehouse with capabilities to support Ecommerce. Amazon, for example, offers anyone selling through their platform the ability to utilize their fulfillment services. B2B sellers can ship in bulk to Amazon, which then manages the operational functions of shipping to the end customer (See Chapter 7: The Amazon Chapter for more about selling through Amazon). You can learn more about this at https://services.amazon.com/fulfillment-by-amazon/benefits.html.

Alternatively, you can work to outfit your own warehouse operations for Ecommerce, but expect this route to take longer, and require investment in capital equipment, people, and processes.

Ongoing Costs to Consider

Once a company invests in digital transformation, they are typically committed to the path and reversing course can be difficult. The good news is that B2B Ecommerce ROI models are usually so favorable that most businesses are happy to make these investments to achieve the associated benefits. All costs for enabling Ecommerce are not upfront, however, and ongoing costs should be incorporated into your ROI model.

Ongoing costs typically center around people and technology, as well as incremental marketing investments (see Chapter 8 for details on digital marketing). Initially, outsourcing some functions, such as creative, technology, and marketing, to agencies is a good path to accelerate efforts. Typically, the Ecommerce function will grow to the point where you can scale back the use of outside resources and insource roles. Eventually, for example, you can hire a designer to manage graphical updates to the web site. You can hire product managers to ensure product data is complete, uploaded to the web, and associated correctly to related products. Lastly, ongoing training is an essential ingredient for maintaining and refining all the new processes and policies a digitally transformed company has created. Because digital touches every part of how a company operates, and because employees come and go over time, training is important to ensure a uniform customer experience. We will cover the roles required for Ecommerce in the following chapter.

Note that you should also incorporate an assumption about additional overhead costs required across the balance of the organization to support your new Ecommerce operation. These costs can include accounting, human resources, rent, office furniture, and equipment for any new employees managing the Ecommerce business. Many companies already maintain significant infrastructure, and this becomes a matter of layering on additional tasks, responsibilities, and people. Luckily, this can happen over time as you grow your Ecommerce business.

Tying It All Together

The cost and return elements described in this chapter should make their way into a profit and loss projection that will provide a set of milestones you can measure against as you execute. Following is an example of how this might look for a mid-market B2B company, integrating the components of revenue improvement, gross profit enhancement, and cost savings (efficiencies) to calculate something called Net Present Value (NPV) of an investment in Ecommerce over a five year period. NPV is a measure of the value of an investment in current dollars, and is commonly used in financial organizations as a way to determine the worthiness of an investment.

Ultimately, all ROI drivers stem from making the buyer's job easier, and thus all investments need to contribute to this goal. When done correctly, with a solid understanding of customer's needs at the center of the effort, this a win-win situation. Buyers win because they get their work done faster, and sellers win because they are earning higher gross margins and incremental revenue, while realizing efficiencies across the organization.

Example ROI Model

	Upfront Costs	Year 1	Year 2	Year 3	Year 4	Year 5
Upfront costs						
Ecommerce Platform Requirements and Selection process	$150,000					
Web site – design, development, integration, data prep, licenses	1,500,000					
Total upfront	$1,650,000					
Revenue and Gross Margin Enhancements						
Revenue						
Incremental Ecom Sales (share of wallet, new customers)		$5,000,000	$7,500,000	$11,250,000	$15,187,500	$18,984,375
Total Direct Costs (product, shipping, returns, etc.)		$1,750,000	$2,625,000	$3,937,500	$5,315,625	$6,644,531
Gross Profit – Incremental Sales (including GP improvements)		$3,250,000	$4,875,000	$7,312,500	$9,871,875	$12,339,844
% GP		*65.0%*	*65.0%*	*65.0%*	*65.0%*	*65.0%*
Operating Costs						
Incremental Marketing Costs		$375,000	$562,500	$843,750	$1,139,063	$1,423,828
Headcount and Resource Costs		970,313	1,242,000	1,863,000	2,173,500	2,484,000
Infrastructure and Technology Costs		500,000	750,000	1,125,000	1,518,750	1,898,438
G&A Load (including fulfillment enhancements)		1,050,000	1,575,000	2,362,500	3,189,375	3,986,719
Total Incremental Expenses		$2,895,313	$4,129,500	$6,194,250	$8,020,688	$9,792,984
Operating Profit – Incremental Ecommerce Sales		$354,688	$745,500	$1,118,250	$1,851,188	$2,546,859
% of Revenue		*7.1%*	*9.9%*	*9.9%*	*12.2%*	*13.4%*
Organizational Efficiences						
Customer self service / reduction in call center volumes		5%	10%	15%	18%	20%
Cost savings		$52,500	$105,000	$157,500	$189,000	$210,000
Cash Flow	$(1,650,000)	$407,188	$850,500	$1,275,750	$2,040,188	$2,756,859
Net Present Value at 10% discount rate	$3,169,837					

Key Chapter Takeaways

- Before developing an ROI model, businesses need to gain a better understanding of their customers and their needs and expectations for digital experiences.

- It is useful to conduct qualitative and quantitative research with the goal of developing buyer personas and customer journey maps to understand the role digital channels play at every step in the customer experience.

- There are three distinct ROI drivers of B2B Ecommerce:

  - Increasing share of wallet

  - Development of new markets

  - Gaining organizational efficiencies

- ROI drivers are as much about organizational efficiencies as they are about technology.

- ROI for product manufacturers is also driven by higher prices and resulting increased gross margins available to them when selling direct to buyers via Ecommerce.

- Investments are both upfront and ongoing.

- Investment in people is as important as investment in technology, if not more.

- Operational investments are also required, including fulfillment capabilities to support Ecommerce.

The Organizational Evolution

4

This Is an Evolution, not a Revolution

B2B Ecommerce operations don't run on their own. When establishing B2B Ecommerce, organizations need to create and fill a number of new important roles—or risk failure. Many B2B companies, especially firms that have been around since before the invention of the Internet, do not have any existing Ecommerce expertise or competency within the organization. Obtaining the incremental revenue and efficiencies available through Ecommerce is an exciting prospect, but it takes time to develop. As a result, Ecommerce for B2B firms is more of an evolution versus a revolution. If you are planning to launch an Ecommerce initiative, it is best to consider a crawl-walk-run approach. Ecommerce will touch every department in your company, and it is not as simple as hiring a few people to manage the function. A large component of a successful digital transformation is a clear presentation of the vision for the company as it relates to Ecommerce, and alignment among departments on tactics to achieve the vision. The good news is that we can look to B2C Ecommerce models to identify what a successful organizational structure looks like, and then emulate the parts of this approach that apply to B2B.

In the previous two chapters, I discussed the need for investment in personnel at all levels—from board members and C-suite level executives all the way down through the organization. I also touched on the need to bring in outside resources, principally to accelerate efforts. In this chapter, I will discuss in more detail what the roles and functions a company needs, how to determine which ones to outsource, when to insource, and how to build out competencies in these areas.

Critical Organizational Roles for Ecommerce Success

So what are the roles and functions an organization needs for Ecommerce success? The chart below shows the roles I have

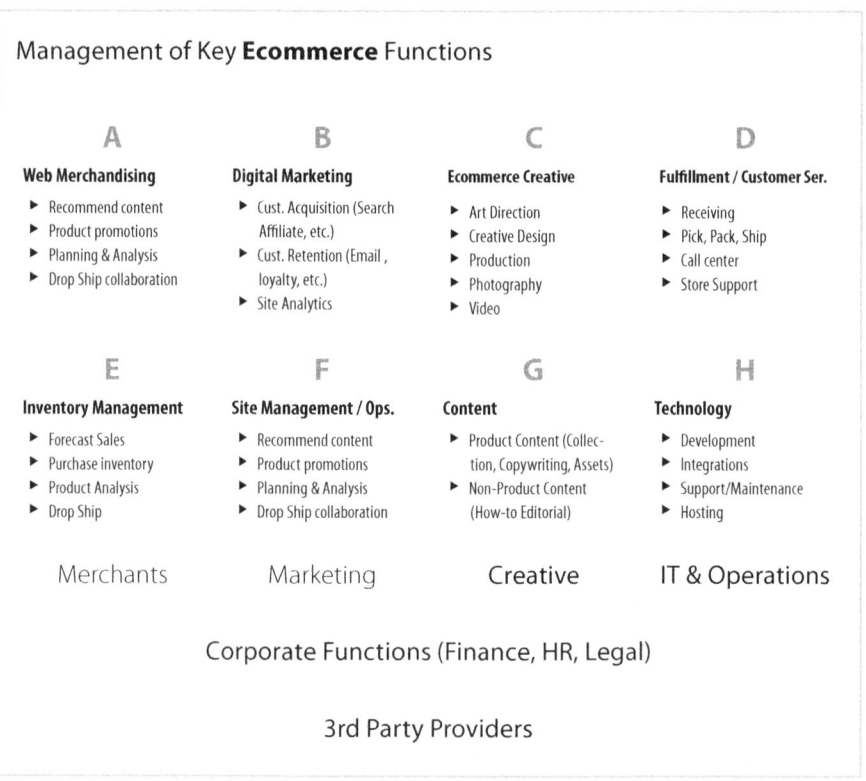

Management of Key **Ecommerce** Functions

A

Web Merchandising
- Recommend content
- Product promotions
- Planning & Analysis
- Drop Ship collaboration

B

Digital Marketing
- Cust. Acquisition (Search Affiliate, etc.)
- Cust. Retention (Email, loyalty, etc.)
- Site Analytics

C

Ecommerce Creative
- Art Direction
- Creative Design
- Production
- Photography
- Video

D

Fulfillment / Customer Ser.
- Receiving
- Pick, Pack, Ship
- Call center
- Store Support

E

Inventory Management
- Forecast Sales
- Purchase inventory
- Product Analysis
- Drop Ship

F

Site Management / Ops.
- Recommend content
- Product promotions
- Planning & Analysis
- Drop Ship collaboration

G

Content
- Product Content (Collection, Copywriting, Assets)
- Non-Product Content (How-to Editorial)

H

Technology
- Development
- Integrations
- Support/Maintenance
- Hosting

Merchants   Marketing   Creative   IT & Operations

Corporate Functions (Finance, HR, Legal)

3rd Party Providers

found to be necessary across organizations with high degree of digital competency, both in B2C and B2B. We will take a look at each of these.

Web Merchandising

Merchandising for Ecommerce can be a foreign concept to B2B firms. When we hear the word "merchandising," we typically think of someone putting clothes on a mannequin in a store window at Macy's or Nordstrom. For B2C retail merchants, this translates into their Ecommerce sites; web merchandising is the foundation of how product is presented on a retail web site, on the home page, category pages, product detail pages, and in other areas. It starts with strong product imagery (see Content below), and includes how products are categorized, described, and sold together via cross- and up-selling. This even includes the post purchase customer experience from a packaging perspective (e.g. how a product arrives and is presented inside of its packaging after being shipped to a customer's home or office). Solid web merchandising competency is critical in B2C Ecommerce, but many B2B firms don't realize the importance of this function. It is not a skill set traditional manufacturers, brands, and distributors maintain. However, product associations, details, and other merchandising tactics are necessary to drive buyer engagement and transactions via B2B web sites, as much as they are in consumer retailing. As a result, people that are familiar with your products and how to best present them to potential buyers are a critical component of your Ecommerce organizational structure.

Following is an example of a well-merchandised Ecommerce web page from one of my clients, Erin Condren, a manufacturer of printed products that sells to both businesses and consumers. Notice the compelling item image, multiple alternative images, product description and details, associated products, value pricing, and benefits statements. These efforts have helped the company to generate an Ecommerce conversion rate that is twice the industry average for their product category.

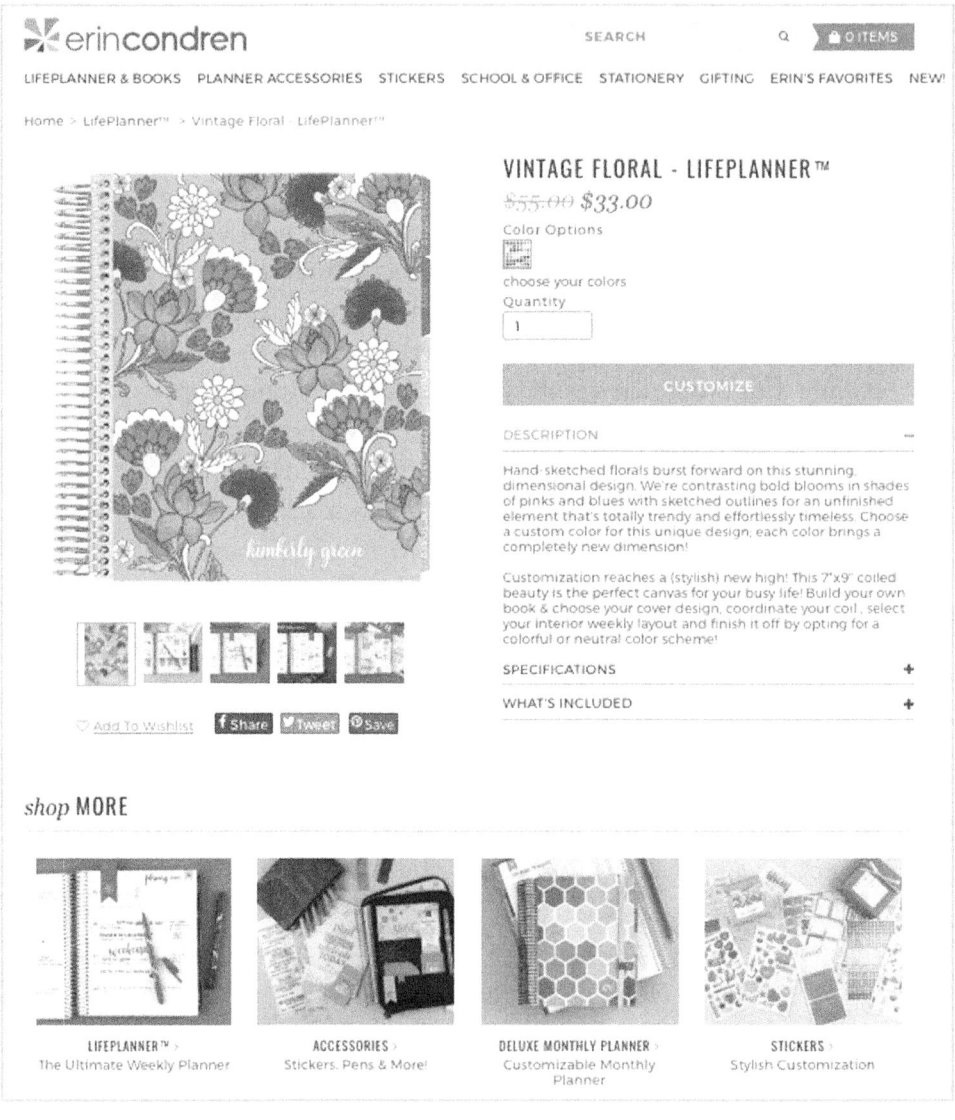

Digital Marketing

Most B2B organizations already have a marketing department, but marketing and driving web traffic to an Ecommerce web site requires a distinct skill set and expertise that traditional marketing departments may not have. This can include (but isn't limited to) knowledge of search engine optimization (frequently called "SEO" or "Natural Search Optimization"), paid search, digital display advertising, email marketing, social media marketing, affiliate marketing, and loyalty programs, to name a few.

Digital marketing is an extremely data-driven endeavor and, as such, knowledge of web analytics is a top skill needed. This goes far beyond simply knowing how many visitors your site is getting, where they are coming from, and what web pages visitors are looking at. Digital marketing demands a more detailed and rigorous marketing analytics capability, one that can manage testing of content (generally referred to as A/B testing), real-time pricing analysis and fluctuations, and deeper understanding of customer buying behaviors and preferences. Each digital marketing channel (such as Google, Facebook, or Email) is highly technical and requires expertise to get the most out of advertising campaigns in each marketing channel. B2B firms do not typically have this competency in house. The good news is that digital marketing agencies can be retained that have this expertise, and they can accelerate efforts here. A list of these firms can be found by simply searching Google for "digital advertising agencies." Refer to Chapter 8 for a more detailed discussion of digital marketing.

Ecommerce Creative

Not to be confused with *Content* (see below), the creative function is responsible for creating all the assets associated with each and every product that is needed by an Ecommerce web site. This includes photography, videos, and digital product spec sheets, as well as site design and layout, banners used on the web site, advertising campaign landing pages on your site, and the overall web site user experience from home page to checkout. The creative function is not only design (making it look attractive), it also requires user experience (UX) expertise. This function is critical to ensuring your web site elements not only look good, but are easy to use and lead to conversions—both on desktop and mobile. UX best practices are well established in the B2C world, and can be leveraged by B2B operators. Again, this is an area where digital agencies can help you get started.

Fulfillment and Customer Service

This is possibly one of the most overlooked aspects of Ecommerce. Many companies focus a large amount of their attention on the web site front end look and feel (site design) and digital marketing, but remember—the online experience is only half of the customer journey. The other half is what happens after an online order has been placed, much of which the customer does not see, namely, fulfillment and customer service. This function includes warehousing products (receiving, stocking, replenishment, etc.), picking, packing and shipping, post-sales customer support, order support, and possibly technical support (especially if your products are highly technical and require a help desk). Support comes in many forms, and can be delivered via email, web site, or phone. It is important for B2B companies to recognize that the fulfillment and customer service skill sets required for Ecommerce sometimes differ from traditional capabilities in this area. In other words, smaller order sizes, new shipping carriers (no longer just Less Than Truckload (LTL) and full truck load shipments—get ready for FedEx and UPS and the associated workflow complexities), and possibly new customer types that need to be accommodated by the shipping and customer service teams.

Inventory Management

Just as the name implies, this function is responsible for making sure a company has the products it is selling in stock when they are ordered. This function needs to know how to forecast sales and manage product supply. In some industries, this role needs to be performed in real-time, as buyers will make split-second decisions about their purchases based on stock, how fast they can get their products, and other factors. B2B firms can often leverage existing inventory management functions as Ecommerce capabilities are introduced, including people, processes, and systems. However, supporting Ecommerce orders is likely to require different approaches to inventory management and forecasting, driven by differences in typical order size, delivery speed, and frequency of ordering. At times, B2B firms can benefit by bringing seasoned inventory professionals from the retail world onto the team, at least on a consulting basis to help legacy teams adapt to the pace and structure of Ecommerce inventory management.

Web Site Management

You can think of launching an Ecommerce site as opening a physical store or distribution center (or "branch" as they are often referred to in the distribution world) to sell your products. The web site functionality and operations are the "four walls" of the store or branch, and the team that manages the physical infrastructure of the web site plays a similar role to a store or branch manager and their workers. They are responsible for the site functioning efficiently, like the way a store manager makes sure the lights are on, that the number of people walking in and out of the location is tracked, that the aisles are clean and easy to navigate, that the shelves are stocked, and that it is simple for customers to find what they are looking for.

The web site management team covers these types of functions, but in the digital realm. They are responsible for the day-to-day management of the site itself, including how and when product information is uploaded or removed, how well the site is running (remember: having a fast-loading web site is integral to success), managing downtime recovery, and performing general site maintenance. This function is also often responsible for maintenance and optimization of on-site search, web analytics and reporting on web site performance, traffic, and other metrics, and A/B testing of web site elements to optimize user experience (frequently conducted in conjunction with marketing). They must communicate with the fulfillment, supply chain, and warehouse teams to ensure that the information on the web site reflects what is available in inventory (unless robust integrations to back end systems exist that automatically update the web site), and that orders are being processed as promised by the web site.

Content

As marketing has moved increasingly towards digital formats over the past two decades, content has become more and more integral to delivering a great web site experience. With the introduction of B2B Ecommerce, content moves beyond support and simple downloadable product flyers. Typically, the content role is responsible for producing marketing content such as blogs, videos, product demos, as well as web site copywriting, product descriptions, specifications, product attributes, and non-product editorial content such as tutorials. Integrating traditional content types, including support literature, product configurators, and how-to guides, is a very powerful approach when used in conjunction with Ecommerce, and resources are required to produce and manage this information.

Technology

Technology is the foundation of a successful Ecommerce web site. The resources that manage this function need to be both flexible and conservative, walking a fine line between supporting the business objectives and managing risks, while communicating practical system limitations. This function also needs to provide solutions and "work-arounds" to technological and systems integration complexities that will impede achieving business goals. The technology team is responsible for the Ecommerce platform as well as integrating systems required for processing orders, managing inventory, reconciling financials, and other key functions. This often includes technical site development, hosting management, integration with inventory tracking, the Customer Relationship Management (CRM) solution, customer service systems, web site security, and analytics software. Often, this function will reside within the Chief Information Officer's (CIO's) or Chief Technology Officer's (CTO's) organization, with dotted line accountability to an Ecommerce leader.

Auxiliary Functions

While these eight functions are the main blocks of responsibility needed to successfully manage an Ecommerce operation, there are also corporate functions that are required to support other aspects of the Ecommerce business. Typically, these include Human Resources, Finance, and Legal. Here is a brief description of each role as it pertains to Ecommerce:

- Human Resources: If you are hiring people to manage the above functions, then you will need support from an HR department or partner in filling those roles, as well as helping to administer employment policies and in creating programs to retain employees.

- Finance: This is an essential role for Ecommerce to function properly. Finance is needed to ensure that inventory is accounted for properly, vendors are paid on time, customers are paying you on time, and that a profit and loss statement is produced to enable goal setting and tracking of Ecommerce performance

- Legal: Legal resources can assist in producing and maintaining terms of service and privacy statements for your web site, as well as ADA compliance, GDPR compliance (if you have customers in Europe, you can find more information here: https://ec.europa.eu/ commission/priorities/justice-and-fundamental-rights/ data-protection/2018-reform-eu-data-protection- rules_en), and other standard legal support for online presentation of information. The Ecommerce team will also require contracting support for software providers, agencies, and other third-party resources that are inevitably employed in the course of building an Ecommerce operation.

You may have noticed that I didn't mention the sales role in any of these functions. That in no way implies that sales is not important; in fact, alignment and support from the sales function is integral to B2B Ecommerce success. This is the reason why I have included an entire chapter to discuss the impact of Ecommerce on the sales process and how Ecom- merce can be a game changer for this function when aligned properly. See Chapter 5: Alignment of Sales Channels for a more in-depth discussion of this function.

Bringing Them All Together

Digital transformation incorporating Ecommerce requires a shift in cultural mindset, following the example of the leader, as I described in Chapter 2. Simply creating the functions listed above without a collaborative framework that holds teams accountable, one that drives changes in thinking and process, will result in failure. This is actually the hardest part of developing an Ecommerce business. And this is especially true in companies that have been in business for many decades, most of which maintain a long-established culture and processes. Too often, I see companies that cannot get out of their own way, even if they recognize the opportunity to embrace digital. As a result, opportunities outpace these firms' ability to take advantage of them. These companies are at risk of losing customers to competitors who are ahead of them in tackling the challenge of evolving the organization. Again, this is why I highlight leadership as the essential core element of digital transformation.

The key to success here is linking all of the functions together, with a clearly communicated vision, specific goals, and metrics. This requires leadership from the top, and spreading responsibility for success across the entire company. It is important to note that this is the one thing a third-party vendor can *never* accomplish; this shift has to happen from inside the organization.

For some businesses, it is not necessarily intuitive that collaboration will create a powerful customer experience in digital channels. In fact, lack of cooperation can take a negative toll on an Ecommerce deployment. When the vision isn't shared, goals are not clearly communicated, and rewards are not aligned, legacy organizational silos and traditional thinking will suffocate attempts at transformation. In this environment, new digital and Ecommerce efforts lead to fear, uncertainty, and even subversion sometimes. People in the organization become afraid of losing their jobs, worried about being replaced by automation, or just generally resistant to change. As a result, the opportunities are missed and the customer experience ultimately suffers. Companies that can't figure out how to align and execute an Ecommerce initiative end up missing the opportunity and lose their competitive advantage (go back to Chapter 1: The Time Is Now if you need more evidence).

However, this does not have to be your company. I can't stress this enough.

The planning phase is a prime opportunity to kick-start collaboration. This is your chance to begin identifying and challenging organizational silos, cultural roadblocks, and traditional thinking. By examining and involving all the functions described earlier in his chapter, an organization can also begin to identify individuals within the firm who may have skills that can be leveraged in developing the new Ecommerce operation (e.g. deep product expertise, marketing, and web merchandising skills).

Many companies I have worked with have utilized a cross-functional steering committee to formulate and oversee the plan for the move into Ecommerce. The steering committee can be a model for the rest of the organization in its cross-functional makeup, involving representatives from all different operating functions of the business (e.g. product, sales, service, marketing, finance, IT, etc.)

As I mentioned above, the good news is that you don't have to build a huge team right away. The crawl-walk-run-fly approach works in organizational development, as it does to the entire Ecommerce development process. The trick is finding the two or three things your organization does master-fully, and then outsourcing the rest (at least at the beginning). In my work with B2B firms, I have seen this approach work quite well. However, note that you still need to have someone in a leadership role internally leading the charge, communicating vision and strategy, and being held accountable for results.

The following graphic highlights the stages of organizational development for B2B firms, following a crawl-walk-run-fly paradigm, where "flying" represents a true digitally transformed business.

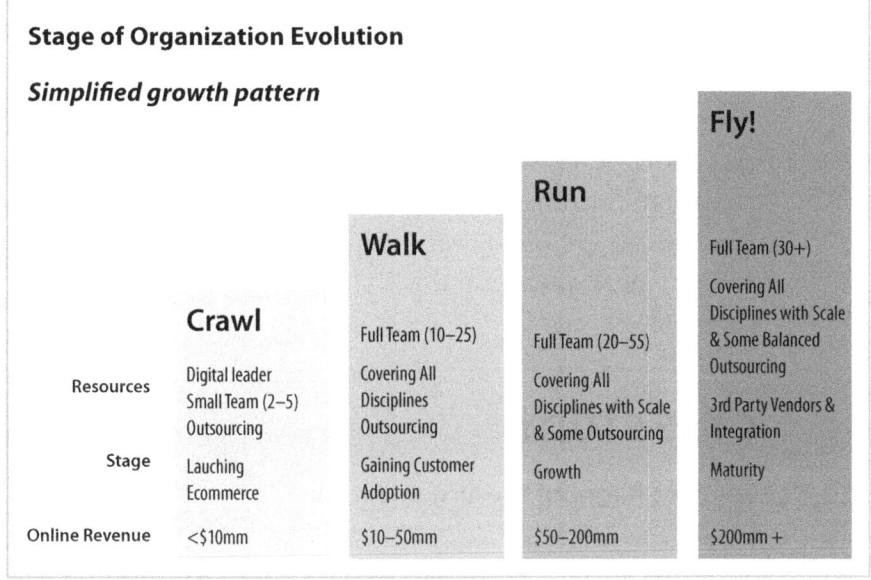

Stage of Organization Evolution

Simplified growth pattern

	Crawl	Walk	Run	Fly!
Resources	Digital leader Small Team (2–5) Outsourcing	Full Team (10–25) Covering All Disciplines Outsourcing	Full Team (20–55) Covering All Disciplines with Scale & Some Outsourcing	Full Team (30+) Covering All Disciplines with Scale & Some Balanced Outsourcing 3rd Party Vendors & Integration
Stage	Lauching Ecommerce	Gaining Customer Adoption	Growth	Maturity
Online Revenue	<$10mm	$10–50mm	$50–200mm	$200mm +

For many of the functions necessary for Ecommerce, such as digital marketing, technology, and even fulfillment, third parties can help you accelerate your efforts without incurring exorbitant fixed costs. I typically recommend looking to outsource the following functions at the "crawl" phase:

- Web site development (technology) and hosting

- Web site design and ongoing creative

- Digital marketing

- Some web site management (e.g. UX optimization, analytics, and testing activities)

Sometimes firms will outsource the fulfillment, inventory, and customer service components for Ecommerce at the "crawl" phase, however, this is dependent upon existing infrastructure and internal capabilities in these areas. I rarely recommend that web site merchandising and content be outsourced, as these are product and customer related functions, and internal resources usually understand these areas better than any third party ever can. Planning is critical here, as well as internal leadership to hold third-party agencies accountable, but learning from other companies that have been through the process is very helpful and will lead to greater success, more quickly, and with lower risk.

CASE STUDY

Lenovo: Aligning the Organization

With the sales team's involvement, Ecommerce efforts are far more effective

Lenovo is a $40+ billion multinational technology company with headquarters in Beijing, China and Morrisville, North Carolina. The company designs, develops, manufactures and sells personal computers, tablets, smartphones, servers, and numerous other electronics products. Lenovo is among the world's largest personal computer manufacturers and sellers.

Ajit Sivadasan is Lenovo's General Manager of Global Ecommerce Sales and Marketing. He has the ongoing task of leading the digital transformation for this massive organization, and with size comes complexity. He knew that putting the customer first would help him align the company's many disparate teams and departments.

"We started by putting the customer first in the process," notes Sivadasan. "By taking this approach, the rest of the organization could then understand why we were doing certain things with Ecommerce. We also involved the sales team early on in order to align them with the Ecommerce effort, as they were very close to the customer's needs."

Aligning organizational incentives and having a shared structure for collaboration has also been critical for Lenovo. The company looks at each customer holistically, and seeks to meet their needs, regardless of selling channel. This takes alignment on sales incentive structures, including, in some cases, incentivizing the sales team with commission on Ecommerce sales for their named accounts. This encourages the sales team to promote the Ecommerce channel to their customers.

"Our B2B customers are asking for Ecommerce," says Sivadasan. "By aligning the organizational incentives, we meet both the customer's needs and provide additional tools to our sales force to enhance their effectiveness."

One example is the introduction of Lenovo's Small and Medium Business online store, which focuses on customers with unique needs that are not effectively met by other sellers. Says Sivadasan: "Our expectation is to provide these customers with products and services that allow them to focus on their core business. In the future, we hope to be able to support these customers through subscription based services to take care of their hardware and software needs."

Today, Lenovo clears billions of dollars in annual transaction volume through its Ecommerce sites and other electronic means, and are clearly reaping the benefits of putting the customer first in the process.

Start with an Overarching Plan

Ecommerce success and organizational alignment begins with a solid, carefully considered plan that provides clarity on revenue and growth potential, and outlines costs and explicit milestones. Before a company does anything else in Ecommerce (besides potentially investing in someone to lead the Ecommerce initiative), it needs to hit the drawing board and come up with a workable plan. This document should be both strategic and tactical in nature, including an overall vision as well as elements needed for execution. Important elements to include are:

- Overall vision and goals for Ecommerce

- ROI model and capital expenditure plan (see Chapter 3 for key components of ROI and investment)

- Customer needs analysis: defining what the customer needs from your Ecommerce web site

- Sales team alignment: Making sure your sales team understands and embraces the new role digital will play in the organization (see Chapter 5 for approaches)

- Customer adoption: Internal/external marketing plan to drive adoption of the new Ecommerce web site

- Selling channel alignment approach (see Chapter 6 for approaches to managing channel conflict, pricing, and more)

- Digital marketing plan (see Chapter 8 for details)

- Ecommerce platform/technology selection (see Chapter 9 for details)

- Organizational and resourcing plan: Outlines how to resource each role defined earlier in this chapter, both in the near term (e.g. through outsourcing some functions) and longer-term (typically insourcing)

- Overall organizational alignment and governance plan, including leadership and roles of each party

- Approach and timelines: Tying each of these areas above to specific target time ranges

The Ecommerce plan must consider how the new initiative will be funded. It should also be centered on the needs of your target customers and consider your relationships with suppliers, distributors, and other resellers. In addition, the plan should contain very specific milestones, with actions to be taken along the way. Break it down into digestible chunks—three, six, and 12 month goals—and make sure the near-term activities are tied to the long-term vision to put it all into context.

Tools for Organizational Alignment: KPIs and a P&L

Specific metrics are critical to ensuring alignment and giving organizational actors their marching orders. A set of well-defined Ecommerce key performance indicators (KPIs) are critical to enabling cross-functional collaboration. When KPIs are combined with a P&L statement, these tools can be used to hold each department accountable and ensure the Ecommerce operation is performing to expectations.

KPIs can be broken down by functionality and frequently include:

- Web Site Operations

    - Web site speed (across devices) in seconds

    - Page load time (by page type, including home page, search results, category pages, checkout, and other key site pages)

    - Site availability (this measures web site "uptime," and target availability time should be set at well over 99%)

- Customer Service/Support

    - Contact volume (tracked to goals for contact reduction from customer self-service activities via the web site)

    - Customer service cost per order

    - Average time to handle a customer service inquiry, by contact method (including email, phone, and online chat)

- Fulfillment

    - Ecommerce order fulfillment success rate

    - Average time to ship

    - On time delivery rate

- Shipping profitability (also possibly including delivery cost per order)

- Inventory Management

  - In stock to out of stock ratio

  - Ecommerce order cancellation rate

- Sales

  - Customer adoption rate (number of customers utilizing Ecommerce for purchases, percentage of total orders and revenue coming from Ecommerce transactions)

  - Incremental sales per customer for Ecommerce adopters (typically measured on a per month or per year basis)

  - Sales team commissions earned from Ecommerce orders

  - Average order size for each ordering channel, including Ecommerce

  - Lifetime customer value (which is also useful to measure for customers that use both online and offline ordering channels; often customers that use multiple ordering channels have higher lifetime values)

- Marketing

  - Web site traffic by digital and offline marketing channel (vs. goals)

- Ecommerce conversion rate (by landing page and/ or marketing channel)

- Leads generated by the web site

- Web Site Bounce rate (by web site landing page and/or marketing channel)

- Web site visits by customer or account

- Repeat visitors

- Unique visitors as a percent of total site visits

- Number of days or visits before purchase

NOTE: See Glossary for definitions of these terms.

In addition to KPIs, companies should set up a profit and loss (P&L) statement to measure Ecommerce performance. KPIs measure statistics, but don't necessarily tell us anything about profitability and ROI. Even if a P&L is not shared outside of the organization, it provides real accountability for the Ecommerce leader, and gives a standardized format to track progress of the Ecommerce function. The Ecommerce P&L should be structured with online revenue and associated direct costs of revenue, e.g. cost of goods sold, payment processing fees (e.g. credit card processing costs), and shipping costs for Ecommerce orders. It should also include direct operating expenses, as well as allocated support costs such as finance, IT, human resources, and other operational expenses required to enable the Ecommerce function. See the previous chapter for an example of a P&L for Ecommerce.

KPIs and the P&L are used to establish a clear structure that all participants can reference throughout the Ecommerce launch process and after the new site is live. The Ecommerce plan should include rewards for performance, such as bonus incentives that are built into team members' compensation. Consider applying incentives across the organization, as Ecommerce touches many areas, and also to the steering committee members, who are doing much of the heavy lifting to ensure success of the program.

Evolution not Revolution

The most important thing to remember in all of this is not to try to boil the ocean right away. Doing too much at once is a recipe for failure. Many B2B organizations are steeped in history, and have earned success with well-established processes and relationships. Ecommerce challenges these traditional ways of doing business. As a result, an evolution—versus a revolution—is a more appropriate approach for many companies. Developing a plan is a key step toward ensuring a successful digital transformation. You cannot expect to build a well-oiled B2B Ecommerce engine overnight. Like anything else in business, success will involve a combination of hard work and patience. Stick with it. With enough planning, commitment, and elbow grease, your company can reap the benefits of Ecommerce. The opportunity is available to you, and a careful balance of thoughtful leadership and planning will lead to the gradual changes needed to capture the benefits for your company.

Key Chapter Takeaways

- Because Ecommerce touches every part of the company, establishing an Ecommerce operation requires firms to evolve how they are structured, creating new roles and responsibilities.

- Success lies in strategically linking all of the roles and functions together, integrating them into the organization in a strategic way.

- Firms new to Ecommerce should take a crawl-walk-run-fly approach that gradually and carefully introduces Ecommerce to the firm's employees and customers. This will ensure long-term success while minimizing disruption.

- Organizations should develop a plan to align all internal and external stakeholders, focusing on customers' needs.

- Using measurable Key Performance Indicators (KPIs) and Profit and Loss (P&L) statements, firms can track their progress as well as hold key project participants accountable.

Aligning
Sales Channels

5

S o far, I have discussed the various functions, skills, and leadership that are fundamental to the development of digital transformation in a B2B environment. You have probably noticed that I have not spent much time discussing a critical aspect of all B2B businesses: the sales function. A common perception is that launching a B2B Ecommerce operation is a surefire way to draw the ire of the sales team. And if done without careful planning and alignment, this can be the case. After all, doesn't an investment in Ecommerce signify the cannibalization of more traditional sales functions? Is this "Death of a Salesman" in digital garb?

Not exactly.

In reality, for most B2B companies, Ecommerce dramatically enhances the efficiency of the sales function. Ecommerce can actually multiply the sales team's efforts by unloading routine tasks to online channels and allowing the team to be more focused and strategic with key accounts. Don't think about Ecommerce as an alternative to traditional sales methods. Instead, in order to take your business to the next level, think about Ecommerce as a way to reinforce all of your existing selling channels by making them more focused, effective, and efficient.

The Internet has opened up a new competitive landscape in the world of B2B buying and selling. It is easier than ever for business buyers to launch a quick search on Google (or, more and more recently, on Amazon; see Chapter 7 for a detailed discussion) and find products they have never used, as well as suppliers with whom they have never done business. B2B selling channels have forever changed in the age of the Internet and always-present mobile devices. Traditional selling models have shifted, and the central communication point for business value propositions has now become digital in many industries.

According to one recent study by Acquity Group, a digital consulting firm, 94 percent of B2B customers research purchases online before making a purchase, regardless of sales channel.[35] Research shows that as much as 70 percent of the buying process is already completed before the buyer even contacts a potential supplier.[36]

The brutal reality is that if your business isn't well-represented on the web, you are losing relevance among your buyer base, particularly as younger, digitally-native buyers come into procurement and buying roles. You are slowly dying a death by a thousand cuts, and may not realize it. Do you really want to sacrifice your entire business because your sales team—or anyone in your organization for that matter—is afraid of change? Of course not.

Yes, Ecommerce can be perceived as a threat to traditional sales channels. But this is also an exciting opportunity that can be seized by leadership and translated into a sustainable competitive advantage. When B2B Ecommerce is implemented successfully, it enables businesses to reinforce their existing selling channels while simultaneously entering new markets and capturing new customers. The end result? Increased market share and an expanded customer base.

And yet, this trend has caught many manufacturers, brands, and distributors by surprise. Most remain ten years or

---

35 http://www.brafton.com/news/94-percent-b2b-buyers-research-online-purchase-decisions/
36 https://hbr.org/2018/03/how-digital-natives-are-changing-b2b-purchasing

more behind where they should be in terms of digital transformation and Ecommerce capabilities. A clear call to action is being sounded by B2B buyers (*your customers*) for vendors and suppliers to meet expectations for digital interaction, product research, order support, service, and purchasing. I've said it in earlier chapters, but it bears repeating: B2B firms not acting now are jeopardizing their very existence. Those that are acting are reaping large benefits.

The Sales Process Has Evolved

In the past, the B2B sales chain had three steps, as shown in the graphic below and listed here:

1. Manufacturers and brands produced goods.
2. Resellers and wholesalers bought the goods in bulk from manufacturers.
3. Business customers (the end users) bought these goods from the stock of resellers and wholesalers.

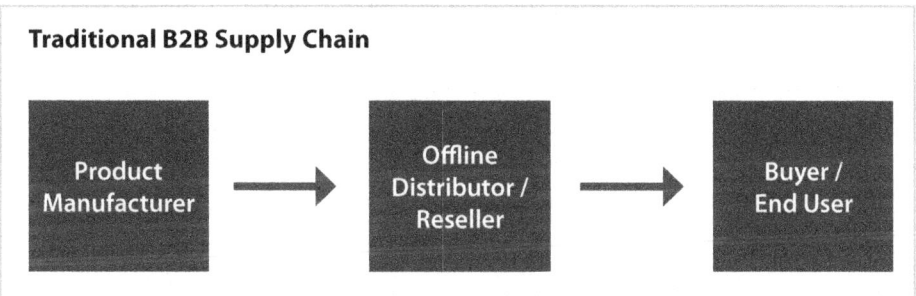

Traditional B2B Supply Chain

Product Manufacturer → Offline Distributor / Reseller → Buyer / End User

Consider a car repair shop, for example. The shops servicing vehicles are the final business buyer and end user of products. Manufacturers of automotive components produce replacement and aftermarket parts, which traditionally would be sold to distributors with a local presence. The repair shop then would order the parts from the distributor when needed, and they would get delivered quickly, usually within a few hours, to the shop by a local delivery vehicle. Simple, right?

Traditional sales channels have evolved, driven by changes in buyer behavior, and the disintermediation of channels is the result. That auto repair shop is now using multiple ways to research and buy parts and supplies, with digital and Ecommerce at the center of much of it. As perhaps the biggest sign of change (and forthcoming disintermediation), Amazon recently announced a move into the B2B automotive aftermarket industry, and the company is expected to become a large player in this sector.[37]

This is just one example. Today's B2B customers across a wide spectrum of categories expect a broader selection, faster delivery, and deeper product information.[38] They expect to be able to access and buy whatever they want, when they want it, through any channel that's convenient to them at any given moment (e.g., mobile, desktop, mobile apps, marketplaces, catalogues, and other channels). They are not wedded by default to any particular channel, even with long-standing personal relationships with traditional suppliers; these matter, but less than they used to. Customers are also showing less brand loyalty than ever before; according to a Gallup business survey, the majority of customers of B2B firms are "at risk of taking their business elsewhere."[39] Convenience trumps many other factors in the modern B2B buyers' decision process. Online channels are now trusted and preferred sources of information and purchasing.

What is considered convenient is fluid, entirely based on the buyer's specific situation at the time the purchase is being

---

37   http://www.businessinsider.com/amazon-is-expanding-into-the-auto-parts-market-2017-1

38   https://www.marketo.com/cheat-sheets/the-changing-b2b-buyer/

39   https://news.gallup.com/businessjournal/220475/why-b2b-leaders-rethink-true-cost-large-accounts.aspx?g_source=BUSINESS&g_medium=topic&g_campaign=tiles

considered. Is the buyer in his or her office or on the road at a convention? Are they on a mobile phone or a laptop? Are they meeting with a supplier in person, and want to make a quick comparison in the parking lot? When a business doesn't have a sales channel that is convenient to the buyer *at the precise moment they want it*, the sale is less likely to happen and the customer can quickly and easily jump ship to another supplier. The barrier for changing suppliers today is much lower than has historically been the case.

Today's sales chain is much more complex, and involves many different possible channels for research and purchase, including pure play Ecommerce distributors, marketplaces such as Amazon, traditional distributors with online and offline selling channels, and manufacturers selling direct to end users. This is illustrated in the following graphic.

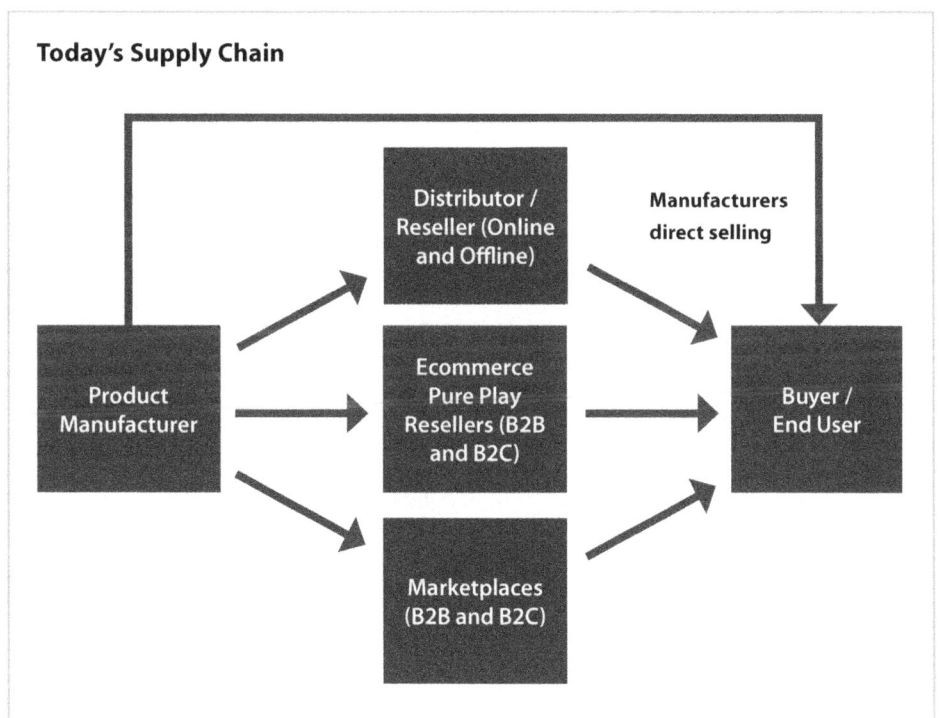

What does sales channel alignment mean in light all of these changes? It is not only about bringing your sales team on board with your digital efforts, though that is a crucial step. More broadly, alignment means ensuring that your customers' perception and experience of the business is consistent and convenient across all selling channels. Consistency is important in terms of how your sales team sells, and how distributors, resellers, and your Ecommerce web site function as an ecosystem. Convenience is about meeting customers where they are at any given moment in time. Once aligned, your business will be positioned to experience the efficiencies and revenue improvements I discussed earlier in this book. Now let's look at how a company should go about setting themselves up for success from a sales channel alignment perspective.

CASE STUDY

Henry Schein: Evolving from Order Taker to Strategic Partner

"Ecommerce is a pie-growing activity"

Henry Schein Inc. is a distributor of healthcare products and services with a presence in 34 countries and over $12 billion in revenue. The company is a Fortune World's Most Admired company and is ranked number one in its industry for social responsibility. Founded in 1932, Henry Schein has very well-established selling channels and deep industry relationships that have existed for decades. But one area where the firm found it could improve was with re-orders. They simply weren't getting customers to make repeat purchases. And as any business can tell you, repeat purchases are essential to long-term growth. The truth was that the firm's sales team didn't always have the time to capture re-orders from existing customers.

To address this, the company launched an auto-replenishment program that allows customers to receive products without having to deal with a sales rep or even place a repeat order. The new system automatically places re-orders based on parameters chosen by the customer at the time of the original purchase, making the repeat order process easy and fast. The sales reps also win credit for all the orders a customer places, even those placed through auto-replenishment. In other words, sales reps can build a regular commission income without having to do additional work.

"Ecommerce is a growing channel for us, our customers are asking for it," says Anoop Kulshreshtha, VP of Digital Technology. Henry Schein has found Ecommerce to be a tremendous opportunity to allow its sales force to become less transactional and more strategic in how they manage their accounts.

"Ecommerce is a pie-growing activity," continues Kulshreshtha. "This is a channel that allows our sales team to become more consultative with our customers, versus just taking orders. By offloading routine tasks, Ecommerce frees up their time to think strategically and more effectively meet our customers' needs."

At Henry Schein, Ecommerce and the sales team work together to benefit all stakeholders. The firm also relies on digital information delivery, such as preventative maintenance alerts for equipment that customers own.

"We help our customers, who are mainly healthcare providers, run their practices better by providing this type of information," says Kulshreshtha. "This deepens our relationships with them." Henry Schein eases the burden on the sales team in the process, generating incremental revenue opportunities while reinforcing decades-long customer relationships in all new ways.

By empowering its sales team through digital methods, Henry Schein ensures the company as a whole acts as a strategic partner to its customers.

Your Sales Team Will Actually Love Ecommerce . . . If You Do It Right

People are comfortable with the status quo. Maybe they dislike change. Or maybe, in the case of the sales team, they suspect that Ecommerce will render them irrelevant. Too often, I find that sales teams will actively work against an Ecommerce initiative, preventing companies from meeting their customers' expectations. In my experience working with a broad mix of manufacturers, brands, and distributors, fears about being replaced by Ecommerce do not play out in reality. If concerns about technology replacing your sales team are blocking you from taking action on Ecommerce, then it is time for you and your team to work past this fear.

So how do you overcome fear and inertia? By demonstrating leadership, confronting concerns directly, and involving your sales team from day one. Sales leadership should be included in the Ecommerce planning process early on and throughout each phase. If an Ecommerce Steering Committee exists (and I highly recommend forming one), the sales team needs to have a seat at the table. Aligning economics and incentives is important, too. Companies can leverage incentives for the sales team to encourage use and promotion of the Ecommerce system, such as paying commissions on Ecommerce sales that occur in sales reps' traditional geographic territories or on sales from their named accounts.

Business is and forever will be about relationships, and your sales team is the main touch-point with customers. Placing sales leaders at the center of a company's digital transformation brings both the customers' needs to the forefront and amplifies sales teams' capabilities to effectively manage relationships. With proper alignment, the sales team can be a large component of Ecommerce success for your organization, and they will embrace digital channels once they see the benefits.

What if you could build an effective Ecommerce site that allowed your team to become more productive? What if you could let them act strategically and target larger orders with bigger accounts? What if your sales executives had more time to spend with the right accounts, capturing more share of their overall purchases, rather than spending time manually processing orders, following-up with smaller clients, and checking order status and inventory levels for customers? The 80/20 rule usually comes into play here. You probably earn 80 percent of your revenue from 20 percent of your clients, your largest accounts. The question becomes: What percentage of your salesforce's time is spent with those largest clients, and what percentage is spent chasing small accounts, pushing paper, or doing other tedious tasks that can be handled through Ecommerce and online self-service? If your salesforce spends more time pushing paper than closing contracts, then implementing an Ecommerce solution that manages routine orders and frees up your salesforce is ideal. And your sales people will see it that way, too, as long as it is presented in this manner.

Here is an example where this approach has worked: I highlighted a client of mine, Kelly/Spicers Paper, in Chapter 3. As you may recall, buying decisions in the commercial paper industry are made based on instant access to critical product data, such as inventory availability and pricing information. Spicers built and deployed an in-house mobile app for their sales force that enables their selling teams to see real-time information about products, including what is in stock, how long delivery will take, detailed product specifications, current pricing, and other data essential to their customers' purchasing decisions. In the past, this information was only available from the back office, and would be obtained by the sales rep through phone calls, emails, and in-person follows ups. Information was not available in real time, or not available at all, particularly while the teams were operating out in the field. The sales rep usually couldn't close the sale on the spot, as they were waiting on stock and delivery details before the customer would finalize a purchase. But now, with this information at their fingertips via a mobile app, the reps are able to close more sales, more quickly. They are able to add value to their customer's decision-making process, versus waiting around for someone in the back office to tell them if their customer can get their order on time.

The results? This company's proprietary mobile app now accounts for almost half of their Ecommerce revenue (which itself is almost 50 percent of total sales), and does so at three percent higher gross margins. Speed outweighs price in the buying decision, and by providing critical information the instant it is needed, the company wins more business, more profitably. The key to their success (and potentially yours): They involved their sales team early in the process of developing the app, listened to their needs and challenges, and then deployed a digital tool that amplifies their sales reps' strengths and lets them operate more efficiently.

As in this example, when your web site allows customers to find what they are looking for quickly and easily, presents those products in an appealing and intuitive way, offers the information buyers need to make a purchase, and enables a simple buying process, you will have eliminated time-consuming work for your customers and also for your sales team. Moreover, if you build in the capability for your sales force to get credit for Ecommerce orders, they will be Ecommerce's biggest cheerleaders, versus grumbling and worrying about the status of their jobs.

Additionally, a well-oiled Ecommerce web site facilitates orders from small accounts, extending the reach of the sales team, and provides an efficient channel for completing routine orders. It allows members of your sales force to spend more time focusing on and maturing the highest value sales opportunities, where solutions-based selling is critical. A modern B2B Ecommerce web site enables you to effectively address your customers' demands for a "consumer-like" experience, shopping for your products the same way they shop on Amazon and other retail web sites for their personal needs.

CASE STUDY

SHI: Leveraging the Web as Powerful Sales Enablement Tool

"When customers are self-sufficient, I can become strategic"

SHI is a global provider of information technology products and services, with more than $8 billion in annual revenue. The company views Ecommerce as a core sales enablement tool and has put web site functionality in place to support this approach. SHI earns hundreds of millions of dollars in Ecommerce revenue as a result of these efforts, and it is a fast-growing part of the business.

SHI's Director of Ecommerce, Arleen Goldberg, notes, "The web frees up time for our sales force. They can better focus on higher value sales cycles and activities, and spend time with customers in areas where personalized attention is more critical."

A number of web site tools enable SHI to achieve these results, including:

- Easy Reordering: Using a feature called "Laptop Standards," the company's web site allows sales reps to track the specific laptop computers a customer typically orders for new employees. This enables either the sales team or the customer to add all products for a new hire to the online shopping cart in just one click. A process that was cumbersome and time consuming in the past now takes only a few minutes.

- Rapid Approvals: SHI's web site allows procurement teams within the customer's organization to ensure product selections are within budgets and cost standards. SHI's system recreates traditional workflows via a web approval routing system. Electronic notifications by email and other means make it easy for procurement officers to know when an order is in queue for approval, and enables them to enact the approval in just a few clicks.

- Streamlined Quote Creation: SHI's system allows sales reps to quickly create sales quotes, or customers can use a self-service feature to obtain quotes on their own, all without sales team interaction.

- Self-Service: Customers can log into their web site account to collect data on metrics like accuracy and speed of order processing, to email invoice PDFs, and to view order and shipping status. This provides better visibility into order status without having to contact the sales team.

These functionalities have delivered real business results that have made the sales team more efficient. For example, SHI estimates that the streamlined quote creation tool alone saves the sales rep on one large account over 40 hours per month. That's 40 hours that can be used for more strategic activities.

And the sales team loves it. One SHI sales team member noted, "When customers are self-sufficient, it gives me time back in my week and allows me to be proactive in my business versus reactive. I am so busy on a day-to-day basis that if I were spending hours just placing orders and creating quotes, I would be doing nothing to strategically grow my overall book of business. I have been successful because our Ecommerce platform makes it simple for all parties involved."

SHI.com helps the company's sales team win and retain customers, while saving time. It does this without the sales team giving up any commission; sales reps earn commissions on their accounts regardless of the source of the sale.

That's true sales enablement where everyone wins.

Aligning Existing Channels

At this point, you might be thinking, "O.K. I can get my salespeople on board. But I have existing channels that I need to pay attention to. I don't want to make customers angry!"

Yes! If you are a manufacturer or brand, you will have existing relationships with resellers. But here's the truth: these resellers' own operations and markets are also being impacted by the digital revolution. It therefore should be clear that these relationships need to evolve as well. This doesn't mean these relationships have to be adversely affected, as long as you confront the realities of what is changing, and have a plan of action.

As I illustrated at a high level earlier in this chapter, the variety of channels where B2B buyers may shop is breathtaking and evolving quickly. The new, digitally-centered selling landscape includes:

- Traditional Resale Channels: These include distributors, jobbers, value added resellers, Original Equipment Manufacturers (OEMs), retailers, and other resellers of your product. If you are

a manufacturer or brand, you likely have these
traditional resale channels in place, and they may
be your largest source of revenue. Many of these
companies have their own sales teams as well as
Ecommerce sites to enable sale of products to their
customers.

- Digitally Enabled Sales Teams: Companies (like
  the Kelly/Spicers Paper example I shared earlier)
  are increasingly arming their sales teams with real-
  time information that is critical at the point of sale:
  when they are sitting with the customer. This can
  include make-or-break details like instant inventory
  information, product specs and compatibility details,
  instant ordering and delivery timeframes, and other
  data. Remember, this isn't about replacing sales teams,
  it is about empowering them to be more effective.

- Ecommerce: Many businesses have enabled
  Ecommerce functionality on their web sites. This
  includes many distributors, who are further ahead
  in this area than their manufacturer and brand
  counterparts. Digital Commerce 360's 2019 B2B
  Ecommerce Market Report found that nearly two-
  thirds of distributors in the United States have a
  B2B ecommerce site, compared with only about
  40 percent of manufacturers. The study also found
  that as customers' demands for buying products and
  services online continues to increase, the number
  of Ecommerce sites for both product makers and
  distributors, wholesalers, and others will grow.[40]

---

40   https://www.digitalcommerce360.com/2019/05/07/distributors-are-farther-along-
with-ecommerce-than-manufacturers/

- Direct from Manufacturer: More and more manufacturers and brands are selling directly to the end customer via Ecommerce, thereby bypassing distributors. Data from Forrester Research suggests that customers are willing to pay **20 percent more** to buy directly from manufacturers. What's more, **43 percent of customers prefer buying from manufacturers**, whom they consider experts.[41]

- Marketplaces: Amazon is one of the major forces here, and, with Amazon Business, the company has added significant business buyer features that will certainly impact any industry they target. (See Chapter 7 for the full story on this 800-pound gorilla and their B2B efforts.)

Collectively, these channels are being impacted by digital transformation that is taking place across industries. The landscape of selling channels has changed, which creates opportunity, as well as risks, for you.

CASE STUDY

VF Corporation: Using Digital Technology to Align Sales, Marketing, and Ecommerce

Digital tools make sales teams more effective

VF Corporation is one of the largest and most prominent apparel designers and manufacturers in the world. The company's brands include The North Face, Lee, Dickies, Wrangler,

---

41   https://www.digitalcommerce360.com/2017/03/08/b2b-buyers-want-brand-manufacturers/

Vans, Timberland, Jansport, and numerous others. VF operates in many channels, including selling to large national and global retailers such as Cabella's, Dicks Sporting Goods, and Nordstrom, independent specialty retailers, small boutiques, online resellers, and through its own stores.

VF Corporation has proactively pursued digital channels as a way to support its customers, and increasingly to empower every step in the selling process. For example, one of the company's flagship brands, The North Face, enjoys a 100 percent adoption of B2B Ecommerce for orders placed by dealers (amongst those dealers not utilizing traditional EDI ordering). By making it faster for buyers to purchase via the web, this division of VF now enjoys the benefits of orders processed digitally, including considerable efficiency gains on processes that historically were managed manually.

Realizing the power of digital tools, VF has further extended these capabilities to enable its sales force. This includes an online merchandising and assortment planning tool, which allows The North Face's merchandisers and sales teams to create targeted, personalized assortments for presentation to its dealers during sales meetings, all using a digital dashboard. Sales representatives also have the ability to create digital visualizations of how a customers' fixtures can be stocked and will appear in the physical store. These customized and merchandised assortments can be downloaded to PDF and shared with customers via iPads during sales meetings.

"Our sales representatives are empowered to choose the most relevant products from The North Face's line for specific customers," says Julie Dixon, Coalition B2B Manager for VF Outdoor and Action Sports. "This helps sales rep more effectively communicate with their customers and really brings it home for them. The in-store visualization tool makes it real."

And once customers visualize what the brand's products will look like, they can then utilize The North Face's B2B Ecommerce system to quickly purchase the products.

"Our sales reps now use these digital tools in the majority of their sales presentations," says Dixon. "The adoption among our team has been terrific, as it makes them more effective."

Neither dealers nor the sales team miss the print catalog The North Face formerly used in sales meetings. The North Face's Senior Sales Planning Manager Pat Fitzmaurice notes, "Our dealers love it [the digital catalog], and we receive minimal complaints about not having a printed catalog."

In addition, these digital selling tools enable better alignment of the sales and marketing functions within The North Face's organization. "No longer is marketing fighting with sales on what to show customers," Dixon says. "North Face's marketing pros will load the products, price lists, brand story, promotional spotlights, and in-store visualizations right onto the iPads in advance of the sales teams' meetings."

In the past, the product information and assortments in printed catalogs would often be out of date by the time the sales team got in front of the customers to share them. Digital has entirely eliminated this issue.

Other business benefits have been numerous. By moving to a digital custom catalog solution, VF has realized considerable cost savings on printed old-style catalogs. And, by extension, The North Face has also reduced its carbon footprint. This dovetails well with the company's overall ethos related to environmental sustainability.

By learning lessons from its Ecommerce success and digitally enabling all of its selling channels, VF is creating mutual benefits for customers, its sales team, and the company's overall growth.

Managing Traditional Resale Channels

How can your business accommodate these shifting preferences? It starts by acknowledging that channel preferences are
changing, and accepting that digital has become a central point
of research and transactions for every industry. It starts with
not only understanding your direct customers who resell your
products, but also the end users of those products, their needs
and buying preferences. I always advise talking with the end
users of your products to objectively understand how digital is
impacting their buying processes; you may not get a clear story
from your resellers alone. Using end users as a starting point,
you can work backwards to analyze each channel and understand how end users buy through them. In other words, you
want to develop a complete picture of how your products move
through various sales channels at each stage.

It is important to note that these are not mutually exclu-
sive selling channels. Traditional resale channels will likely
continue to exist in most industries, however volumes may
shift to other areas, such as towards Ecommerce and marketplaces. As some channels become less relevant over time, they
need to be managed down, while simultaneously investing in
new channels that are growing. Acknowledging the reality of
what is happening is the first step.

Companies can utilize a number of different tactics to
manage existing selling channel relationships in this new,
digitally-centered world. The most important thing you can
do for your business is to understand how other channels are
selling your products, and then organize your own sales process—digital or otherwise—to maximize the value of those
channels. A manufacturer's or brand's Ecommerce and marketplace efforts can be competitive to these channels, however, digital efforts can also support traditional channels. A

detailed review of approaches to managing channel conflict can be found in Chapter 6.

If you are a manufacturer or brand, distributors and resellers will likely be a part of your sales channel mix for a long time. However, depending on the industry category, this mix will probably change. It is important for you to understand the value that your resellers add to their customers, as this will help inform your perspective on how important these resellers will be to your business over time. Channel conflict, specifically over pricing, is always a concern. Multiple approaches exist to manage this effectively, which I will cover in the next chapter.

The Internet is the great equalizer, especially when it comes to traditional competitive differentiators like price, selection, and convenience. Resellers who differentiate solely on these factors will inevitably be fewer in numbers in the not too distant future. The largest distributors and marketplaces are likely to capture much of this business over time. By contrast, if your resellers are adding value through service or application expertise, and are providing high-level solutions for their customers, they are more likely to persist. I recommend evaluating each of your resellers on the basis of the value they add to their customers' experience and creating a channel alignment strategy based on this.

What All This Means for Distributors and Resellers

Distributors and resellers need to be honest (*really honest*) about the value they add for their customers. Don't just assume that you add value because you have been in business for 1,000 years and have great personal relationships with your customers. Ask your customers why they buy from you to figure out precisely how you add value to every transaction.

If you can't realistically and objectively do this yourself, hire a consultant to help you.

Figure out how to differentiate yourself from your competitors, and keep in mind that your suppliers may be competitors on some level. Maybe you provide better solutions, superior product application knowledge, faster delivery times, amazing customer support, proprietary products, or better content. Maybe you combine products in a unique way to meet customer needs. Whatever it is, be honest with yourself. The traditional value components of distribution—price and selection—are those being disrupted by digital transformation, led by Amazon.

As an example of a company adding real value, I work with a fast growing mid-market seller of industrial fans called Big Ass Fans (yes, that's really their name). The company's products are used in factories, stadiums, airports, and other intensive applications where high volume movement of air is important for efficiency of HVAC (heating-ventilation-air conditioning) systems and overall environmental control. And these fans really are BIG. Some of the products have blade diameters of over 30 feet. Thus the company name.

The selling process to end users of Big Ass Fans' products is extremely consultative. It is a high-touch activity, requiring in-depth product knowledge and expertise to make a decision on the right mix of products for the customer's application. This typically includes consultations with electricians, architects, and contractors, and complex measurements and facility system tie-ins that are required for installation. Each installation is in a unique environment with its own challenges, and the company's salespeople are trained to help customers through each step of the purchasing and technical design process.

This is real value, and it's the value that stems from the technical understanding of the product and its deployment.

A 24' Wingspan Big Ass Fan installed in an industrial distribution facility

It goes far beyond simply making a product available at a competitive price. Ecommerce is not going to replace every aspect of the selling solution in this case. But it can enhance it through delivery of the right information at the right time during the process, and by providing an easy transactional method for relevant support products, such as installation brackets, repair components, and parts that are needed after the fans are installed.

As a traditional distributor or reseller, you should think about making shifts in your business model, if you haven't already. If you are a sizable player and have your own proprietary products (as many distributors have introduced in recent years), think about doubling down in this area. You can capitalize on areas where you have deep knowledge and expertise, and your product can stand on its own. Acquiring one or more of your suppliers is another avenue that could be pursued to accelerate your positioning. For example, Cardinal Health, the large medical products distributor I highlight several times in this book, acquired Medtronic's Patient Care, Deep Vein Thrombosis and Nutritional Insufficiency business in 2017. This acquisition provided Cardinal with a broad product portfolio across a number of important brands and categories, as well as considerable product manufacturing capabilities.

Regardless of the business model, B2B companies need to honestly review their value to the end customer and market approach, and align selling channels. Ecommerce is a change agent and enabler, and one you can use as a catalyst to better serve your customers.

Key Chapter Takeaways

- Sales teams must be aligned with the Ecommerce effort in order for it to be successful; the sales team should be involved in the planning and execution of Ecommerce initiatives.

- Sales teams can be made more effective through Ecommerce. Online selling pushes the burdens of low-value tasks such as order status checking and routine reorders to digital channels, and allows the sales force to spend more strategic time with key accounts.

- Ecommerce can allow the B2B organization to reach into markets it otherwise cannot effectively serve with a sales team, such as smaller accounts.

- A digitally-enabled sales force armed with real-time information that saves time and effort can be even more effective while in the field.

- Selling channels have evolved to become more digitally focused, with many brands and manufacturers now implementing direct-to-end-customer strategies for selling, including their own Ecommerce web sites and marketplace listings.

- Traditional resale channels, such as distributors, will likely continue to be a part of the selling channel mix for many manufacturers and brands, but product manufacturers should understand the value these resellers add to their end customers, and understand that traditional channels may diminish in importance in some industries with the advent of digital transformation.

- Distributors and other resellers must carefully evaluate the value they provide to their customers, in order to thrive and even survive in this new environment; competitive business models focused only on price and selection will be increasingly challenged by new entrants such as Amazon and manufacturers' direct selling efforts.

Managing
Channel Conflict

6

As we covered in the last chapter, the B2B sales channel mix has shifted, and as a result, the customer journey has changed. Any business looking to develop an Ecommerce operation is now going to have to address and proactively manage something called channel conflict. What is this conflict? In its simplest form, it is when two or more selling channels—such as a distributor and a manufacturer's own Ecommerce web site—compete with each other for the same end buyers' dollars. Wikipedia puts it this way:

> *Channel conflict occurs when manufacturers (brands) disintermediate their channel partners, such as distributors, retailers, dealers, and sales representatives, by selling their products directly to buyers through general marketing methods and/or over the Internet.*[42]

Historically, manufacturers have spent quite a lot of time, effort, and money establishing relationships with distributors and other resellers to help them drive sales. When a solid working relationship exists with these channel partners, it can be viewed as self-destructive to undercut sales and profits by marketing directly to buyers. However, this conventional logic ignores purchase preference shifts, which are becoming

---

42 https://en.wikipedia.org/wiki/Channel_conflict

heavily digitized, as we have discussed. So, this topic must be approached carefully and dealt with, but should not be ignored. Experiencing some discomfort from channel conflict is a sign that you are moving down the digital transformation path.

And channel conflict isn't limited to just manufacturers. In fact, many distributors and resellers are launching their own private label products and acquiring manufacturers, which puts them in competition with their traditional business partners. As such, a more accurate version of the Wikipedia definition above would read like this:

> *Channel conflict occurs when* **any participant in the supply chain** *disintermediates* **any other participant in the supply chain**, *including* **manufacturers**, *distributors, retailers, dealers, and sales representatives, by selling their products directly to buyers through general marketing methods and/or over the Internet.*

Channel Conflict Is Largely Centered on Product Price

The main conflict among channels is usually centered around price. When a manufacturer or brand sells directly to the end user of the product, they always have more overall margin to work with. Manufacturers have the ability to sell products at a lower price, as they can now capture the "retail" profit margin on the product. Consider the following table showing a simple example of a manufacturer's gross margins in selling to traditional distribution vs. selling directly through Ecommerce to the end user.

This example over-simplifies the scenario and does not consider other costs of selling via Ecommerce, such as shipping and marketing costs. However, it gets the point across.

	Wholesale Selling (e.g. selling to a distributor)	Direct Selling (e.g. selling via Ecommerce)
Product Cost	$6.00	$6.00
Wholesale Price	$10.00	NA
"Retail" Price (Paid by End Customer)	NA	$25.00
Gross Profit to the Manufacturer	**$4.00**	**$19.00**

The product that sells at a $25 "retail" price to the end customer (the ultimate user of the product) yields more than four times the profit to the manufacturer versus selling this same product to a distributor at a $10 wholesale price. This is powerful math for most manufacturers,and a strong incentive to move into direct selling. This margin gain is somewhat offset by conflict with existing resale channels, as well as any costs associated with adding resources and skill sets necessary to execute a direct selling strategy. That said, these conflicts are being either mitigated or confronted, and direct selling to end customers has become a powerful driver of investment decisions.

This power to disintermediate is the central underlying factor that defines channel conflict, and must be managed by manufacturers and distributors alike to avoid alienating traditional reseller channels. Resellers are often responsible for a very large percentage of a manufacturer's revenues, and this must be respected. In addition, many resellers add real value to the end customer, as we've discussed in the previous chapter. Thus, a balanced approach is necessary.

How to Manage Channel Conflict

As is my mantra for many things related to building a successful Ecommerce operation, the first step is to have a plan for how you will approach channel conflict. That means understanding the value chain for your products entirely, from start to finish, by selling channel, and understanding the value that each player adds. For manufacturers, is also important to understand how distributors or resellers are selling themselves. Your Ecommerce site may actually be able to complement or enhance how a distributor operates. Remember, making all buyers' jobs easier is the key to success with B2B Ecommerce, and this can also include your traditional resale channels.

A good channel conflict management plan includes several components, as highlighted below. Note that I am focusing mainly on manufacturers in this discussion, as these companies tend to have the most acute channel conflict issues.

- A definition of each selling channel's capabilities and value to the end customer, including sales trends in each channel

- A clearly articulated approach to product price, by channel

- A communication strategy for each channel, including defining potential benefits for resellers of a direct to customer strategy via Ecommerce

Let's take a look at each of these.

Define Each Channel's Capabilities and Value

Your channel conflict management plan should evaluate how each current sales channel operates, and what it is capable of doing with additional attention and support. Start by analyzing your current and prospective selling channels (e.g. distributors, OEMs, other resellers, your outside and inside sales force, Ecommerce, and other channels). Within channels, you might consider doing this for individual large customers. For example, one very large building materials company I work with completed this exercise for each of their three largest customers (which happen to include Home Depot and Lowes) in order to form the basis of their channel conflict approach as they considered launching their own B2B Ecommerce channel. The firm concluded that those channels added value by promoting the brand and reaching new end customers. They eventually launched their own Ecommerce site with pricing parity, thus avoiding direct competition with their top sales channels.

Once you have your channel mix laid out, then address the following key questions for each channel:

- How much revenue are you currently driving through each channel?

- Why does the end customer use this channel to buy your products?

- What is the key value that the channel adds to the end user's buying experience? Is it price, selection, speed of ordering, convenience, service/support, or something else?

- Do your channels add product, application, or other expertise that goes beyond just buying a product? E.g. does a reseller help the end customer combine a series of complex products from different manufacturers to create a new solution? I often see this in fields such as engineering, construction, electrical, chemicals, MRO (maintenance, repair, operations), and similar fields where products require technical expertise for application. Product or application knowledge is value the resale channel can add.

- What selling channels do resellers use for your product? E.g. do they have their own sales force in the field, a call center, Ecommerce web sites, etc. By putting additional sales and marketing resources behind products, resellers often extend a brand's market presence, adding value in the long-run.

- For resellers, do they have their own Ecommerce channel? How are your products and brand represented there? How well are they displayed and how prominently?

- What role do personal connections play in channel partners' relationships with the end customer? Be critical of how much this really matters (particularly to younger, digitally-native buyers).

- What systems and investments might the end customer have made with your resellers to ease the friction of doing business, such as electronic data interchange (EDI) or other automated ordering systems?

- What potential does each channel have to increase sales if additional investments are made in your own Ecommerce systems and product data improvements?

When conducting this exercise, it is critical to identify each channel's value while also identifying how each channel is likely to change over time due to digital disruption. The channels ripest for change tend to be the lowest value, where historical lack of information and transparency has led to inefficiencies in the value chain, such as cases where the end customer is paying more only due to habit or lack of a viable alternative channel.

For example, take a look in the B2C world of consumer automotive sales. Once upon a time, car buyers would have to go from dealer to dealer to compare products, prices, incentives, and financing options. Print magazines and word of mouth were the only ways to obtain peer feedback and professional vehicle reviews. This was a lot of work for the prospective car owner, and more often than not, buyers would only visit one or two dealers, and then succumb to an irresistible offer from a skilled car sales person. Car dealers counted on this. There was no transparency in terms of price, real MSRP, real value, etc. Buyers had to take the dealer's word for it that a car was appropriately priced. And usually the buyer ended up paying too much.

Not so any longer. Today, buyers have access to a much larger amount of information about cars. They can look up to see how well a model has retained its value over time. They can look online to compare pricing and offers from different dealers. They can see the MSRPs on both car brands' web sites and also third-party sites like Edmunds.com. Consumers can find what experts would consider a fair retail price for a new or used car, and obtain consumer and professional reviews of every model of car that has ever existed. They can even buy a car online, such as through eBay Automotive, essentially eliminating the need for difficult negotiations.

The truth is that power has shifted from the auto dealers, who used to have full control of information, to the consumer, who is now fully empowered with extensive details about what they should look for in terms of options and price. The consumer's newfound power has had an impact on dealers, too, flattening margins.[43] In fact, according to the National Automotive Dealers Association (or NADA), gross profit to dealers on new automobile sales fell from over 10 percent in 1979 to under 4 percent in 2013.[44] As a result, dealers have been forced to up their game and differentiate in new ways, particularly around things like service, innovative financing offers, extended warranties, and leasing programs. New channels for buying have opened up, complete with a new transparency around price, and as a result the value of traditional channels in this category have changed.

Look at the trends in your business and be honest about what they are telling you. In the case where you find you can't be objective, an independent consultant may be helpful, and can look at the data from an impartial viewpoint. The fact of the matter is that traditional selling channels are typically laden with long-term personal relationships that can also be friendships, and removing yourself from the process is often the best approach to obtain a real picture of what is happening.

CASE STUDY

Avery: Moving Closer to the End Customer

A brand controlling its own digital destiny

Avery Products Corporation manufactures stationery, name badges, labels, dividers, cards, loose-leaf fillers, and related products, and is a worldwide leader in its category. The company

---

43   https://maxdigital.com/blog/internet-changed-car-dealerships-gross-margin-profit-ability/
44   https://images.app.goo.gl/EwzP1RbapEQfpqv27

is a division of CCL Industries, a specialty label and packaging solutions provider to global corporations, small businesses, and consumers. You've probably seen Avery's products in many office supply stores such as Staples and Office Depot, at distributors such as SP Richards, and in online storefronts such as Amazon.

With thousands of businesses and consumers as customers, and many ways of reaching these buyers, Avery has to carefully manage how the company approaches its selling channels. Resellers have traditionally been responsible for the majority of Avery's sales, and most of these companies have their own sophisticated Ecommerce operations. Why, then, would Avery launch its own direct to consumer (B2C) and direct to business buyer (B2B) online selling channels?

There are many reasons.

"We wanted to control our own destiny," says Ricky Hernandez, Avery's Senior Director, Sales and Merchandising, Ecommerce Channel. "We needed to get closer to understanding our ultimate customer, those who actually use our products in their day-to-day life. This helps us not only maintain and grow sales through Ecommerce, but also helps us in product development and enables us to quickly respond to all types of customer needs."

The company has found an innovative approach to managing potential conflict by proactively taking control while being transparent across all channels. Avery works hard to clearly communicate with its resale partners about what it is doing and why, even as the company's own resellers respond to market and buyer behavior changes. For example, retailers like Staples and Office Depot have launched their own private label versions of Avery's products in recent years, selling these store-branded products via their own web sites alongside Avery's offerings. As a result, Avery looked to its own Ecommerce efforts to continue to support the company's position in the market. Avery started selling directly to consumers and businesses via Ecommerce, something they hadn't done previously.

And something surprising happened when they did this. The firm found that the efforts needed to prepare product information and systems for their own web sites allowed them to better support their resale partners. For example, Avery's team can now provide accurate product information in electronic format for use on resellers' Ecommerce web sites. They can gather and provide this information very quickly, allowing them to be responsive to reseller needs. They use this approach in communicating how the company's internal Ecommerce endeavors can benefit resale partners.

By taking control of the Ecommerce sales channel, Avery is now better able to focus on improving products, proactively managing its brand on the Internet, and supporting all sales channels. Today close to 60 percent of Avery's total business happens online, through Avery's own sites and through resellers' web sites. The company's proactive and transparent approach has allowed them to achieve this result.

Clearly Articulate a Pricing Approach, Organized by Channel

Because price is the center friction point that creates channel conflict, it is critical to understand the pricing dynamics in your market. Begin by understanding the gross margin profile on your products, and the economic benefits you can achieve by selling direct via Ecommerce. Some key questions to ask regarding your pricing approach include:

- What "retail" or resale price (the price paid by the ultimate user of your products) has the market supported over the past two to three years for your products through each resale channel?

- What are the pricing trends in each resale channel?

- Based on pricing history and trends, how much overall margin do you have to work with—your cost versus the ultimate resale price?

- How does each sales channel price your products? And do they typically offer discounts on your (or their) list pricing? Do they use promotions and similar tools via Ecommerce/direct channels? If you sell thousands of products, you might approach this at a category level instead of product level to make data analysis more manageable.

- How is the price to the end customer typically determined and managed? E.g. Are there contractual, private pricing relationships that are negotiated, or is the product bought at a published resale price, such as an MSRP, from a web site or catalog?

Your pricing approach for direct selling efforts via Ecommerce can include the following tactics:

- Set a clear Manufacturer's Minimum Advertised Price (MAP) and enforce it. This is a channel-agnostic and well-documented policy that informs all channels what you regard as the pricing that is acceptable to present publicly. Note that MAP policies can be difficult to enforce legally, and need to be deployed in a channel-agnostic manner, but they are clear lines in the sand that help manufacturers and brands manage selling channels. Of course, you should honor your own MAP policy on your Ecommerce site, at least for any public-facing pricing.

MANAGING CHANNELS: APPLE

The classic example of this is Apple, which sells its products across three distinct channels: Online, in Apple-branded retail stores, and through third-party resellers like Verizon, AT&T, Best Buy, and Wal-mart. With each of its channel partners, it dictates the reseller's margin uniformly regardless of the partner's size and volume of sales. They do this by controlling the wholesale discount given, which removes any incentive to offer consumer discounts. In fact, Apple often encourages resellers to go the opposite route, to sell their products at a higher price, using financial incentives to advertise Apple products at a "minimum advertised price." This ultimately encourages resellers to sell Apple products at the uniform MSRP.[45] Apple's example clearly illustrates that when you have a great product that's in high demand, you have channel leverage. Not every manufacturer or brand can do this, to be sure, but it provides a compelling example of how channel conflict can be managed.

- Set public-facing pricing—i.e. the pricing that anyone looking at your web site sees—to a level that is reflective of your other channels' web site pricing. One of my clients does this so that no matter where current or prospective customers look on the Internet, they see the same pricing, so the buyer determines who to purchase from based on other factors, such as service, ease of purchase, and delivery time.

- Consider leveraging Ecommerce functionalities to offer special pricing to specific customers (or groups of customers), only displayed behind a web site login (in essence, a private web site). For example, you can

---

45   https://www.macworld.com/article/2024257/how-apple-sets-its-prices.html

use digital tools to show MSRP pricing on the public-facing web site, but once a customer logs into their wholesale account, they are presented with customer-specific pricing levels, perhaps reflective of contracted discounts. Moreover, if you have different customer segments using the same web site, Ecommerce tools allow you to expose price selectively based on the customer login and account type. In other words, one segment gets to see one price, while a different, unrelated segment is presented with a different price. Some B2B Ecommerce sellers I work with don't even display pricing online until a customer logs in. The point is that there are a variety of ways to use tools to manage pricing visibility on your web site.

- Assortment variation is another tactic that can be very effective in managing channel conflict. You might consider repurposing an existing product line with a different brand name or feature set, or even create a new product line just for direct selling. For example, I work with a well-established manufacturer of a wide variety of garden and home décor products. The company generates over $350 million in revenue per year, and sells its products to numerous major retailers as well as distributors. They recently started selling directly to consumers under a separate brand, but leveraging the same great products. This portion of their business, which is entirely Ecommerce and marketplace driven, has quickly grown to over $20 million in revenue, and continues to grow by 50 percent per year.

Don't forget that when you move into Ecommerce, you have other tools, such as free shipping, that you can use to influence the sale without impacting the price that is displayed or publicly accessible to your channels. Whatever your approach, you must understand and track pricing by channel on an ongoing basis.

A good plan will recognize and anticipate potential channel conflicts around price and address price fluctuations as you go to market. As you execute an Ecommerce strategy, you may find opportunities to be more aggressive within some customer segments or geographies, particularly in new market segments that are not addressed effectively by your traditional resellers. The bottom line is that you need to know where and when you can be aggressive, and where and when you can't.

Develop a Communication Strategy for Each Channel

Managing channel relationships starts with managing the relationship holders in your own firm. As we discussed in the previous chapter, your internal team may fight against Ecommerce efforts, or, at minimum, maintain concerns about its impact on the relationships they have with their customers. This is why it is essential to gain alignment with internal relationship managers before broaching any potential conflicts with resale channels (such as distributors, retailers, and other resellers). It is critical to present a unified front, as this is a major point of friction (see Chapters 2, 3, and 5 to find approaches to gain organizational alignment).

Once you achieve internal alignment, then it is time to get the channel partners involved, and address each selling channel with its own communications strategy. Surprising channel partners should be avoided, and long-term relationships should be respected and managed with a transparent, business-focused approach that clearly communicates why you are starting an Ecommerce operation. The communication should start from the top, with the CEO reaching out to the top people at each channel partner to explain what you are doing, how you are doing it, and how it will benefit the channel. Craft talking points informed by the understanding you gained from the analysis described earlier in this chapter. Consider including the following items in your discussions:

- Observations about the channel partner's purchasing habits and preferences, and how product research and purchasing behaviors are increasingly accomplished via digital means.

- Your "retail" pricing approach, and how it will be managed.

- Your MAP (minimum advertised price) policy, clarifying how you will support the resale price across the market, which will help them maintain margin on the products they sell.

- Improved channel support with enhanced product information, digital capabilities, and systems integrations. As the channel partners' own selling efforts become increasingly digital, you will be better able to support them based on your own Ecommerce skills and capabilities.

- Your expectations and projections caused by the "halo" effect, which tends to lift web site traffic and interest for the entire ecosystem of sellers of a brands' product as manufacturers and brands implement broader digital marketing and awareness efforts. This has been shown for years in the B2C market, where some brands even refer traffic to resellers' web sites for purchases, in addition to selling on their own web sites.

- Better sales team support in the field using digital means, such as access to real-time pricing and inventory data.

- New versus existing markets, and how Ecommerce may impact each. As a brand or manufacturer entering direct selling via Ecommerce, you may target a different market segment than your resellers have traditionally focused on. For example, when one plumbing supply company I work with went to market with Ecommerce, they focused on their desire to enter the Maintenance Repair Operations (MRO) market when discussing their Ecommerce approach with resellers, which is a market that their traditional retail partners do not focus on.

Ultimately, channel partners will come to recognize that the world is changing, and digital is now at the center of customer behavior and the buyer's decision making processes. The perception of the risks of channel conflict is often larger than the reality, and the fear of retaliation by channel partners is typically much greater than what actually occurs. An easy way to gauge this is to simply ask channel partners (in private, where public huffing and puffing is not necessary) about trends they are seeing among their other suppliers. In the B2C market, you will be hard pressed to find a manufacturer or brand that is not selling direct to consumer. This is coming to B2B markets, and resellers generally know it.

CASE STUDY

Bollman Hats: Evolving to Transparency

"Our channel partners ultimately welcomed our direct selling approach"

Bollman Hat Company is America's oldest hat maker. Founded in 1868 in Adamstown, Pennsylvania, Bollman manufactures men's and women's hats under multiple brand names, including Baily, Kangol, Helen Kaminski, Country Gentleman, Betmar, Pantropic, and others. It is a market leader in its category, both in the United States and globally. The company has multiple sales channels, including B2B wholesale selling to resellers such as boutique retailers, department stores, and online retailers. The company also has its own Ecommerce sites and retail stores.

As you might imagine, with so many selling channels come many potential channel conflicts. As an early entrant into Ecommerce in the late 1990s, the company has an interesting story of evolution.

When Bollman first launched an Ecommerce site, the company did it by leveraging an alternative brand name.

"We bought the web site Hats.com as the first step," says Denise Foley, Bollman's Ecommerce leader. "We were worried our retailers would react negatively if we were engaged in direct selling to end customers, and we were concerned about a potential backlash, that they would stop buying our products."

As a result, Bollman set up Hats.com as a separate company, even establishing a separate legal corporate structure. The company established a minimum advertised price (MAP) policy, and stuck to it on their own web site. This approach was designed to create an arm's length relationship to their own direct to consumer operations, and a level playing field for their retailers.

"We were not trying to hide what we were doing but we also didn't make a big announcement to our existing customers," says Foley. "Hats.com sold our brands online before most of our wholesale customers even had an online presence."

Over the years, the company grew its Ecommerce sales on Hats.com, and it added considerable revenue. After some time, retailers and resellers learned that Bollman was operating Hats. com. Surprisingly, there was very little backlash.

"We eventually learned through experience that our resale channels expected us to control our presence on the Internet as the leading manufacturer in the category, and Ecommerce is a part of this," says Foley. "By exposing our entire catalog online, we can present more assortment than is available through our resale partners, and this helps us drive more demand across all channels. We manage retail pricing carefully, and we found that our channel partners respect this and ultimately welcome it."

Bollman has also developed strong fulfillment capabilities, shipping smaller orders directly to customers. This has helped the company move into drop shipping on behalf of its resale partners, in which Bollman ships smaller orders taken on its retail partners' web sites directly to the retailers' customers. Adding this service has strengthened Bollman's partnerships with resellers, and has also helped them expand Bollman's product offerings on their own Ecommerce sites while simultaneously easing the inventory burden on its partners.

Today, Bollman sells through multiple web sites and is open and transparent with its resale partners on how it approaches and manages the Ecommerce channel. As a result, the company is well-positioned to continue to grow as buyer purchase preferences accelerate their shift towards Ecommerce channels.

If You Can't Beat 'em, Build 'em.

The old adage, "If you can't beat 'em, join 'em," somewhat applies to issues surrounding channel conflict, though many companies today are not "joining," but rather building their own marketplaces. This helps manufacturers to maintain control over their online sales while also supporting traditional resellers. Often, these online marketplaces are more complex than a basic, transactional Ecommerce web site.

The strategy here is two fold: 1) to build an online portal for selling your products (including potentially reselling products from other manufacturers), and 2) to become the central locus where anyone in your industry can buy and sell products, including resellers who can operate storefronts within the manufacturer's marketplace. In some ways, this is becoming the "Amazon" of your industry. Leveraging your deep industry knowledge and authority to become an online destination for products in your category. This approach has been used successfully in B2C Ecommerce; Best Buy, for example, allows resellers to sell products on Best Buy's site. B2B firms are now catching on.

Case in point: Honeywell Aerospace. This $14 billion division of Honeywell International built a B2B aviation marketplace, where at least six other aerospace companies have set up storefronts. It calls the marketplace "GoDirect Trade." Their goal in doing this was to "provide more details on products and pricing than has been traditionally available in the industry." And so far, it appears to be gaining traction. For example, the firm reported the sale of a $100,000 jet engine completely transacted online.[46] Honeywell hopes to grow this marketplace to at least 100 marketplace sellers by the end of 2020, filling a B2B Ecommerce need they identified in their

---

46   https://www.digitalcommerce360.com/2019/03/27/a-sky-high-ecommerce-sale-1-1-million-for-a-jet-engine

industry. While this might not seem like anything new to B2C marketplace shoppers, this approach is a revolutionary idea in an industry where business has been traditionally conducted via email or phone. The move made a lot of sense to Honeywell, given that many manufacturers in their space do not have Ecommerce capabilities themselves. By offering a platform where these firms can sell their products, Honeywell has made buying and selling avionics parts more transparent and efficient, and has positioned itself to become a central hub in its industry.

While this sounds more complex than simply building your own Ecommerce web site, you might be surprised to learn that an entire segment of Ecommerce software is devoted directly to providing marketplace platform capabilities. One such company is Mirakl, which offers both B2B and B2C versions of its marketplace platform. In deploying numerous B2B implementations for companies such as Hewlett Packard Enterprise, Toyota Material Handling, and Siemens, the company has found three distinct use cases for its platforms in the B2B arena:

- Distributors: Online marketplaces allow distributors to extend their product assortment without having to maintain a larger stock. Sellers typically ship products sold on the marketplace directly to buyers using their own inventory, not stock held at the distributor.

- Manufacturers (like Honeywell): Marketplaces allow product manufacturers to avoid competition with their channels by providing a place for distributors to resell both the manufacturer's products as well as complementary and even competitive products. This enables the marketplace operator to gather information about potential competitors as well as deeper customer data, while also maintaining the customer relationship and attracting more traffic to the company's web site.

- Procurement: Marketplaces can help companies more rapidly digitize their businesses by easing the process of onboarding suppliers; pushing the considerable work of creating great online content to outside suppliers speeds digital transformation and procurement of new products for the marketplace operator.

It is important to understand that in each of these situations, the business building the marketplace is not trying to simply outsell their competition. In fact, the marketplace approach can be somewhat counter-intuitive. Enabling more competition within your product category can actually lead to additional competitive intelligence and stronger overall strategic position for the marketplace operator. By opening a marketplace where buyers can find superior information and procure more products, these firms are creating a destination that buyers will likely turn to more frequently, and thus positioning the marketplace in a central role in the industry. Marketplaces can be a source of incremental revenue for the firms that manage them, as they typically are structured to collect commissions on sales completed through the platform. While this may not be a solution for every B2B company, it certainly can be an effective—and lucrative—way to manage channel conflict.

Recognize the Reality and Act

Many companies that are exploring B2B Ecommerce are rightfully concerned about channel conflict, and there should be no question that it needs to be managed during the execution of an Ecommerce initiative. B2B companies need to pay close attention to the end customer and prioritize their needs above traditional relationships.

Confront the reality of what is happening across channels, and do not be a slave to traditional selling channels. Without the desire and accompanying action to evolve into a digital-first company, you risk losing relevance altogether. Your competitors will be there to take advantage of the changes I have described, regardless of your own action or inaction.

There's one other channel that I haven't addressed yet, and it's an 800 pound gorilla. It is a channel that's changing the way almost every Ecommerce or would-be Ecommerce business operates. I am talking about Amazon, of course, which is the subject of our next chapter.

Key Chapter Takeaways

- Channel conflict is a valid concern for manufacturers, brands, and distributors, and is typically centered around price.

- However, channel conflict is not a reason to avoid pursuing a digital transformation strategy, including Ecommerce, as it can be managed.

- A plan for managing channel conflict for manufacturers and brands should be part of the overall Ecommerce deployment plan, consisting of three components:

  - Definition of each selling channel's capabilities and value

  - Clearly articulated approach to product price, by channel

  - Communication strategy for each channel

- Multiple methods exist for a manufacturer to manage price, including Minimum Advertised Price policies, managing publicly displayed pricing, and alternative selling brands and product line variations.

- Communication to channels should be clear and respect channel relationships, while also acknowledging business realities and highlighting benefits to channel partners that will result from a manufacturer's own digital and Ecommerce presence.

- A marketplace strategy provides an additional, innovative approach to managing channel conflict, as it allows both manufacturers and resellers, such as distributors, to sell via a central online hub offering a broad assortment of products targeted to specific industries. Software packages are now commercially available to enable B2B companies to more easily and quickly deploy these marketplaces.

The
Amazon Chapter

7

I t should be painfully obvious that it's impossible to discuss any form of Ecommerce—B2B or otherwise—without discussing Amazon. Amazon is a dominant force in Ecommerce and beyond. No other company has had such a profound impact on how consumers and businesses purchase products. Amazon has transformed how people shop and set the bar for online experience, post-purchase fulfillment, digital merchandising, and marketing. In many ways, Amazon is the spark that has ignited the fires of change in the B2B world.

At its core, Amazon is a disruptive juggernaut that is disintermediating traditional sales and distribution channels. In 2017, it accounted for a whopping 60 percent of all online sales growth in the United States, and in 2018, it accounted for over 40 percent of overall growth.[47] Its impact is being felt on traditional resale channels. As an example from the retail sector, just take a look at Circuit City, Borders Books, Toys 'R' Us, CompUSA, Linens 'n Things, Sports Authority, Sears, and many other big box retailers—all of which have been forced to shutter their doors, in great part due to Amazon. Similarly, Amazon emerged in 2018 as the largest apparel retailer in the United States, surpassing Macy's and Walmart. There is a growing list of apparel retailers that are falling off the map or are severely threatened, including The Limited,

---

47 http://www.marketwatch.com/story/amazon-accounted-for-60-of-online-sales-growth-in-2015-2016-05-03

Charlotte Russe, American Apparel, Wet Seal, BCBG, Diesel, True Religion, and numerous others. From sports equipment to consumer electronics, from department stores to specialty products, and many more categories, Amazon is disrupting nearly every retail industry.

Consider the following graphic, which shows Amazon's percentage of total retail Ecommerce sales in the United States as of early 2019 in various product categories.

Amazon Retail Ecommerce Sales Share, by Product Category
US, 2019, % of total

% of Total Retail Ecommerce Sales

Apparel & accessories — 37.5%

Auto & parts — 15.8%

Book music & video — 79.5%

Computer & consumer electronic — 55.5%

Food & beverage — 32.7%

Furniture & home furnishings — 43.7%

Health, personal care & beauty — 41.0%

Office equipment & supplies — 51.2%

Other categories — 61.6%

Toys & hobby — 54.1%

Source: eMarketer, February 2019

In another staggering statistic, Amazon Prime, the company's highly successful loyalty program, is expected to be in almost 60 percent of *all* U.S. households by 2021.

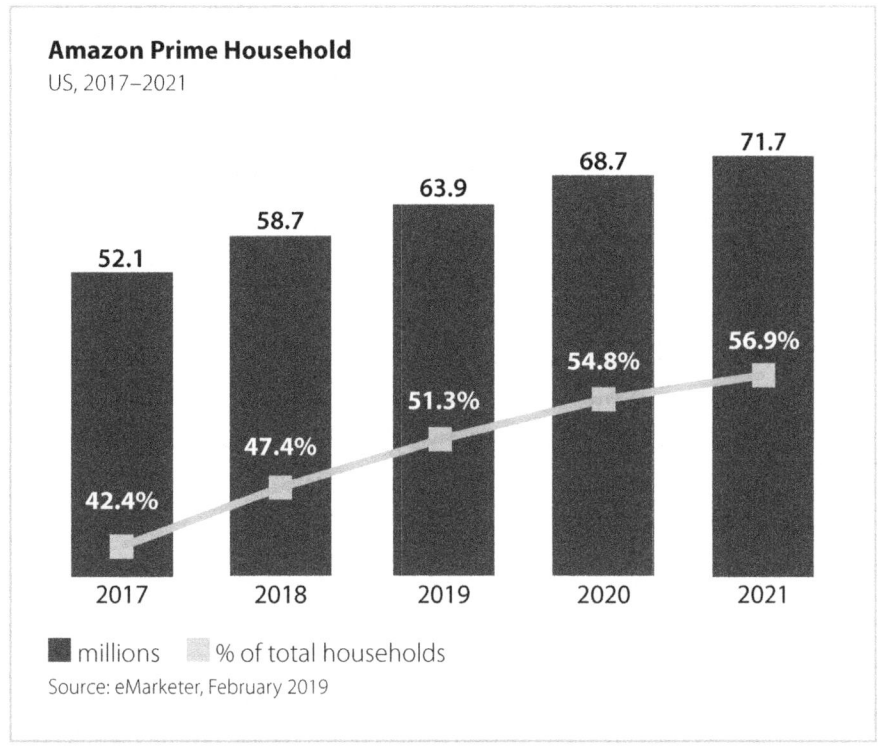

If you are a B2B manufacturer, brand, or distributor you might be thinking, "So what? Amazon is where people buy books, electronics, batteries, kid's clothes, and toilet paper." The truth, however, is that Amazon has not only changed your customers' expectations of how Ecommerce should work, but it is also investing heavily in B2B selling online.

In 2015, Amazon created Amazon Business, dedicated to capturing and growing the burgeoning demand for buying business-related items. This includes everything from a $1 box of staples to high-end commercial printers that cost thousands of dollars, from janitorial supplies to rack-mounted servers, food service equipment, and medical supplies for hospitals.

Anyone who sells products online—be they B2C or B2B—inevitably must ask themselves a question: Should we sell on Amazon or stay away? It is a tricky question to answer, but the truth is that every product merchant in today's digitally-centered world must have an Amazon strategy. Ignoring Amazon is not a strategy for success. In 2019, the company announced it had exceeded $10 billion in annual revenue for its Amazon Business unit in the prior year. That's nearly unthinkable given that it had only launched three years prior; very few businesses have ever grown this rapidly. In late 2019, RBC Capital Markets, a leading Wall Street investment bank, issued a projection indicating that Amazon Business' sales will surpass $52 Billion by 2023.[48] This puts Amazon's B2B volume ahead of all but only the largest of traditional distributors. This growth can't be ignored.

Trading Places: Amazon Is the New Google

Once upon a time, in the mid-2000s, Google was the home of ALL online search (well, the vast majority of it). It didn't matter if you were looking for a new pair of shoes, your favorite band's song lyrics, or an academic paper on Botswana's economic system. Google was the place to go. It still is, for the most part; Google has captured more than 90 percent global market share of search.[49]

However, today things have shifted, and Amazon is now the top online destination for buyers to search for products. In a Raymond James study published in 2017, 52 percent

48 https://www.cnbc.com/2019/12/06/amazon-business-a-b2b-unit-to-reach-31-billion-revenue-by-2023-rbc.html
49 https://www.businessinsider.com/how-google-retains-more-than-90-of-market-share-2018-4?IR=T

of people said that Amazon is now their first choice to begin product searches.[50] A more recent BloomReach study found that the percentage of people who start their product searches on Amazon is even higher, at 55 percent, while Google's share of product search has dropped to about 28 percent.[51] This continues a more than four-year trend for Amazon, suggesting that their share of product searches will continue to grow.

Amazon is where a huge chunk of consumers—and increasingly B2B customers—head when they are thinking about making a purchase. For that reason alone, you might think it is a no-brainer to sell your products on Amazon.

Consider this: Amazon converts buyers at a far superior rate than the average Ecommerce web site. According to a study by web site traffic measurement firm Millward Brown Digital, the average conversion rate for Top 500 Ecommerce merchants is 3.32 percent.[52] Amazon, however, converts at 13 percent for non-Prime customers and an astonishing 74 percent for Prime customers. While these numbers are impressive, they shouldn't be a shock: the buying intent of visitors to Amazon.com is extremely high.

Looking into the B2B arena, it is clear that Amazon is accelerating its efforts. It is doing this to build off of current business buyer activity on the marketplace. The number of B2B buyers beginning their product searches on Amazon is growing. A 2018 survey by B2BecNews revealed that eight out of ten business buyers were using Amazon to research and make corporate purchases online. The same study showed that only 40 percent of manufacturers and 50 percent of

---

50   https://www.geekwire.com/2017/amazon-continues-grow-lead-google-starting-point-online-shoppers/
51   http://www.prnewswire.com/news-releases/amazon-grabs-55-percent-of-consumers-first-product-search-set-to-dominate-2016-holiday-shopping-300334545.html
52   https://www.digitalcommerce360.com/2015/06/25/amazon-prime-members-convert-74-time/

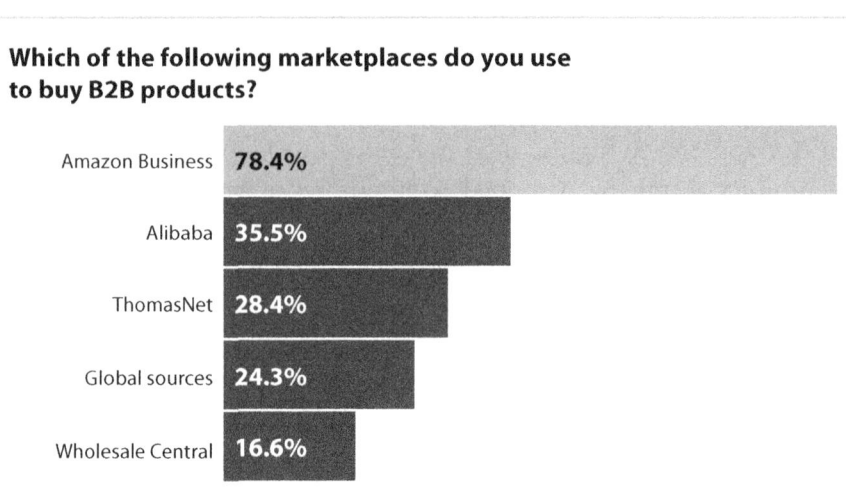

Which of the following marketplaces do you use to buy B2B products?

Amazon Business	78.4%
Alibaba	35.5%
ThomasNet	28.4%
Global sources	24.3%
Wholesale Central	16.6%

(respondents can choose multiple answers)

8 of 10 business buyers use Amazon to research and make a corporate purchase online, according to a B2BecNews survey of 110 buyers from a wide range of industries including automotive, consumer electronics, healthcare and industrial products.

distributors currently sell on Amazon.[53] B2B buyers are on Amazon, but the majority of sellers are not.

This trend is impacting traditional distribution channels in B2B. Forrester Research reported in 2017 that the number of business-product related searches starting on Amazon has now grown to equal the number of searches that begin on distributors' sites.[54] An increasing number of business buyers are finishing their shopping journeys on Amazon as well. In 2015, the percentage of B2B buyers who indicated they fin-

---

53   https://www.digitalcommerce360.com/2018/08/28/infographic-b2b-sellers-lag-behind-buyers-using-amazon/
54   *Insights into the Behavior of the Modern B2B Buyer*, 4th Annual Survey, Forrester Research, March 2017; https://cloudcraze.com/thank-you/thank-you-for-downloading-the-2017-b2b-survey-results-analysis/

ished their purchases on distributor sites was 30 percent. In 2017, just two years later, that number had plummeted to 16 percent, with 40 percent saying they use Amazon to complete purchases.[55] Business buyers are flocking to sites that are easy to use, are fast loading, have broad selection, do not have complicated login requirements, and maintain built-in trust. Amazon does these things better than anyone and is seizing market share from traditional channels in the process. It is quickly becoming a major distribution channel that product sellers can leverage to drive sales. According to Forrester, by 2020, it is expected that B2B buyers will make over half of their purchases online—a trend that is only beginning, but accelerating quickly.[56] What is important to note are the drivers for this shift: convenience, speed, and price. And Amazon is exceptional in delivering customer value in all three areas.

This has a vital implication for brands, manufacturers, distributors, retailers, and other resellers across the B2C and B2B spectrum: not being listed on Amazon creates risk of obscurity and irrelevance for your company. The rate of return on "traditional" internet marketing methods for products—using Search Engine Optimization and Paid Search tactics to drive traffic to products on a branded web site experience (for details on these marketing approaches see Chapter 8)—is decaying. Yes, branded product web sites remain relevant and should provide a powerful customer experience, and are the central component of a digital transformation strategy. However, the role the site plays in product discovery is less prominent than it once was as customers' product search behavior shifts in favor of Amazon.

---

55 Ibid.
56 Ibid.

The Amazon Conundrum

Product sellers face a conundrum. Sell on Amazon, and you get access to the enormous Amazon customer base and the sales it can provide. But Amazon limits your ability to directly re-market to customers buying your products through the marketplace. You do not "own" the customer relationship, which also means you cannot necessarily grow it.

Some companies choose not to sell on the platform due to fear they are "teaching" Amazon their business. By selling as a marketplace merchant, these companies believe they may be enabling Amazon to become a highly capable future competitor by providing product, sales, market, and customer data, all without Amazon needing to take any inventory risk.

Additionally, some merchants are concerned with the commission Amazon takes when selling their products. Depending on the specific products offered, Amazon takes somewhere between eight percent and 15 percent on each transaction.[57] Some product categories command even higher rates, up to 45 percent.

Still, a large percentage of Amazon's shipments are products that are owned and sold by third-party merchants, running storefronts they control on the Amazon marketplace (vs. selling to Amazon as a wholesaler, called "first party selling"). According to Business Insider, third-party merchants are responsible for as much as 83 percent of the sales made on the Ecommerce platform.[58]

Jeff Bezos' the founder of Amazon, publicly celebrated the growth of third-party merchants, noting in his 2018 letter to shareholders, "Third-party sellers are kicking our first-party butt. Badly." He went on to highlight the emphasis Amazon has put on growing third party selling. "Why were

---

57   https://services.amazon.com/selling/pricing.html
58   http://www.businessinsider.com/third-party-merchants-drive-amazon-grow-2015-10

independent [third-party] sellers able to grow so much faster than Amazon's own highly organized first-party sales organization?" asked Bezos, rhetorically. He continues, "There isn't one answer, but we do know one extremely important part of the answer: We helped independent sellers compete against our first-party business by investing in and offering them the very best selling tools we could imagine and build. There are many such tools, including tools that help sellers manage inventory, process payments, track shipments, create reports, and sell across borders–and we're inventing more every year."[59]

Amazon's business model is highly reliant on merchant-provided assortment in third-party selling accounts, and as Bezos highlights in his letter, the company is constantly innovating to make it easier for sellers to manage orders through their platform. In fact, as of mid-2019, Amazon was making considerable and deliberate efforts to shift its product assortment towards third-party merchants versus products it buys from manufacturers and resells via its first party approach. The company was converting traditional wholesale first-party manufacturer relationships to marketplace sellers, where Amazon doesn't purchase products at wholesale, but instead allows manufacturers to sell themselves via the Amazon marketplace. This may feel like bad news to traditional wholesale suppliers to Amazon. However, I strongly believe that third-party selling is a "better deal" for brands and manufacturers, as it is a more profitable way to sell on the marketplace, though the transition from first-party to third-party can be a bit painful and takes time.

So, if you are just starting to consider Amazon, should your business dive into Amazon to take advantage of the sheer number of customers there? Or are you better off sticking

---

59   https://blog.aboutamazon.com/company-news/2018-letter-to-shareholders

with your own web site and possibly other marketplaces out of fear of Amazon deciding to compete directly against you?

Amazon's Investments in B2B

Let's take a closer look at what Amazon is doing in the B2B space. Since 2015, the company has been investing heavily in enabling business buyers to purchase online using the same tools and user experiences that they have become accustomed to as consumers. The company calls this Amazon Business, and it is now digitally supporting traditional B2B workflows and customers' purchasing expectations.

Amazon's efforts include:

- Hiring People: Amazon is a metrics-driven execution machine that hires very smart people. Over the last few years, Amazon promised to add 100,000 jobs— from engineers and software developers to warehouse workers—between 2017 and 2020 in order to meet growing demand.[60] This is important to B2B segments, as many of the people they are hiring are right out of traditional industries. These are people who are familiar with channel dynamics, product differentiation, and the nuances of B2B selling; e.g. people who understand where inefficiencies lie in traditional selling channels and how to capitalize on them.

- Acquiring Business Buyers in Key Sectors: For example, in 2017 Amazon secured a major public sector contract that enabled procurement processes at public agencies and nonprofit organizations to be

---

60   https://www.nytimes.com/2017/01/12/business/economy/amazon-jobs-retail.html

handled through Amazon. The multi-year contract is worth as much as $5.5 billion.[61] Amazon has a growing sales team that is out in the field recruiting both business buyers and sellers just like you and your competitors to its platform, building out its B2B marketplace ecosystem. *Putting sales people in the field is new for Amazon* and a sign that the company now understands what it will take to build out Amazon Business.

- Integrating with Procurement Systems: Amazon is integrating with a number of the most common procurement software platforms utilized by corporate and institutional buyers (more than 40 platforms to date). This enables business buyers to use their enterprise systems, such as the ERP (enterprise resource planning system), to buy products through Amazon. In other words, procurement teams can now buy things using Amazon in the same way that they buy something from other vendors through their ERP.

- Creating B2B Workflows and Functionalities: Amazon has added key functionalities that are required by business buyers and sellers, such as support for tiered pricing and purchase approval processes. They are even extending business credit terms to buyers, enabling buyers to obtain traditional payment terms such as Net 15, 30, 60, or 90.

- Amazon also recently extended Amazon Prime to business buyers, allowing businesses to become Prime members and take advantage of free shipping and

---

61   https://www.opi.net/business/large-resellers/amazon-businesss-5-5-billion-public-sector-land-grab/

other program benefits, such as streaming music and other content.

And these investments have been paying off. After only three years operating, Amazon has grown its business division to eight countries and more than $10 billion in revenues.[62] Combine these investments with the fact that Amazon is probably ten years ahead of most other companies in terms of how they use data to personalize digital experiences, and the evidence that many business buyers are *already* buying on Amazon, and you have a brutal reality to confront. Disintermediation has started.

This Is Good News for Brands and Manufacturers

. . . if you confront the brutal reality!

If for some reason you have skipped ahead to this chapter, you may have missed this key point: traditional sales channels are changing. The digital world is quickly moving to the forefront, and companies that ignore these changes are putting themselves in peril. Nowhere is this more apparent than by looking at the impact of Amazon on multiple B2B industry categories.

Consider the following examples:

- Amazon is making considerable inroads in the janitorial/sanitation category. One of the largest traditional distributors in the category, $5 billion company Essendant, reported an 8.9 percent drop in sales in this product category in 2017, largely

---

62 https://www.digitalcommerce360.com/2018/09/11/amazon-business-surpasses-10-billion-in-annualized-sales/

attributed by industry analysts to competition from Amazon.[63]

- In the Maintenance Repair Operations (MRO) category, Amazon has been attributed to taking volume from some of the largest players. Notably, in 2017, Grainger—widely considered an industry leader in Ecommerce—reported its first downward earnings trend in many years, and reduced pricing on many products to help drive top line revenue.[64] Analysts have been predicting this for a number of years, and expect Amazon Business to continue to exert increased pressure on long-time industry leaders.[65]

- Amazon generated about $3 billion in sales of auto parts in 2017, growing at close to 20 percent per year. O'Reilly Automotive, AutoZone, and Advance Auto Parts have all slipped from their highs in the stock market since Amazon's push into this category.[66]

While these impacts can be viewed as negative to resellers, Amazon's impact to traditional distributors is actually a huge opportunity for manufacturers and brands. If you are one of these two types of businesses, launching on Amazon Business will give you the immediate opportunity to:

- Drive incremental revenue and capture new customers.

---

63 https://www.digitalcommerce360.com/2018/03/07/jansan-distributors-grasp-digital-commerce/

64 https://seekingalpha.com/article/4073097-w-w-grainger-amazon-effect

65 http://investcorrectly.com/20150701/amazon-com-inc-amzns-amazon-business-impact-margins-fastenal-company-fast-w-w-grainger-inc-gww/

66 https://www.ratchetandwrench.com/articles/5175-report-details-how-amazon-is-disrupting-the-automotive-aftermarket

- Stay relevant to existing customers, many of whom are already loyal Amazon buyers who use Amazon for their businesses.

- Position yourself ahead of your competitors. The window of opportunity is open now but it likely will not last. For evidence of this, you can reference Amazon's closed categories on the retail side of their business, where they have enormous assortment and are not allowing new suppliers/sellers to launch on their marketplace. B2B sellers have some leverage at this moment to capitalize on Amazon's efforts to build out their B2B marketplace. It is an advantage to get there before your competitors do.

- Take control of how your brand is positioned on this rapidly growing channel. As a fun and somewhat disturbing exercise, try searching for one of your products right now on Amazon. I do this with CEOs all the time, and it immediately and invariably causes instant anxiety when the CEO sees how their brand shows up on the number one place people are looking for their products. Most of the time, the brand does not present well. Poor product information and rogue sellers the company has no knowledge of often make up the majority of search results, and prices are likely below where the company would like them to be. By leveraging a Seller Central (third-party Amazon Marketplace) account, you can control the pricing of your product and your brand on Amazon.

- Ignore Amazon's B2B efforts now, and you will be playing catch up later. If you are a brand or manufacturer, you need to control your destiny on this marketplace. In my opinion, there is no reason not to, especially if your products are truly differentiated and can't easily be replaced by a substitute. Any potential threats that Amazon may pose can be limited or even avoided by taking control of your brand on the platform; overlooking it will almost certainly have a negative impact on your business.

Key Questions for Determining the Best Approach

How should you approach Amazon? As a business owner, brand, manufacturer, or distributor, there is no single right answer. The correct path for you will depend on your business model, your product, the products' strengths and weaknesses, your risk tolerance, and your willingness to invest resources into managing sales on Amazon. Consider the following:

Does your product stand on its own?

To be differentiated on Amazon (or any marketplace, for that matter), your products need to stand on their own, i.e. they must have enough unique user benefits, so that customers understand they are buying something that is yours—not Amazon's. You do not have as much of an opportunity to differentiate based on service or experience when selling through Amazon, as you might using other channels. The more your product and its benefits are clear, the better positioned you are to take advantage of the brand building opportunities of selling through this channel. If you control the manufacturing of the product (i.e. you are the sole source), you will be in the driver's seat in terms of leveraging Amazon's power to expand sales and brand recognition.

On the other hand, if you make a product that is a commodity, or your differentiation is something other than the product itself (e.g. service or support), leveraging Amazon's platform may pose a challenge. It will be more difficult to differentiate your product, but more importantly, you may experience downward pressure on price and profit margins, as well as expose yourself to risk if Amazon becomes a high percentage of your revenue. For example, should Amazon change their selling terms or even directly enter the market as a competitor by directly sourcing private label products, it will increasingly be difficult to retain the same revenue and profits you have enjoyed. This is particularly risky if you have invested heavily in personnel, processes, and technology to support the marketplace.

Do you have enough resources?

You need to understand and be ready to cover the expenses for managing product information, order flow, shipping updates, marketing activities, and other overhead needed to effectively sell on Amazon. This includes staffing to support ongoing platform management and fulfillment, as well as content optimization, marketing, and other related expenses. You also need to be able to meet their very strict performance guidelines for customer service, which often means additional resources. The good news is that there are third-party agencies available to help you accelerate your efforts to enter the marketplace (a self-serving side note here: one of these firms is called Enceiba, which is a company I'm involved with and can recommend without reservation. See: www.enceiba.com for details).

These questions aside, there is enormous potential for revenue growth when you work with Amazon. A well-managed presence on the marketplace is a proven channel that many companies have used to profitably drive revenue and expand brand awareness.

CASE STUDY

Crescent Electric: Selling on, Competing with, and Learning from Amazon

As an industry-leading distributor of electrical supplies, Crescent Electric Supply Company (CESCO) knows its industry and what it takes to succeed. It has maintained its leadership position by keeping its eyes open to changing customer preferences and new distribution channels, and this self-awareness has fueled the company's evolution in the digital age.

Founded in 1919, Crescent is one of the largest electrical suppliers in the United States, with $1.5 billion in annual revenue and over 160 locations in 29 states. The company serves contractors, utilities, institutions, and industrial customers with a broad line of electrical, lighting, automation, and data communication products. It has been conducting Ecommerce for well over a decade and views online selling as a key element in providing superior customer service.

And Crescent knows that Amazon is setting the online experience expectations for its customers.

"Amazon doesn't raise the bar, it IS the bar," quips Steven Annese, Crescent's Director of E-business Strategy and Commerce. "We admire what they do and study their approach. We view Amazon as a partner, a competitor, and, perhaps most importantly, a learning experience." Crescent uses a mixed strategy of selling on the marketplace to learn first-hand how Amazon delivers value to customers, while proactively looking for ways to differentiate itself.

Annese cites several components of Amazon's strategy that Crescent emulates, including

- Putting the customer first in all decisions, over the desires of suppliers and other stakeholders.

- Trying new things, without fear of failure, and learning from mistakes. Annese cites Amazon's early unsuccessful attempts to launch auctions and later in the B2B market with Amazon Supply (the precursor to Amazon Business).

- Setting high benchmarks for customer satisfaction, including on-time shipping and ratings provided by customers on products and quality of service, and holding themselves accountable to meeting and exceeding these goals.

Crescent has adopted each of these tactics in its business and believes this has been key to its own successes in Ecommerce, which is the company's fastest growing selling channel.

As for selling on Amazon, Crescent offers a limited part of its assortment on the marketplace as a third party (3P) seller. This allows the company to keep its hand in the marketplace at a detailed level and learn how Amazon interacts with suppliers and customers.

"We have adopted tactics that Amazon uses for our own Ecommerce web site as a result of this approach," cites Annese. These include:

- Working with vendors for competitive and favorable terms (e.g. learning from Amazon's approach to managing its suppliers).

- Getting orders out the door very quickly, exceeding customer expectations for delivery; CESCO ships within a two day window.

- Minimizing product defect rates and quickly reconciling issues when they do occur.

By participating in the marketplace, Crescent can also clearly identify ways to differentiate from Amazon. "We go far beyond what Amazon will provide to buyers in terms of customer service and support," says Annese. "This includes installation and application expertise that we provide to our customers for the products we sell."

For example, Crescent maintains an expert in-house technical support team that will assist customers with their projects, including researching product compatibilities and working with product manufacturers to create technical solutions for customers. This is not something that Amazon provides.

And with this clear differentiation based on service and expertise, Crescent uses Amazon as a way to expand its own brand recognition. "A very large number of online product searches are starting on Amazon these days, and we see new customers becoming aware of our business through Amazon, based on product searches that are conducted there." This is a somewhat unexpected benefit for the company of selling on the marketplace.

In this digitally-centric age, B2B firms cannot afford to ignore Amazon. Crescent's balanced strategy allows it to learn, analyze, and most importantly, act.

How to Succeed on Amazon

Once the decision has been made to take advantage of Amazon, the question becomes how can you succeed in the marketplace. Amazon's marketing tools for sellers work similarly to other online advertising platforms (not yet to the level of Google's advertising tools, but getting there!). Following are five tips to ensure your business succeeds on Amazon. It is important to note that some of these require a significant investment in resources and advertising. However, the payback can be substantial, and the capital investment required to launch and manage a successful Amazon presence is an order of magnitude lower than launching your own Ecommerce web site. As such, it is often a great first step for your firm to dip its toe into the Ecommerce world before building your own Ecommerce web site and full-fledged operations. Additionally, it can help build knowledge and overall confidence within your organization.

1) Determine your Selling Approach (1P versus 3P)

Amazon offers several ways to sell your products on their platform. The first is called First Party (1P) selling, also known as "Vendor Central." In this approach, Amazon buys your products from you in a traditional wholesale model. They then warehouse your products, set the price, and take and ship orders to customers. You earn your typical wholesale margin, similar to what you would receive from other wholesale channels, and you do not control the price of your products on Amazon. In 1P selling, Amazon typically initiates a wholesale buying relationship, but you can also contact them to be considered. You may even encounter Amazon buying representatives at industry trade shows, where the relationships are often initially established.

The alternative way to sell on Amazon is called Third Party (3P) selling, which is also known as "Seller Central." In this approach, you set up a storefront on Amazon that you manage yourself, or a third-party agency manages it for you. In this case, you are responsible for the pricing, brand presentation, product information, fulfillment, and overall account management on Amazon. While this takes more work on your part, the 3P approach also gives you more control over how you sell your products on Amazon, including the retail prices for your products on the marketplace, and it helps you better control potential sales channel conflicts with distributors, your sales team, and your own web site.

Now, it is possible that one or more of your existing resellers are already selling your products on Amazon. This presents a unique situation that needs to be carefully handled. You can either:

- Request the reseller to not sell your products on Amazon.

- You can declare them an official "Authorized Reseller."

- You can do nothing and compete with them directly on Amazon.

How you choose to handle this situation is entirely up to you, but today, many brands and manufacturers are opting to become the sole Amazon seller in order to maintain brand and price control on this highly visible channel. Taking the 3P approach to selling, while simultaneously establishing channel resale controls for Amazon, allows brands to directly address and manage any potential channel conflict issues that arise.

It is important to note that in the 1P model, Amazon famously does not honor MAP (minimum advertised pricing) policies, and for good reason: they are laser focused on bringing value to their customers, not to their suppliers. To counter this and help to manage channel conflict, many sellers opt for the 3P approach. And, as of this writing, Amazon is beginning to dictate to manufacturers and brands which selling model they will be able to use, and is proactively removing some brands from the 1P model. These brands will be forced to implement a 3P selling approach if they wish to continue offering their products on Amazon.

2) Invest in building a foundation of great product data

Many digital marketing managers have invested a lot of time, energy, and budget into developing robust product data for their web sites. The good news is that a lot of this data is extremely relevant to Amazon's system, and can be used in setting up products for sale in the marketplace. Amazon is a data-driven company, and products with better quality data will perform at a higher level. Unfortunately, too many product listings on Amazon don't go far enough, only including a basic product photo, title and description. That simply is not sufficient.

Each product listed on Amazon needs to have a strong, highly descriptive title which incorporates product benefits, an extremely detailed product description, technical product data like size, weight, and other details, five or more images,

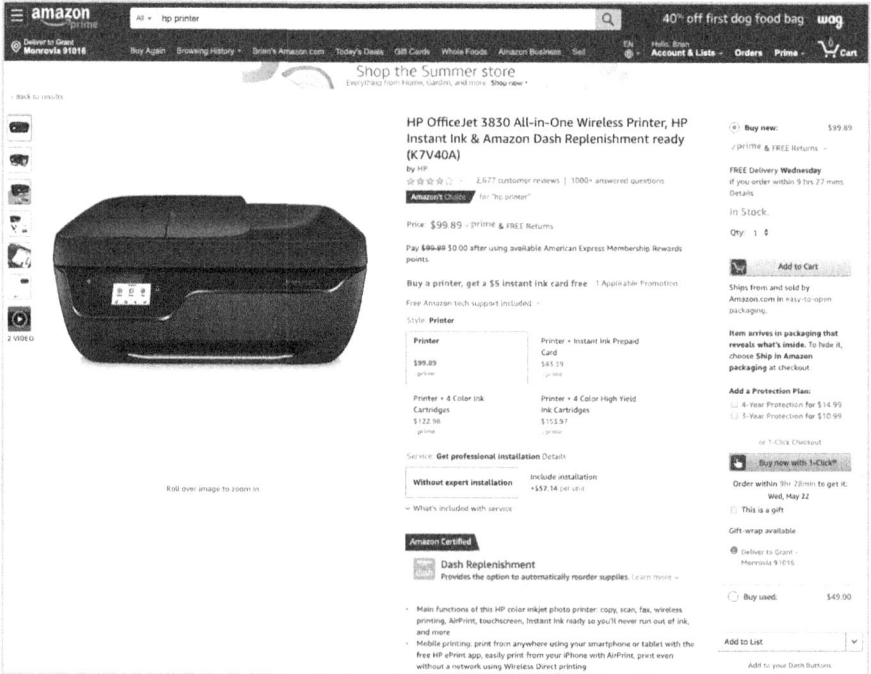

and ideally at least one video. This means that staff with excellent product knowledge is required to produce high-quality videos and photos. Over my many years in Ecommerce, I have learned that great images sell products online, and this holds true on Amazon as well. The bonus here is that you can leverage all of these assets across other selling channels. Amazon calls these great product listings "A+ Pages," and you should aim for nothing less for your listings. An example of an A+ product page from Hewlett Packard, a long time and very high volume Amazon seller, is shown in the graphic.

3) Spend time on customer engagement

You might think Amazon is simply an Ecommerce web site; it isn't. It is a consumer engagement platform and massive product search engine. And the more engaged you are in the selling and optimization process, particularly for 3P sellers, the more prominently your products are going to rank in Amazon's search results. This means:

a) *Encouraging positive product reviews:* Amazon weighs the number and ranking of product reviews very heavily in deciding what to present in search results and within category listing pages. Anything you can do to encourage satisfied customers to write a review will help your overall rankings and visibility. Tools exist in the marketplace to assist with generating reviews on your products, including Amazon's "Early Reviewer Program," which enables sellers to generate more review content, faster (for a fee, of course). Reviews should be solicited after every customer makes a purchase.

b) *Rapidly responding to all feedback:* The quality and speed of your responses is extremely important, as it impacts your seller rating, which in turn impacts visibility. Amazon sets a high bar here for response time from sellers, and you need to comply in order to achieve and retain good rankings.

c) *Monitoring competitors, testing content, and taking control of your brand:* See how your pages compare to your competitors and test micro-adjustments to the title and description to increase visibility and conversions. For 3P sellers, ongoing price monitoring is also important, particularly for manufacturers and brands who are looking to ensure resellers are not eroding selling prices on Amazon (including Amazon itself). Obtaining brand control on Amazon requires a multi-faceted approach, including:

- Registering your brand(s) on Amazon, which allows legitimate brand owners to confirm their status as the legal brand owner inside of the marketplace ecosystem. This includes supplying trademark certifications and other supporting documents, and can take as little as a few weeks, but it can take much longer if you do not already own your trademark.

- Creating a written Amazon policy that outlines your company's approach as it relates to selling in the marketplace, and then sharing it with all of your resellers. In this policy, you must identify who is eligible to sell on Amazon, and who is not. You may opt to retain this right only for your company. This type of policy should be part of an overall Internet policy document that is updated and shared on a regular basis.

- Identifying all the sellers that are offering your products on Amazon so you can understand who they are and if they have been authorized (you may be surprised to find your products being sold by someone you don't know). Consider ordering from the sellers to see how they handle the sale and deliver the products. The goal here is to clean up the channel and gain better control of who is selling, how they are selling, and align them with your Amazon policy.

- Putting an internal policing procedure in place to consistently monitor sellers and pricing on your products; software and agencies are available to help you do this.

d) *Develop a brand page:* Amazon gives brands the opportunity to build branded pages on their platform

to create a brand-appropriate experience within the marketplace. There is significant payoff to be had here: the more sales volume you do on Amazon, the more benefits you can get from them (if you get big enough, you may even qualify for "Strategic Seller" status). For examples of good brand pages, check out GE Lighting,[67] or the B2B page for Fluke Multimeters.[68] See the screen shot for a great brand page example from Black and Decker. Note the prominent use of brand imagery, lifestyle photography, and clearly laid out product categories in a menu format just below the company logo.

4) Take advantage of the advertising tools Amazon offers

Amazon offers a number of paid advertising tools that can boost product visibility, generally under the umbrella of something called Amazon Advertising (note: until September 2018, it was called Amazon Marketing Services or AMS). These tools are critical for having your products stand out amidst the millions of listings on Amazon, and can give a nice boost to sellers new to the platform. These marketing tools include:

a) *Sponsored Products:* Paid search advertisements in which a seller can purchase keywords to present relevant products at the top of the search results page when a search is executed for the purchased keyword (a similar approach to Google AdWords for those of you

---

67   https://www.amazon.com/GE-Lighting/b/ref=w_bl_hsx_s_hi_web_2592442011?
field-lbr_brands_browse-bin=GE+Lighting&ie=UTF8&node=2592442011
68   https://www.amazon.com/fluke

who have advertised on Google). Sellers pay for this
visibility on a cost per click basis (i.e. when someone
clicks an ad, the seller is charged). This drives more
visibility for your products, helping them garner more
reviews, which ultimately improves organic visibility.
Additionally, Amazon offers analytics to help users
understand and manage ad spend to improve what
is called Return on Advertising Spend (or ROAS;
see glossary for definition), or as Amazon reports it,
Amazon Cost of Sale (or ACoS, which is the percentage
of cost against revenue from the sale, and Amazon's
reporting metric for ROAS).

b) *Sponsored Brands* (banner ads, formerly known as
Headline Search Ads): These ad units are also based on
keywords, and allow sellers to showcase several products
in a single banner advertisement at the top of search
results and category pages. Sponsored Brands also
provides the ability for sellers to create targeted landing
pages on Amazon for each ad, which improves their
effectiveness.

c) *Product display ads:* These advertising units are closer to
the point of purchase, displaying on Amazon's product
pages. These ads highlight a single product, and are
displayed near the "Add to Cart" button. In theory,
marketing dollars can be more effective with this ad
unit because they are typically more targeted and there
is higher buying intent. Note, however, that at this time
Product Display Ads can only be used by 1P Vendor
Central sellers.

d) *Amazon Sponsored Display:* As of mid-2018, Amazon
offers the capability to drive traffic back to your
Amazon store by using display ads served across the
web.

Following is a graphic showing where each of these ad types show up on Amazon.

Amazon Advertising Examples on Search Results Page

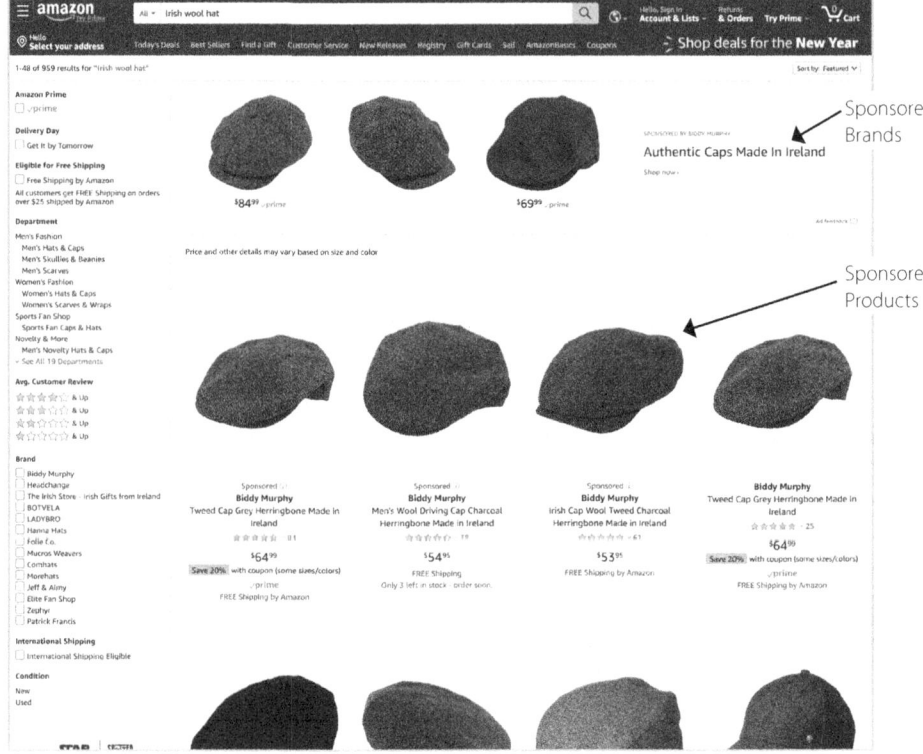

With any of these advertising tools, it is critical to have a well-organized strategy and experienced resources executing for you, just as you would for a traditional search engine marketing program. The good news here is that higher Return on Ad Spend levels are still available to sellers on Amazon, even for non-brand specific terms (similar to the advertising efficiencies that were available on Google in the mid-2000s).

Amazon Advertising Example on Product Listing Page

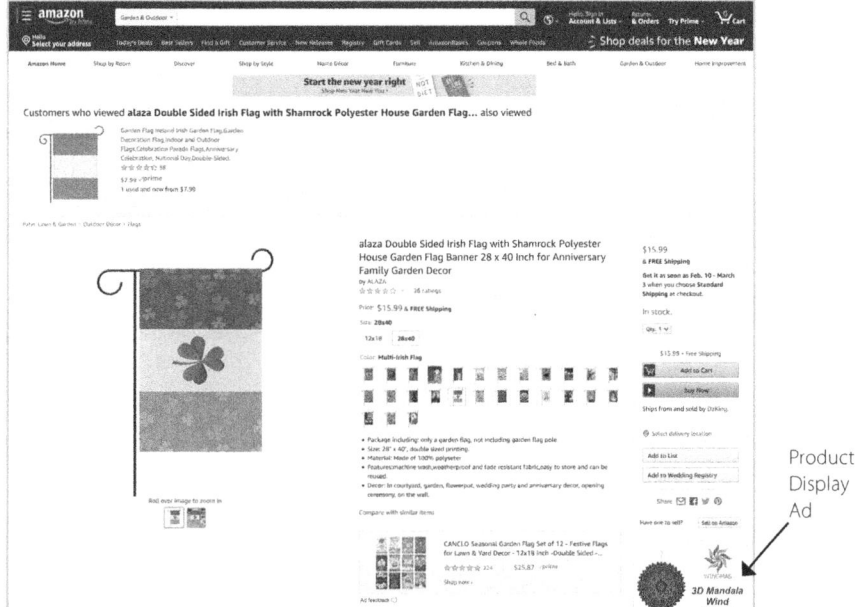

Product Display Ad

5) Make sure your fulfillment is on-point

If you are selling via 1P on Amazon, you just need to get the product to Amazon in bulk, and they take it from there, shipping individual orders to buyers. However, if you are operating as 3P seller, you are responsible to ship the product to the buyer. Several options exist for 3P marketplace sellers for fulfillment on Amazon. These include merchant fulfilled, where sellers ship orders directly to the buyer, and Fulfilled by Amazon (FBA), where sellers ship products in bulk to an

Amazon warehouse. Amazon then stores the products and ships individual orders on the seller's behalf.

There are two reasons why you need to ensure your fulfillment system works flawlessly. First, you are more likely to receive positive product and company reviews when your shipments arrive on time and the contents are accurate. Second, depending on how fulfillment is handled, your products may be eligible to be listed as eligible for Amazon Prime, the company's two day (soon to be one day) shipping program. For your products to be eligible for Prime, you either have to sell products directly to Amazon as a 1P Seller or you can leverage Fulfilled by Amazon (FBA). Amazon also recently began authorizing highly capable sellers as Prime-eligible shippers in a program called Seller Fulfilled Prime (see https:// services.amazon.com/services/ seller-fulfilled-prime.html for all the relevant details). Note that this program, as of late 2019, was not accepting new applicants and its future is in question. The bar to qualify for and operate in this program is very high, and only the most seasoned direct shippers meet its requirements. Unfortunately, some shippers already in the program have not met Amazon's fulfillment standards, which may cause a roll back of the program in the future. Being visible to Amazon Prime

Prime traffic converts

6x higher

than non--Prime traffic

Prime Members spend

4.6x more money

than non-Prime customers

Amazon Prime eligibility can increase sales on a product by as much as

30–50%

Source: Enceiba

members increases the likelihood that your products will be found and purchased.

The overriding point is that if you launch an Amazon program, you want to ensure the bulk of your products are eligible for Amazon Prime. As mentioned previously, Prime members convert at a 74 percent rate, and are estimated to number over 105 million people globally as of late 2019. Prime customers also spend 4.6x more than non-Prime members on Amazon. This is a market segment you do not want to miss capturing.

Sellers can also apply what they learn on Amazon to their own Ecommerce operations. Remember that Amazon sets the expectations for your buyers, as the vast majority of the people that buy from you, also buy from Amazon, either in their personal lives as consumers or as business buyers (or both). Smart B2B companies are not reinventing the wheel with Ecommerce. Instead, they are stealing smartly from Amazon.

Case in point is a leading manufacturer of safety supplies, Ergodyne (www.ergodyne.com). This firm constantly looks to pull ideas from Amazon.

"We see that Amazon tests digital experiences at scale, and we use this as a benchmark," says Theresa Kuske, Ergodyne's Senior Digital Marketing Manager. "If they implement something—a new feature or functionality—it has been proven to be effective by their customers. It works."

Ergodyne then adopts Amazon's approaches on their own site, such as offering free shipping and adding enhanced content on product pages, such as videos and detailed images. Ergodyne sells on Amazon as a 1P seller, and they think about Amazon as both a way to grow their brand awareness and as a way to learn. As a result of these efforts, the company has improved conversion rate on its own product pages by more than 50 percent.

Making the Decision: So Should You Jump In?

If you have a product or brand that you manufacturer or own—and it is unique, stands on its own merits, and is in-demand—I believe you should strongly consider getting yourself on Amazon. Sure, you may be concerned that Amazon will leverage what they learn about your industry category by selling your products and then enter your business by sourcing directly. Perhaps there are some categories where this is truly a threat (e.g. Amazon Basics for commodity products such as batteries, and in the apparel category, where Amazon has dozens of private label brands). However, the highly complex nature of the products in many B2B industry categories, combined with the continued importance of product and application knowledge (often delivered by human beings, not computers), makes this a much lower threat for most B2B industries. Additionally, if you are truly an innovator in your field with fantastic product—and that product is your core competency—I believe the risks are limited.

Note that Amazon Business also brings real time-to-market benefits for your own Ecommerce presence, particularly if you are new to online commerce. A typical manufacturer or brand can be up and running on the Amazon platform in one to two months, normally at a nominal cost. Compare this to development and deployment of an in-house Ecommerce web site, which can consume 9 to 18 months with associated capital costs ranging from $250,000 to multiple millions or more. Amazon's programs such as Fulfilled by Amazon also make it easier for sellers to ship quickly to business customers and to meet Amazon's fulfillment and service requirements without having to invest in their own warehouse, picking/packing, and shipping operations for smaller order sizes.

Business buyers are shifting their buying to Amazon. A report released by Digital Commerce 360 in late 2019 revealed that over 50% of business buyers were making at least 10% of their work purchases on Amazon Business.[69] Amazon is aggressively recruiting sellers for Amazon Business. As of this writing, they are hungry for B2B companies, but this will likely change over time as product categories get filled. If your company is not represented on Amazon, you are at risk of losing volume to a competitor. At minimum, you should be protecting your brand presence on Amazon with a well-organized and complete program and learning Ecommerce best practices from Amazon. My advice is to confront the reality and act.

CASE STUDY

Medelita: Growing with—and Learning from—Amazon

A happy Medelita customer

Medelita is the definition of a digital-first brand. The designer and manufacturer of medical uniforms launched in 2008 with an Ecommerce-first approach. The company is a high-growth industry disruptor, taking on the likes of Cardinal Health (whose case studies are also prominently featured in this book) and traditional hospital supply stores, selling high-quality, stylish scrubs, lab coats, and other apparel items to

---

69 Source: https://www.digitalcommerce360.com/2019/09/24/b2b-buyers-are-primed-for-more-amazon-business/

doctors, nurses, and large health care institutions such as Kaiser Permanente, Mayo Clinic, and others.

Medelita knew early on that Amazon was not only a sales channel, but also critical to growing their brand presence in their industry. The company looked directly at Amazon as a place to learn, adopting best practices and tactics used by the marketplace to improve its own Ecommerce selling both on its own site and on Amazon.

"We invested in launching an Amazon presence in year two of our business, and it has paid off for us," notes Dan Stepchew, Chief Ecommerce Officer at Medelita. "Selling medical uniforms directly to buyers via Ecommerce was unheard of prior to us entering the market. We leveraged Amazon's reach to millions of customers as a way to make our target customers aware of our products and brand. We use Amazon's pay-per-click advertising vehicles such as Sponsored Products to create awareness, so that when someone searches for 'medical scrubs' on Amazon, we show up in the search results."

For its next step in building its Amazon presence, Medelita made the move to sell the majority of its products as a third party (3P) Seller Central merchant on the marketplace, while keeping its traditional first party (1P) account for a limited number of products (where Amazon buys on a wholesale basis from suppliers).

"The third party approach gives us more control over price, brand, content, and inventory on key items," says Stepchew. "And we are able to obtain more profit as a result of this approach, versus selling as a first-party vendor to Amazon."

Medelita also adopted tactics from Amazon. For example, by shortening delivery times, the firm found a way to capture a larger market share.

"In the past, doctors and other medical practitioners would need to wait at least a month for their custom scrubs and lab coats to arrive after order," observes Stepchew. "By shortening the delivery cycle to just days, following Amazon's model, we have been able to beat customer expectations and obtain a premium price in the process."

Clearly a win for both customers and for Medelita.

Today, Amazon is one of Medelita's fastest growing sales channels. The company credits Amazon with helping to drive more than 20x increases in its own direct Ecommerce sales on the Medelita web site since 2010, making them a fantastic growth story and a lesson for other B2B brands.

Key Chapter Takeaways

- Amazon is a dominant force in the Ecommerce business that can't be ignored, and it is increasingly penetrating B2B categories.

- Amazon is now the number one place that buyers go to research products online, having surpassed Google and other web sites; if you are not well-represented on Amazon, you are risking irrelevance.

- Amazon is investing heavily in B2B channels, including hiring seasoned people (out of B2B industries), building tools to accommodate traditional B2B buying workflows, and drawing the U.S. Government, large corporations, and universities to the platform.

- Companies cannot ignore Amazon—having a strategy on how to approach the marketplace is critical.

- If your product is the core of your competitive differentiation (vs. service or some other differentiator), you should be selling on Amazon. If not, you should still be selling at least some products on the marketplace to protect your own branding and pricing, and to learn and adopt best practices.

- To succeed in selling on Amazon, you will need to take the following steps:

    1) Determine your approach.

    2) Invest in a foundation of great data/content.

    3) Invest in customer engagement via Amazon.

    4) Take advantage of Amazon's advertising tools.

    5) Ensure your fulfillment and customer support is set up to meet or exceed Amazon's requirements, and that your products are eligible for Amazon Prime.

Digital Marketing and B2B

8

The Digital Marketing Revolution

Just as digital has changed how consumers shop—and therefore how B2B buyers expect to shop—over the past 20+ years, so too have the methods and channels for reaching buyers evolved. While these digital marketing channels have been well-established in consumer Ecommerce for many years, these are generally new approaches for most B2B sellers. As a result, digital marketing can be challenging and confusing for B2B companies that are dipping their toes into digital for the first time.

The marketing function at most B2B companies has traditionally been driven by offline media: content (such as thought leadership publications), trade shows, print advertising in industry publications, sponsorships at industry events, and other methods. But the world has evolved. Today's B2B firms that are serious about success must develop the marketing function to include significant digital components in order to remain relevant to the modern B2B buyer. This is evident when we look at how B2B companies have shifted their marketing budgets toward digital channels. B2B marketers are putting more money into improving their web site, digital marketing, and social media.[70] According to Hubspot,

---

70 https://www.emarketer.com/Article/Mixing-Digital-B2B-Marketing-Approach/1016753

a leading marketing technology firm, more than half of B2B marketers allocated 50 percent or more of their marketing budget to digital channels as of 2018, including web site development, digital marketing, and social media.[71] This isn't a brand new trend. A 2016 survey of 295 global business leaders by Selligent, a global marketing automation solutions provider, revealed a dramatic shift in marketing spend away from traditional channels, such as print, trade shows, and

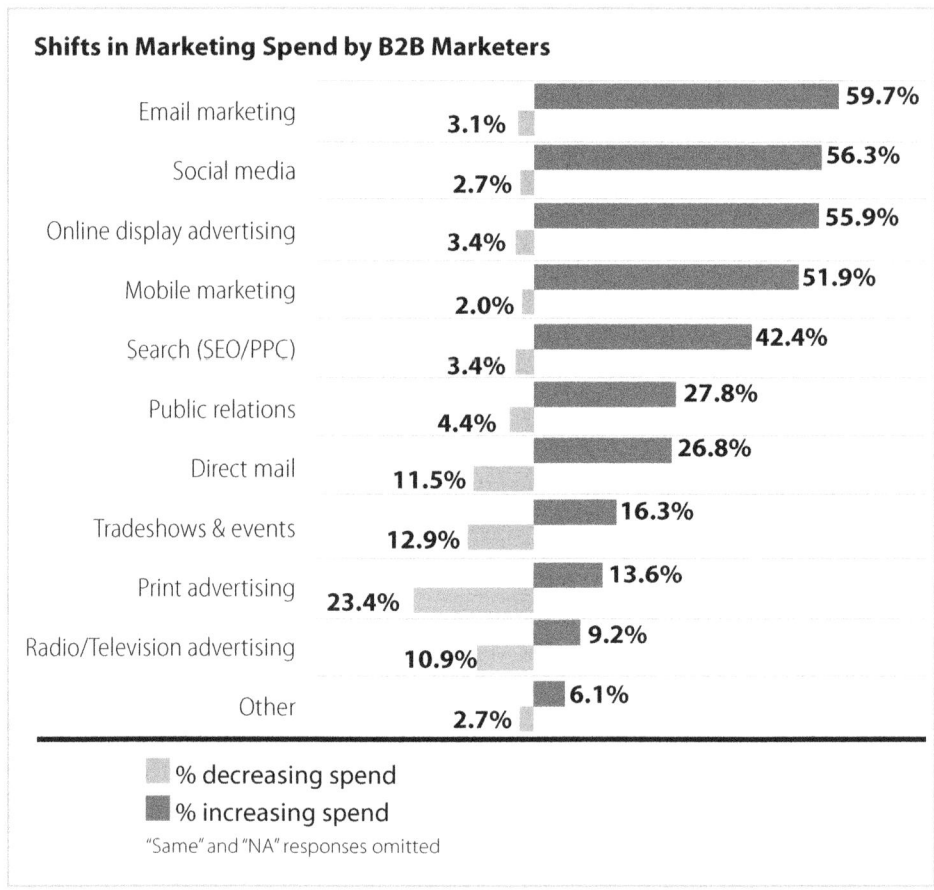

Shifts in Marketing Spend by B2B Marketers

Channel	% decreasing spend	% increasing spend
Email marketing	3.1%	59.7%
Social media	2.7%	56.3%
Online display advertising	3.4%	55.9%
Mobile marketing	2.0%	51.9%
Search (SEO/PPC)	3.4%	42.4%
Public relations	4.4%	27.8%
Direct mail	11.5%	26.8%
Tradeshows & events	12.9%	16.3%
Print advertising	23.4%	13.6%
Radio/Television advertising	10.9%	9.2%
Other	2.7%	6.1%

% decreasing spend
% increasing spend
"Same" and "NA" responses omitted

71   https://cdn2.hubspot.net/hubfs/455263/Marketing_Mix_2018_Report%20v3.pdf?t=1513614524815

television, and towards digital media, such as email, social media, and display advertising.[72]

While channels and methods have evolved to become increasingly centered on digital, many marketing goals have remained the same. A survey conducted by the Safefrog Marketing Group and reported by eMarketer found that lead generation remains the top priority among B2B marketers, while converting leads is the second priority.[73] With the addition of Ecommerce capabilities, converting online leads now has a place where those activities can be directed. In fact, digital

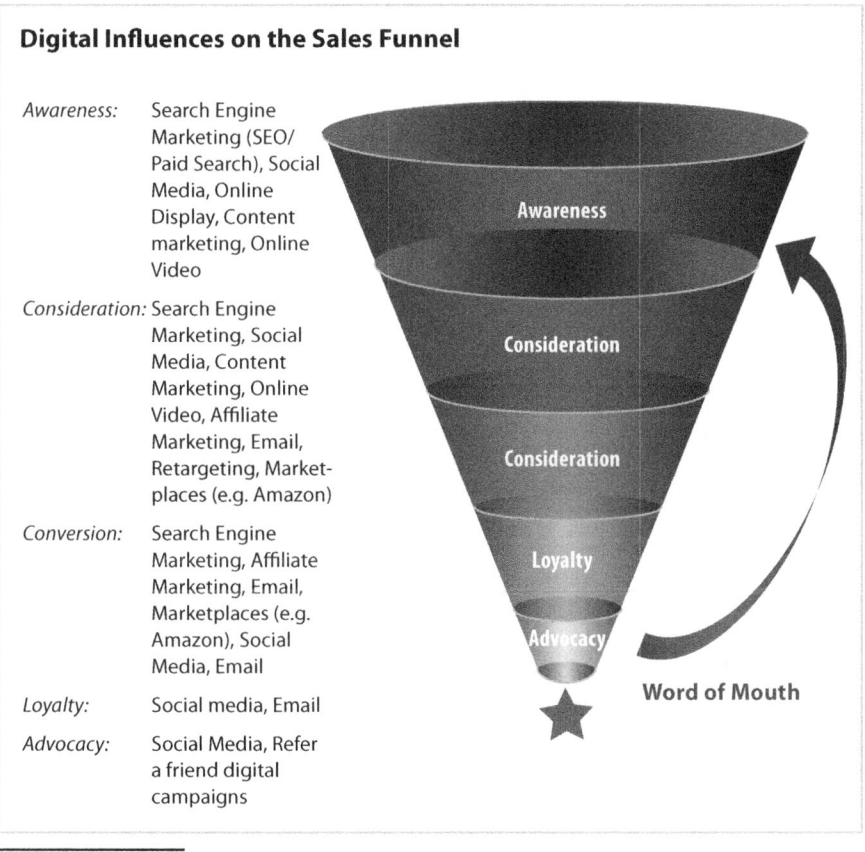

Digital Influences on the Sales Funnel

Awareness: Search Engine Marketing (SEO/ Paid Search), Social Media, Online Display, Content marketing, Online Video

Consideration: Search Engine Marketing, Social Media, Content Marketing, Online Video, Affiliate Marketing, Email, Retargeting, Marketplaces (e.g. Amazon)

Conversion: Search Engine Marketing, Affiliate Marketing, Email, Marketplaces (e.g. Amazon), Social Media, Email

Loyalty: Social media, Email

Advocacy: Social Media, Refer a friend digital campaigns

Awareness

Consideration

Consideration

Loyalty

Advocacy

Word of Mouth

72 http://www.cloudanalysts.com/percentage-revenue-companies-spending-marketing/
73 Ibid.

marketing has evolved to become a key component of the B2B purchase cycle.

If you're a B2B marketer, it is time to re-examine your sales funnel, paying close attention to how digital tactics can and should contribute at each stage. At each step of the funnel, digital marketing plays a role in informing the buyer's journey. Consider the graphic on the previous page, which shows a traditional sales funnel and how various digital marketing tactics map to each stage of the funnel. I will define each of these tactics as we move through this chapter.

The good news is that a good portion of the marketing collateral used in traditional marketing can be repurposed for digital channels. However, there are also unique skills and approaches necessary for success in digital marketing and cross-channel selling. Your marketing message must be adapted to digital media and formulated to reinforce both online and offline selling. There are more opportunities than ever to leverage digital marketing, and many B2B companies are still early in deploying digital advertising. As a result, the return on marketing spend in digital can be very high because it is not yet as competitive as it is in B2C. Additionally, digital marketing is measurable in ways that most traditional marketing approaches are not.

Many of the tried and true methods used by B2C retail marketers are now leveraged by their B2B counterparts in an effort to generate leads and reach new markets. Traditional online marketing tools like paid search, social media, display advertising, email, and more have long been a part of the playbook for consumer-facing companies. Let's take a look at each of the tactics in more detail.

Search Engine Optimization

Search engine optimization (SEO) is the process of improving a web site's visibility in a search engine's unpaid listings. Usually called "natural," "organic," or "earned" results, the goal is to have your web site listed near the top of the search results page when a relevant keyword search is executed (at minimum on the first page of results). Note these are not paid clicks, distinct from paid search advertising, often referred to as SEM or PPC, which I discuss later in this chapter. Following is an image of a Google search results page for the term "iPhone Charging Cable," highlighting organic search results versus paid results.

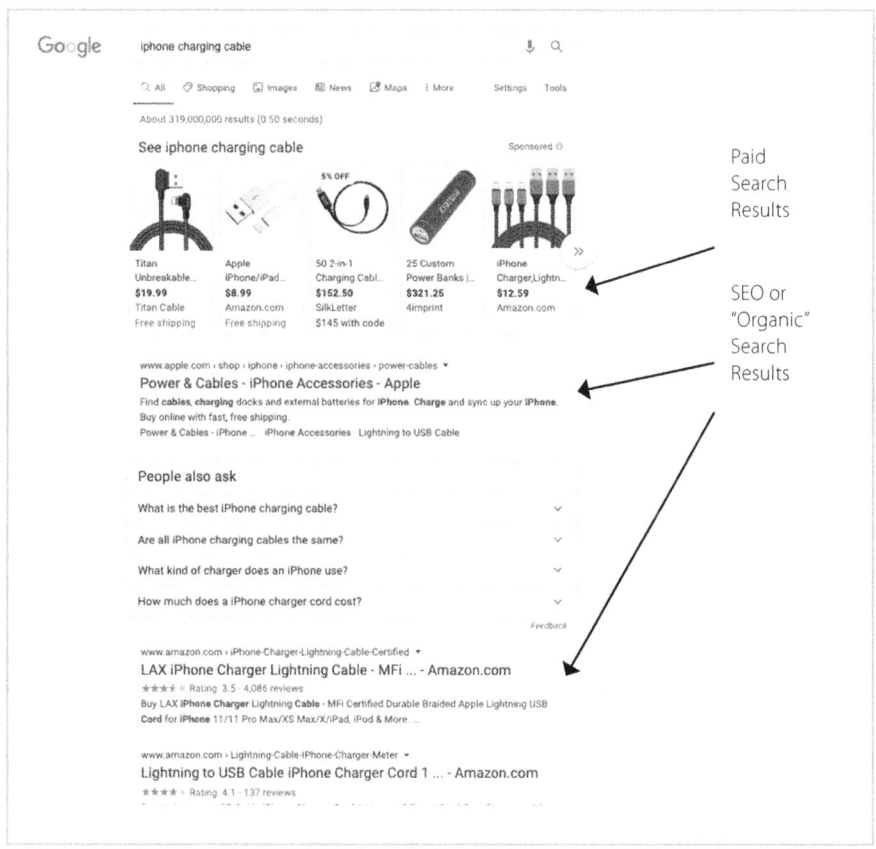

Typically, the higher a web site is ranked on a search results page, and the more frequently it appears in search results, the more visitors the site will receive. SEO can target many different kinds of search, including keyword search, image search, local search, video search, academic search, news search, and industry-specific vertical search engines.[74] Google maintains nearly 95 percent of all search traffic, and as a result, most web sites focus their SEO efforts on ranking well on this search engine.[75] As noted in the prior chapter, Amazon has taken a significant portion of product search volume for products from Google, however, Google remains a very important digital presence for B2B marketers.

There are entire books covering the topic of SEO and improving search engine rankings. Some of these titles include *The Art of SEO, SEO Made Simple*, and *Search Engine Optimization (SEO): An Hour a Day*. I am not going to attempt to duplicate these fine works here, but I will provide some basics, so that you will have a solid grounding in the essential elements of a good SEO program.

There are three main factors that affect a site's rankings in organic search engine results (See Glossary for term definitions):

1. Web Site Structure (including, but not limited to the following elements)

    *   Basic site crawlability: How easy it is for search engines to read the data on your web site.

---

74 https://en.wikipedia.org/wiki/Search_engine_marketing
75 https://www.statista.com/statistics/220534/googles-share-of-search-market-in-selected-countries/

- URL structure: This is the structure of your web site page "addresses" that show up in the web browser address bar.

- Site map: This is the map of your web site that displays all of the pages of your site in logical categorizations.

- Site longevity: How long your web site has been live on the Internet; typically the longer it has been live, the more authority search engines attribute to its content.

2. On-site Content

- Product and category level content: This includes both text as well as rich media, such as videos and images.

- Content tags: web page titles, keywords, header tags, and other content tags.

- Articles and videos: Beyond basic product and category level content, this is rich content about your products, applications, answers to common customer questions, and more.

- Customer reviews, commonly asked questions with answers, and other customer-generated content.

- Company blog: The place where you regularly post content of interest to your audience; your "voice" on the Internet.

- Locally-optimized content: Content related to your company's local presence (such as offices, distribution centers, stores, or other locations).

- Other content: Information about your company, a press room with press releases, leadership biographical information, etc.

3. Inbound Links:

    - The number and type of other web sites linking to your site is a measure of your virtual popularity score (often referred to as PageRank). This helps search engines understand how important your web site is to the broader Internet for specific search terms.

    - Links from the web sites of industry authorities, influencers, and other sites are of particular value, e.g. links from educational institutions, social media, industry web sites, and blogs can positively impact your rankings.

SEO is an important digital marketing program on its own, however, the power of SEO can be enhanced and extended when combined with other digital marketing programs. Content, email, and paid search programs, when executed well, are highly integrated with SEO campaigns. Each of these types of programs can provide data and insights into how your customers shop, and can help you improve your advertising programs' effectiveness. Leveraging this data within SEO is important, but extending that leverage and data across programs is even more powerful. For example, you could use SEO reports to inform paid search bid strategies on specific search terms, and vice versa.

While marketers do not pay for clicks in SEO, it is important to remember that SEO isn't free. It takes time and a dedicated effort to achieve and maintain high natural rankings in search results. There are a few key tactics that need to be undertaken in order to succeed in SEO:

- **Know your key terms:** Understand which keywords have the most potential for your business in terms of traffic, online conversions, and brand value. This must be buyer-focused. What terms do your customers use to find your products and brand? This will provide a starting point for a keyword list. My clients have used this approach successfully many times. For example, for a search on "oversized industrial fans" on Google, my client Big Ass Fans shows up several times in the top SEO results. They garner quite a lot of interest in their products from these searches, even in cases where the person searching isn't already familiar with their brand.

- **Make page content work harder:** Web site page content drives much of your SEO ranking. Add highly converting keywords to the highest level pages on your site; home page, category, product, and static pages. Include visible text on pages, anchor text, alt-text on images, and title and meta tags on every page.

- **Match page content to keywords:** Create landing pages for key targeted search terms, and ensure that the content and products delivered on these pages is reflective of the search term(s) you are optimizing for.

- **Prevent duplicate content:** If your products are in multiple categories on your web site and have the same content on each, make sure that the search engines recognize only one page as the "official" page for relevant keywords. Duplicate content can negatively impact your rankings. (Note that there are methods to accomplish this, such as canonical tagging and use of "no follow" tags that go beyond the scope of this book. More information can be found online on these tactics.)

- **Use social media and external link building to improve rankings:** Social media optimization is an effective way to leverage content through blogs, online link sharing, and other social media tools to increase relevant content and links. Leverage vendors, partners, customers, and other third-party relationships to build backlinks to your web site.

Paid Search/Search Engine Marketing (SEM)

Paid search goes by many names, including pay per click (PPC) and search engine marketing (SEM), but they all refer to the same type of advertising that directs traffic to your web site through paid ad placements on search engine results pages (as distinct from SEO, which are non-paid links). In SEM, advertisers bid in a virtual auction on keyword phrases relevant to their target market and the buyer's purchasing intent. The "winning" advertisement is determined on the basis of bid amount and quality of the ad, among other factors.[76] Like SEO, there are a set of tactics and activities that are essential to success. These tactics require expertise and knowledge. Unless you have (or are willing to invest in) expert in-house paid search staff, I usually recommend retaining a digital marketing agency to help with these programs.

Following are a few high level tips describing what is required to achieve success with a paid search program,

---

76   https://en.wikipedia.org/wiki/Search_engine_marketing

focused on Google (due to this search engine's dominance of the market).

- **Develop a bid strategy and test plan:** It is very easy to spend a lot of money very quickly on SEM. That is why it is essential to have a strategic plan, which includes keywords that are both branded (your brand names, such as "Apple iPhone") and non-branded (more general terms, such as "smartphone"). In addition, you will need to conduct ongoing review of current bids and a test plan for uncovering new opportunities.

- **Focus on conversion:** Do not let Google fool you. This search engine company offers many tools to promote increased clicks, but more clicks may not always be the best for your brand or products, especially if you are achieving a conversion rate below 1 percent. To make SEM profitable, it is more important to receive fewer clicks from highly qualified traffic than more clicks from less qualified traffic. Invest time in testing and analyzing your campaigns and keywords to determine which drive conversions.

- **Make it all match:** Divide your SEM campaigns into as many logical groups as you can feasibly manage. Google rewards the relevance of ads by giving higher positions at a lower cost-per-click. Ensure the content in the ads matches the search term as well as your landing page content. Having a number of ad groups is the best way to take advantage of this. You can even have an ad group consisting of only a single keyword.

- **Use your ad space wisely:** Google gives you a limited number of characters per line; make them count. It is critical to have people with product knowledge write the ad copy; you know what is important about your product. Test different versions of the copy to find the most efficient verbiage, remembering that conversion (versus click volume) is most important metric.

- **Create landing pages for specific ad groups:** Context-specific landing pages are one of the most effective tools in increasing conversions from paid search advertising (as well as from other digital marketing tactics). For example, don't send paid search traffic on a specific product-related keyword to your company's homepage, which may not feature that product. The more relevant the web site landing page, the better your ads will perform and convert.

- **Use your branding:** If your brand is memorable and recognizable, then your marketing will be more effective by leveraging the brand name in your ads.

- **Use both SEO and SEM together to improve your referrals from search pages:** As mentioned above, SEO and SEM can work together to make an effective strategy that should be built in tandem. It is similar to combining print, radio, and television in traditional advertising. Paid search can provide a basis for the SEO program, helping to identify high-converting keywords that should be a focus for SEO efforts, as SEO traffic typically takes longer to build on specific keywords (vs. paid search, where marketers can simply pay for traffic on targeted keywords).

- **Rebalance your budget:** For companies just starting their efforts, they may wish to allocate more budget to SEM (e.g. up to 80 percent of the overall search engine budget, including both SEO and SEM). The goal is to build an understanding of which keywords generate traffic and sales. Once a baseline is established, it is important to analyze how well campaigns are performing and re-adjust the budget regularly, shifting funds to SEO activities as needed. For example, as rankings improve in natural search, you can reduce budgets in paid search for the same keywords. You may no longer find it necessary to pay for visibility, as your organic rankings will send more traffic as they appear higher in search engine results pages.

- **Do not "set it and forget it":** Whether managed internally or through an agency, paid search is a marketing program that should be managed frequently—daily, or even several times a day depending on newness of program, bidding strategies, and other factors. A "set it and forget it" approach is guaranteed to result in wasted spending and sub-optimal results.

Content Marketing and Video

Content marketing has long been an established marketing tactic at B2B firms, and it is a perfect format for digital channels. Approximately 88 percent of B2B companies use content marketing as part of their strategy, according to a recent survey by the Content Marketing Institute.[77] The same survey found that the B2B marketers interviewed believed that content marketing via the web "is the most important technology" for future efforts. This is for good reason. All marketing programs are fueled by content, and in B2B

---

77 http://contentmarketinginstitute.com/wp-content/uploads/2015/09/2016_B2B_
Report_Final.pdf

Example of a great use of online content: Big Ass Fans

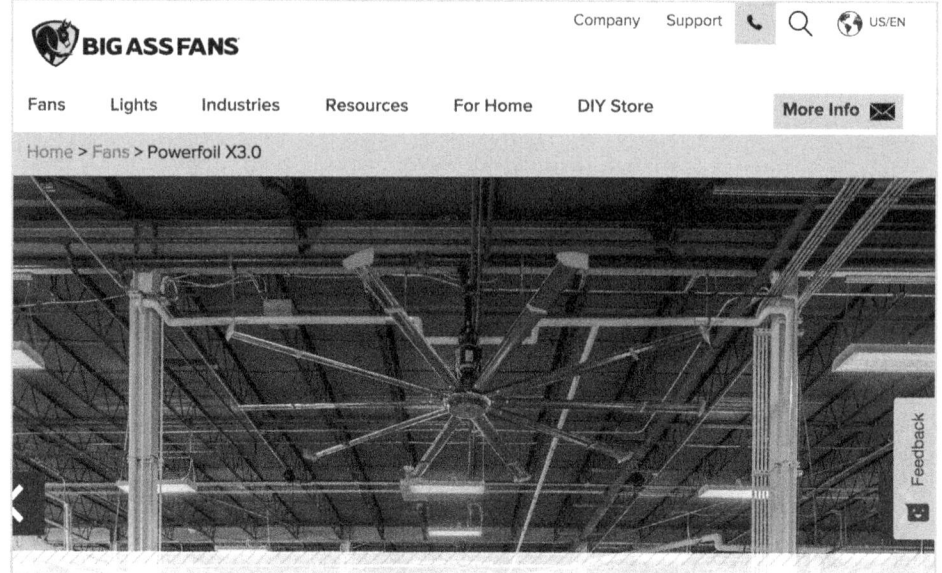

Example of a great use of online content: Big Ass Fans

COLOR CUSTOMIZATION

We like to think every one of our fans is an eye-catching centerpiece. But if you'd like your Powerfoil X3.0 to be something other than the standard silver and yellow, upgrade with any of our 11 classic colors, or specify one of your own. We can paint your fan any color in, over and beyond the rainbow.

Check out the diagram to see which parts of Powerfoil X3.0 can be painted. Then call today for a quote!

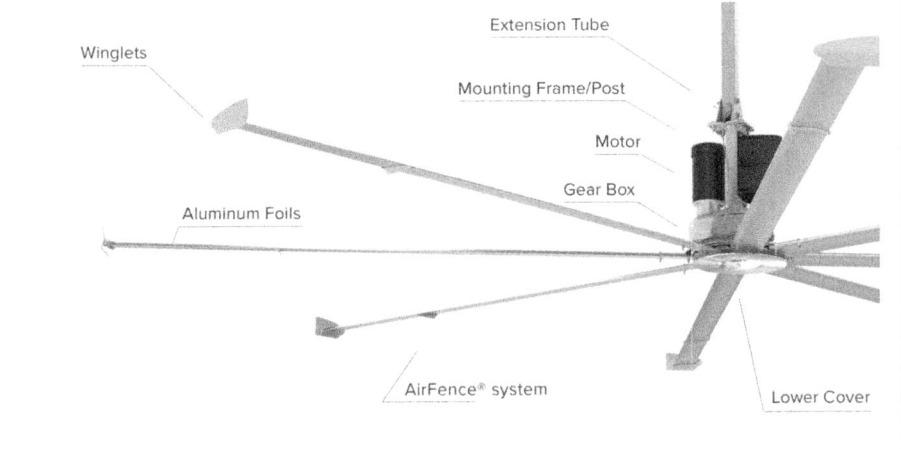

WARRANTIES

U.S.A., Canada, Australia, Singapore, Malaysia

Export

View other product warranties

TECH SPECS

Powerfoil X3.0

Powerfoil X3.0 (Español)

Powerfoil X3.0 (Français)

9k, 13k, & 20.7k LED Kit

Washdown

Classic Colors

INSTALL GUIDES

Pre-install Checklist

Quick Install

Electrical Install

Wall-Mounted VFD

Powerfoil X LED

Power   Chat is Offline [+]

product categories, great content allows firms to stand out as experts and thought leaders in their field. Detailed content, such as product guides, application and installation instructions, compatibility information, customer testimonials, case studies, in-depth product descriptions, and technical specifications, can be used on web pages in a dynamic manner to inform and engage customers and differentiate from competitive offerings. Industry leading marketers taking advantage of advanced web tools will present this content at key moments during the web site experience, including when the customer is using a mobile device. Content can be presented when a site visitor is just learning about a brand, while they are deep diving on product research, or even during the online checkout process to provide relevant and helpful information. Content can build confidence in the buyer that they are making the right purchase decision.

On the prior two pages is a great example of how one of my clients, Big Ass Fans, uses content on their web site to provide prospective buyers with technical specifications, installation guides, and customization options for one of their best selling products.

Great content has uses across all digital channels, even beyond your web site. Content can be leveraged within social media channels, such as Facebook, Instagram, Twitter, and LinkedIn. Posting authoritative and interesting stories about your industry and products to a community of followers on social channels can help to reinforce your authority and generate new customer leads. In addition, content should be leveraged to boost search engine rankings and improve paid search campaign results, by integrating content into landing pages on your web site. Content can also be distributed to bloggers and industry influencers as a way to drive more traffic, and improve your search engine rankings through an increased number of quality links to your site.[78]

Another type of content that has grown enormously over the past few years is the use of online video, particularly in B2B settings. Video can address a wide variety of strategies and tactics, such as online versions of traditional advertising, product demonstrations, branding, thought leadership, and more. The growth in this content type is massive, and as of 2018, approximately 85 percent of businesses have internal staff or other dedicated resources producing in-house videos.[79] Given this level of growth, and the fact that more than half of all marketing professionals name video as the content with the best return on investment, this is an area that needs to be seriously considered for a focused content generation approach. For a good example of how businesses are using video to generate brand awareness, industry authority, and leads, just take a look at your LinkedIn newsfeed, which will likely be ripe with video content.

Online Display and Retargeting

Online display advertising involves presenting image and text-based promotional messages on third-party web sites such as blogs and industry publications, news web sites, and social networks like LinkedIn and Facebook. Typically, these are the digital equivalent of buying advertising in a print trade publication, but with the added benefit of controlling where and when they show up, and who actually sees them. The typical goal of online display advertising is to develop brand

78   https://searchengineland.com/3-b2b-companies-integrate-seo-online-marketing-strategy-183837
79   https://blog.hubspot.com/marketing/video-marketing-statistics

awareness for your products, but this advertising method can also help to enhance brand preference and purchase intent.[80]

For example, following is an online banner display advertisement for Lemo medical devices on the web site of the Medical Product Outsourcing magazine.

Example Online Display Advertisement

"Retargeting" is a form of display advertising, also known as behavioral remarketing, that presents advertising when a web site visit occurs, but the user does not "convert" (make an online purchase or fill out a contact form, for example)

---

80   https://en.wikipedia.org/wiki/Display_advertising

during the web site visit. Retargeting uses tracking technologies such as pixels and cookies to identify web site visitors, and then serves online display ads on other web sites to those who have shown at least some engagement with a web site.[81] For example, if a prospective customer is browsing a particular product on your web site, using retargeting, you can serve ads featuring that product on other web sites they visit. If you have ever browsed products on Amazon, but then later saw an ad for those products on, say, your local newspaper's web site, you have been retargeted! When you notice a brand or product that you have viewed on one web site appearing on other sites you visit, you are being "followed around the web" by retargeting ads.

Display advertising and retargeting often go hand in hand. It can be cost-effective to use display advertising to draw prospects to your site initially, and then retarget these potential buyers on other web sites with more customized and personalized advertising. Retargeting offers a number of technological features that increase its efficacy. These include:

- **Frequency Caps:** Overexposure to a brand or a specific digital ad can result in decreased campaign performance, and a frequency cap ensures marketing dollars are not wasted on individuals who are not likely to make a purchase.

- **Burn Code:** Prevents converted customers from continuing to see display advertising.

- **Audience Segmentation:** Tailors ad messages and creative assets, such as images used in the ads, based on users' stage of the purchase funnel (e.g. researching products versus ready to buy) and areas of interest.

---

81   https://en.wikipedia.org/wiki/Behavioral_retargeting

- **Demographic, Geographic, and Contextual Targeting:** Targets ads based on demographic information, like age or gender, contextual factors like customer profile, buyer preferences, subject matter of the web site, or geographic data.

- **Rotating Creative and A/B Testing:** Advertisers can test ads against each other to see which content and presentation style performs better with different audience segments. The result is the ability to fine tune ad creative assets and copy. Running with the same set of ads for months on end will result in lower performing campaigns. By testing, advertisers can get a stronger sense of what works and what does not. Additionally, this tactic can be employed to test different ads affordably before sinking a heavy investment of marketing dollars in a wider-reaching campaign.

- **View-Through Conversion Tracking:** View-through conversions occur when, after an ad impression is made, the user does not interact with the ad (e.g. click on it), but later converts (buys online). Retargeted ads, even if they are not clicked, can increase brand awareness, and this influence should be considered when utilizing this marketing method.

Social Media

Social media has had a massive impact on how businesses operate and engage with their audiences, and has been used for many years by B2C marketers. Social media also has an impact—and a role—in B2B marketing. At its core, social media marketing is the process of gaining web site traffic and attention (e.g. building brand awareness) through social media web sites and mobile apps. Marketing programs typically focus on creating content that attracts attention, emphasizes industry authority, drives deeper engagement with a brand, and encourages people connected to a company on a social media platform to share content across their own social networks. When the underlying message spreads from user to user, it resonates because it comes from a trusted, third-party source, as opposed to the brand or company itself. This form of marketing results in what is called "earned media" (e.g. it is earned through saying or doing something worthwhile) rather than paid media.[82]

B2B marketers invest in social media to strengthen thought leadership, deepen customer relationships, and raise brand awareness, more so than for direct return on investment from online or offline sales tied to social media campaigns. In fact, according to business media firm IDG, a whopping 75 percent of B2B buyers and 84 percent of C-level executives turn to social media for information regarding purchases. But, only 42 percent of marketers say they can accurately measure the ROI of their social media presence.[83] As a result of these factors, social media is generally included in the marketing mix, but is not the top area of investment. A survey jointly conducted by Deloite, Duke University's Fuqua School of Business, and the American Marketing Association reports that B2B companies are spending about 12 percent of their total marketing budget on social media, though that figure has grown considerably in recent budget cycles.[84]

The most commonly utilized social media platforms by B2B marketers, as reported by the Content Marketing Institute, include (in order of usage by marketers):

---

82   https://en.wikipedia.org/wiki/Social_media_marketing
83   https://www.idg.com/blog/5-statistics-will-change-view-b2b-buyers-journey/
84   https://cmosurvey.org/wp-content/uploads/sites/15/2018/02/The_CMO_Survey-Highlights_and_Insights_Report-Feb-2018.pdf

- LinkedIn (used by 97 percent of B2B marketers)

- Twitter (87 percent)

- Facebook (86 percent)

- YouTube (60 percent)

- Instagram (30 percent)[85]

There are numerous examples and case studies of B2B firms succeeding with social media that you can easily find online, but perhaps my all-time favorite (mostly because I find it hilarious) is the industrial-strength blender company Blendtec's YouTube video series, "Will it blend?" This

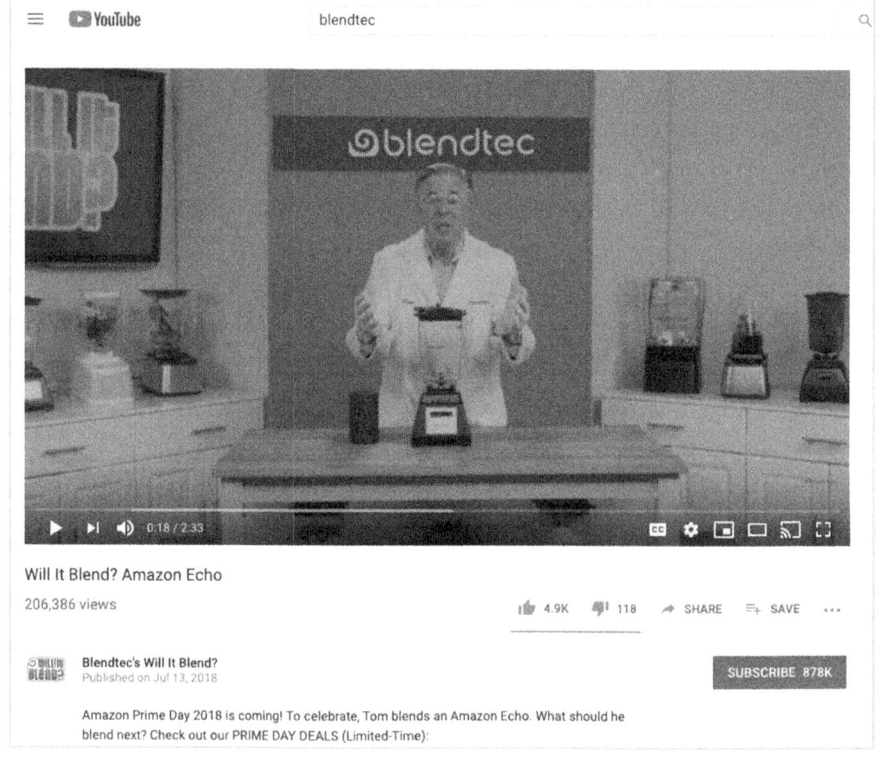

85   https://contentmarketinginstitute.com/wp-content/uploads/2017/09/2018-b2b-research-final.pdf

manufacturer sells its products mainly to resellers and also to consumers directly over the web. The company's YouTube video series takes a light-hearted approach by testing out the "blendability" of various items in their very powerful blenders. They've put iPhones, glow sticks, diamonds, lighters, golf balls, and many, many more items into their blender over the last 13 years, and they continue to make new videos to this day. While the videos are fun to watch, they also do an amazing job of illustrating the quality of their product as well as giving viewers something entertaining that is worth sharing. In fact, its top video received more than 18 million views, and their channel boasts nearly 900,000 subscribers.

Email Marketing

This tactic may already be familiar to many B2B firms, as it is the most used and well-established digital communications vehicle in the marketing toolbox. That said, maximizing email marketing to fully benefit and support your Ecommerce operations is an activity that requires an analytical mindset and a dedication to testing. Email can be used at nearly every stage of the marketing funnel, enabling you to convert and grow your relationship with customers. Email is one of the best performing digital marketing channels, with an industry average Return on Advertising Spend (ROAS) of 40 to 1. In other words, a single dollar spent on email campaigns returns forty dollars on average.[86]

The keys to success with this channel are having an effective medium for capturing email addresses, maintaining a healthy email list, and leveraging customer segments based on a variety of factors, including product purchase history, engagement with web site content, and other factors. There

---

86   https://promorepublic.com/en/blog/grow-email-list-ecommerce/

are a variety of software platforms that make managing your email marketing program easier, and many of these solutions will integrate directly into your Ecommerce platform and related systems. Additionally, many types of marketing emails can be automated, making this essential marketing function considerably easier (more on that later in the chapter).

To plan out your email marketing program, it is important to first understand that there are a variety of types of emails that you may send current and prospective customers. Some of them will be sales-focused, but many of them will either enhance the customer experience of your brand or add value to tasks and activities the customer is already doing. These email types include:

- Promotional content, such as discounts, sales, and closeouts offered at special prices

- Shopping cart abandonment content, focused on ensuring that customers return to your web site to complete orders if they leave the site with items still in their online shopping cart

- Informational content, like product guides and user manuals

- News content, including press releases, blog posts, videos, and more

- Transactional content, such as order and shipping confirmations

- Account management content, including reminders to review order and account information and privacy policy updates

- Product servicing reminders for equipment in the field, replenishment reminders for consumable products

The key is matching up these different types of emails to different customer segments throughout the course of their customer journey (refer back to Chapter 2 if you need a refresher on creating customer journeys). In other words, you want to send the right message to the right customer at the right time. This takes testing and it will evolve over time as your customers' needs become clear. You can develop a starting baseline by using current assumptions about your customers, with the objective of moving prospective and current customers through your sales funnel. An initial plan might follow a process that looks like the following graphic:

Prospective Customers	At Purchase	Current Customers
Email Capture	Welcome Message	Monthly Newsletter Opt-in
Monthly Newsletter Opt-in	Add to Current Customer List	New Product Announcement
Product Tracking	Order Confirmation	Product Information Emails
Product Information	Order Shipping	Promotions
Abandoned Shopping Cart	Request for Product Review	

Let's take a look at a couple of these email processes to fully understand what they are and when they should be sent.

First, for prospective customers, it is important to capture their email address quickly and easily. Concern yourself less with capturing an enormous amount of information about the subscriber upfront (this can be done later). Aim to collect the name and email address, and possibly company name. Ease of sign up is paramount here. Email address collection can be accomplished through a variety of methods, including through a newsletter sign-up box on your web site or more complicated methods such as offering a whitepaper or other helpful piece of content in exchange for an email address.

Pop up web site overlays have become a very common way for companies to collect email addresses, usually from the home page when a prospective customer first visits the web site. For example, power tool and outdoor maintenance equipment maker Worx sells to both B2B and B2C buyers, and deploys a homepage overlay to collect email addresses using an incentive.

Pop Up Web Site Overlay Example: Worx.com

Once you capture a prospect's email address, you can start marketing to them, often in very precise ways. As a starting point, a series of emails should be sent to new subscribers welcoming them to your brand. This email series, typically two to three emails sent over the course of a few weeks, should provide background information about your company and products, and possibly offer the prospective customer an incentive to make their first purchase. This is commonly called a Welcome Series.

Personalized email content is an important way to capture the power of this marketing method. Depending on the sophistication of your email software and its integration with your other systems, you can track which products the prospect has viewed on your web site, how often he or she looks at a particular product (or set of products), and what other content he or she has engaged with. By observing these web site behaviors, you can then deliver an email that speaks directly to the prospect's needs. For example, if a prospective customer has viewed an item on your site but has not purchased it, you might send the prospect an email within 24 hours with information and messaging relevant to that product. Similarly, if the prospect places an item into the online shopping cart, but does not complete the purchase, you might send them a series of emails reminding them that the product is still available and ready to be shipped (these are called "abandoned cart emails"). If the prospect does not respond to these emails, you could begin sending promotional emails with limited time offers to create urgency to make a purchase.

Another common form of email marketing in B2B is referred to as "drip campaigns." These are a series of emails that are intended to nurture a prospective customer's interest in a company's products. A typical drip campaign will begin when a prospect registers to receive a white paper or similar piece of thought leadership content, signalling their interest in a particular topic or set of products. The prospect then will receive a series of follow up emails—a "drip" of consistent communication over a defined period of time, such as a few months, with additional helpful content and product offers to incentivize a first purchase.

Email communication should not stop once a customer makes a purchase. A best practice is to regularly send marketing emails to customers with personalized content based on the products they have purchased. This content could consist of a discount on future orders, user manuals, technical information, real world product application stories, training information, re-order instructions, or promotions for other related products. Transaction-related emails are also important to send to customers, including order confirmation and communication of shipping status. These types of emails are frequently opened, and are a great place to insert offers for related products and complementary product content. Lastly, once the customer has received a product, you may want to send them an email requesting a product review if your web site offers this functionality.

Email marketing is a tool to strengthen and grow customer relationships. Successful B2B email marketers look to balance product information and offers with content that demonstrates industry thought leadership and helpful product application information. This means sending monthly newsletters with targeted information relevant to the products the customer has purchased, timely promotional emails, new product announcements, and other types of communications.

These are just a few simple examples of how effective marketers use segmentation to create relevant emails and enhance the performance of this marketing channel. More advanced approaches include creating highly targeted email communications based on specific customer preferences, size and nature of the customers' businesses, product application and usage preferences, and other personalized factors. Greater relevance of the content of emails equates to higher levels of success in email marketing. Relevancy requires tracking customer activities across all interaction and purchase channels. This is the reason that the most successful email marketing programs are heavily integrated with other systems, such as Ecommerce, Order Management, and Customer Relationship Management systems. The more information you have about your customers, the more you can deliver the right personalized messages to them at the right time. This is also a key component to increasing the frequency with which you can send emails to your customers.

I often find that B2B companies are fearful of sending too much email. However, today's customers, who have been trained through their consumer shopping habits, have become accustomed to receiving as many as two or three emails per week from a single company. Creating a well-thought-out email marketing calendar with a variety of content and offers, and watching your unsubscribe rate (the rate at which people request to be removed from your email list), will help you determine the right cadence for your email marketing program. You can also ask your customers how frequently they want to receive email from you through an online "Preference Center." On the following page is an example of an email preference center from Ferguson, a large distributor of plumbing supplies, HVAC equipment, and other products, and a leading Ecommerce player in its category.

Finally, as I mentioned earlier, testing should play a key part in your email marketing program. This means testing subject lines, images, product offers, marketing messages, layout formats, and more. To get the full benefit of testing, you need to track a variety of metrics that are specific to the channel. Key performance indicators that should be tracked for email marketing activities include:

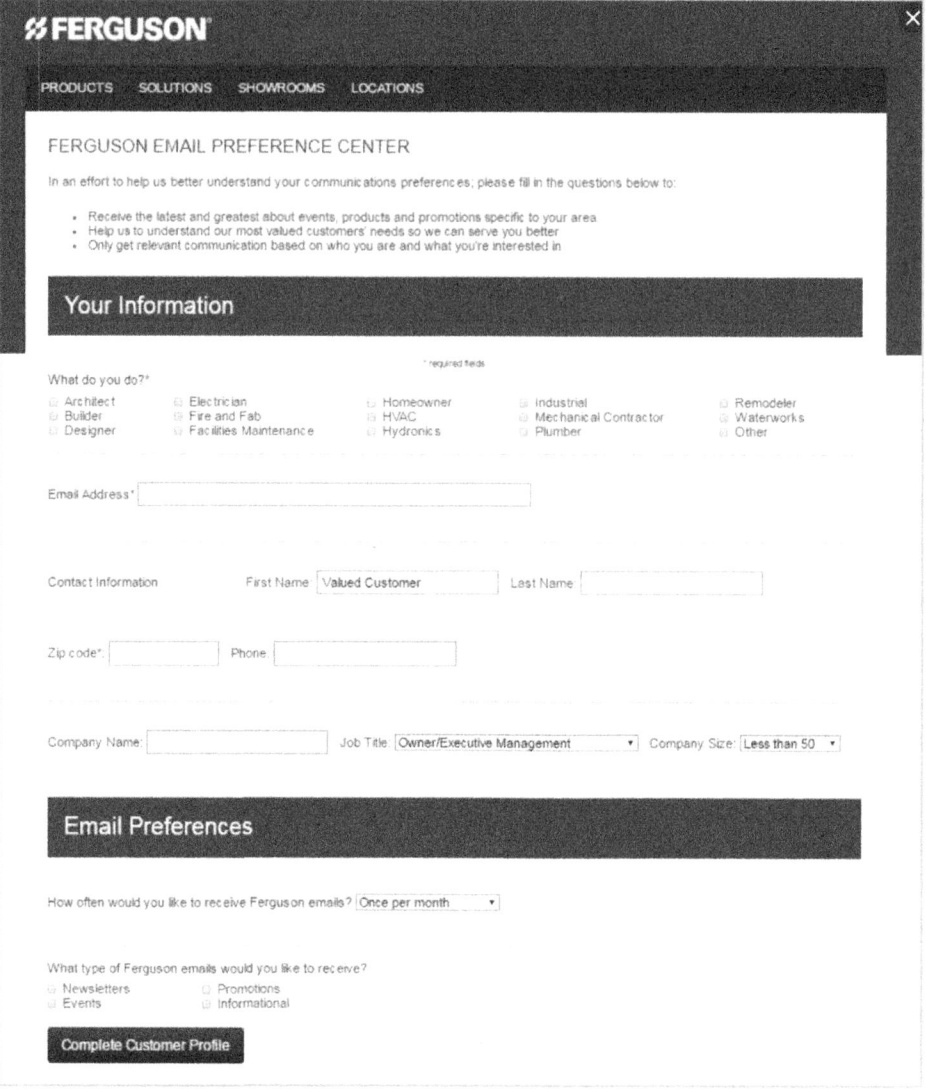

- Email open rate: Percentage of people who open each email compared to the number of emails delivered.

- Unique open rate: The percentage of individuals who opened an email; this excludes multiple opens by individuals.

- Click-through rate: Percentage of people who click on content to go to your web site

- Bounce rate: Percentage of emails that were not deliverable; keeping this rate low is important to the success of your program and it is therefore essential to periodically remove email address that continually bounce back.

- Unsubscribe rate: Percentage of people who chose to opt out of your communications.

- Conversion rate: The percentage of email recipients who went on to make purchases.

A good email marketing platform will track these and other metrics, and provide you with a report with actionable insights on how to strengthen your program. The following table shows a few of these metrics, on average, sourced from dozens of email accounts I have access to, for different types of email marketing campaigns. This will give you an idea of the performance you should aim for with your own program.

Campaign	Average Open Rate	Average Unique Click Rate	Average Conversion Rate	Average Revenue Per Email Sent
Wecome	35.1%	7.47%	11.72%	$ .97
Post Purchase	30.8%	5.74%	7.82%	$ .48
Replenish	21.5%	3.63%	28.59%	$ 1.12
Back in Stock	17.8%	9.34%	4.53%	$ 6.50
Brownse Abandon	37.3%	8.86%	4.11%	$ .43
Cart Abandon	29.9%	8.02%	21.73%	$ 2.39
Recurring Automated Campaigns	10.74%	1.31%	3.32%	$ .05

CASE STUDY

Sonepar: Breaking the Email Misconception

"If you are providing relevant content, they will want to hear from you"

Sonepar USA is a market leader in the B2B distribution of electrical, industrial, safety products, and related solutions. The firm has more than a dozen operating companies, including Vallen, Irby, OneSource, and Crawford Electric, among many others. Sonepar has been supporting its customers in Ecommerce for more than 20 years, and as a result, also maintains an advanced digital marketing function to support selling via online channels.

Some B2B companies are afraid to contact their customers via email more than once every month or two. Sonepar believes this to be an overly conservative approach, born of misconceptions by B2B managers and executives regarding how much email customers want to receive.

"We have found that getting the right information in front of our customers at the right time via email provides value to them and incremental sales to us," says Bill Mortimer, Senior Manager of Digital Marketing for Sonepar. "We have value-added things to say, and we communicate with our customers frequently via email. For example, in our email program we have found it really impactful to provide information about a specific job or task our customer needs to accomplish, adding value to their day to day work, versus just providing a discount or deal."

By understanding the customer's use of Sonepar's products, the company enables its customers to be more successful in their own businesses. And they don't only focus on promotional messages as a result, nor are they afraid to communicate with their customers via email proactively.

"Contacting your customers only once every 1-2 months via email is not enough," says Mortimer. "You need to set a regular cadence for email, and for some of our operating companies, this is as frequently as three emails per week. If you are providing relevant content, they will want to hear from you."

Mortimer recommends enabling customers to select their own preference for frequency of contact via email. "Put the decision in the hands of your customer through an online preference center, where customers can log in and select how often they want to hear from you, and about what." Most modern email software companies provide this capability.

By getting email right, B2B companies have permission to contact customers regularly through this channel, often resulting in an unmatched ROI.

Affiliate Marketing

Affiliate marketing is a type of performance-based advertising in which a business rewards other companies via commission payments for sending visits and purchases to the business' web site. There are four parties typically involved in affiliate marketing: the merchant (the "publisher" or seller), the network that contains offers for the affiliate to choose from and also manages payments, the publisher (also known as "the affiliate"), and the customer, who actually makes the purchase. This type of marketing has been utilized for many years in B2C marketing, and is occasionally used in B2B marketing programs, particularly as a method of rewarding influencers and industry thought leaders for referring web site traffic,

Affiliate Put Your Ad On Their Website

Affiliate Gets A Commission, You Get A Sale

How Does
AFFILIATE MARKETING
Work?

Customer Clicks And Converts

Conversions Are Tracked

leads, online sales, and visibility provided for a seller's products and brand.

There are four types of payment structures in affiliate marketing. The first is called Pay per Sale (PPS), in which the publisher (the affiliate) receives a portion of each sale that results from referred web site traffic (essentially a sales commission). The second form is Pay per Lead (PPL), in which the seller pays a referral fee based on each lead a publisher sends to the seller. The third form is Pay per Click (PPC), where the publisher receives compensation simply on the volume of traffic their web site sends, and is paid for each click. The final form is Cost per Action (CPA), in which a publisher is paid when a visitor sent by an affiliate takes targeted action, such as signing up for an email newsletter or downloading a white paper.

Here are some tips for making affiliate marketing work for you:

- **Resource with experienced people:** Like all marketing disciplines, affiliate marketing requires expert support in order for it to work. Either look for a qualified outside agency (called Outsource Program Managers or OPMs) that focuses on affiliate management, or assign someone on your team to work with affiliates. Successful program management hinges on developing relationships with affiliate partners, and managing performance through data and regular work to ensure visibility is achieved for your products and brand through your affiliate's own marketing efforts (such as their web sites or email marketing programs).

- **Allow affiliates to link deep into your site:** Encourage your affiliates to link directly to content pages, category list pages, or product pages, as these will likely convert at a higher rate.

- **Find potential affiliates through networking or summits:** In selling through affiliates, developing a personal connection with people at publishers is important. Meeting them at industry trade shows, summits, conferences, or through mutual contacts will help gain their trust and allow you to add them to your network. Many of the large networks, such as Commission Junction and Linkshare, have annual conferences that you can attend to develop these relationships. Additionally, consider approaching industry publications, industry experts or influencers, associations and networking groups, and other content-driven web sites that are relevant to your field. This is a way to incentivize and digitize these traditional B2B relationships.

- **Give it time to work:** Starting an affiliate marketing program will take time. Time will be required to secure high-quality affiliates, build traffic, and generate value. View this type of marketing as a long-term plan to help increase sales.

- **Research and plan your affiliate marketing strategy carefully:** Talk with your customers, find out where they shop online and what industry publications or web sites they regularly visit, and see if it makes sense to add those outlets to your network. For example, niche online publishers likely exist who have your target audience's eyeballs already visiting their web sites.

- **Network size may not matter:** Large networks may work well for some companies, but they may not work for you. Some networks may have higher fees, may not give smaller companies the level of support they need, and just may not be the right fit. Smaller networks may be better solutions to start out with, especially if you can find one that specializes in your industry. Consider evaluating networks such as ShareASale as alternatives to the large affiliate networks. Keep in mind that many typical affiliate marketing networks are B2C oriented, but the established networks provide a solid framework for creating referral links to your site, and a structure that can be emulated in a B2B environment.

Marketplaces: Heightened Visibility

The adoption of marketplaces across B2B categories has created a cost-effective way for sellers to reach massive numbers of new customers. Many of the buyers that utilize marketplaces can be difficult to reach via a traditional sales force or physical distribution presence. As a result, marketplaces can be a lucrative incremental sales channel for B2B firms. The perfect example of this is Amazon Business, which we discussed extensively in the previous chapter. However, as big and as relevant as it is to B2B Ecommerce, Amazon is not the only marketplace.

In fact, there are a wide variety of B2B marketplaces, many of them serving specific industries or niches. For example, Alibaba.com has grown to become one the world's largest marketplaces for manufacturers. In fact, Alibaba is now one of the biggest Ecommerce companies on the planet, generating $54.5 billion in revenue in its 2019 fiscal year.[87] Industry specific marketplaces have also emerged. For example, SpecialChem.com helps industrial researchers and product specifiers find the right chemicals for a variety of applications. Joor (jooraccess.com) is a fast growing wholesale marketplace for fashion brands and retailers, accounting for a company-reported $15 billion in annual transaction volume in 2016.[88] For medical devices, 2018 saw the launch of Chamfr (chamfr.com), aiming to become this industry's hub for medical device components across all leading manufacturers. Another example, WholesaleCentral.com, is among the oldest wholesale marketplaces for, well, just about anything. Take some time to do your research, and you are bound to find one or more marketplaces that can play an instrumental role in growing your Ecommerce business.

---

87 https://www.statista.com/statistics/225614/net-revenue-of-alibaba/
88 https://jooraccess.com/Annual-Report

Here is a list of some of the largest and most prominent marketplaces (B2C and B2B) in the world, as of this writing:

- Amazon (including Amazon Business)

- Wal-mart (including Jet.com)

- Alibaba

- JD.com

- Mercado Libre (Latin America)

- eBay

- Buy.com

- Rakuten

- Flipkart (India)

- Newegg

- Bonanza

- Overstock

- Pricefalls (electronics)

- 3tailer.com

- Wayfair (home furnishings)

- Reverb

- Houzz (also home furnishings)

Do your research to find marketplaces that serve your industry vertical. These are analogous to Amazon but for specific industries, where sellers present products for buyers to consider and purchase within the defined parameters of a specific industry's needs.

Loyalty and Referral Marketing

It's quite common to find refer a friend and loyalty marketing programs in the B2C world. And for good reason: They work extremely well. In the U.S. alone, more than three billion consumers are signed up for loyalty programs.[89] And while the rate at which consumers sign up for memberships is slowing, loyalty programs are still growing at a healthy 15 percent each year.[90]

Typically in these types of programs, consumers are rewarded for spending money at a retailer or referring a friend. They can be as simple as a punch card at your local coffee shop to more complicated and involved efforts such as airline mileage programs that provide points (or "miles") that are redeemable for discounts and free trips. These types of programs do not always translate directly into B2B. Business buyers are not spending their own money when they make purchases for their firm, and therefore do not have the same motivations as consumers. Developing a B2B loyalty program needs to take this into consideration.

The goal of any loyalty program is to entice buyers to spend more of their budget with your company. A B2B loyalty program can be implemented to balance both personal incentives for the employee and purchase incentives for the business. For example, some B2B sellers have found that rewarding the purchasing agent (and potentially the purchase influencer) with personalized thank you gifts, such as gift cards or other similar perks, to be effective. Other sellers have found it fruitful to reward the entire company for their loyalty, not only with discounts based on purchase volume, but also incorporating more meaningful and larger gestures such

89   https://www.inc.com/peter-roesler/loyalty-programs-remain-extremely-popular-with-con.html
90   Ibid.

as paid events, industry seminars at desirable locations, and even fully paid vacations. Note that many large buying organizations maintain restrictions around these types of activities and rewards, so you will need to determine how, when, and if you are able to create these programs for your customers (or a subset of your customers).

Eligibility for loyalty rewards must be tied to business results, the most obvious of which is purchases made from your firm. Some boundaries or thresholds need to be set in order to make these types of programs profitable. You don't want to give away $100,000 worth of rewards for company who spends $150,000 per year with you. But you may find that spending $100,000 on rewards for customers who spend more than $1,000,000/year worthwhile, particularly if you can demonstrate how the loyalty program has directly resulted in incremental revenue from that customer.

Maintaining an ROI model for a loyalty program is critical. This model should incorporate metrics like average order value, annual purchase frequency, and customer retention rates, in order to understand your baseline. Then the program should be developed around these metrics, with defined goals and thresholds for each. For example, you might offer rewards for customers who spend 30 percent more than the average customer after enrolling in the program, or for customers who complete a certain number of orders per year over a specified dollar value. As with any marketing program, success will come with testing and analyzing the results. Roll out a loyalty program to a small group and observe how they engage and take advantage of loyalty benefits. Monitor your key metrics over time and compare what participants in the program spend to what non-participants spend. Lastly, adjust your approach and rewards to fuel program expansion.

CASE STUDY

Augusta Sportswear Group:
Learning from B2C

Double digit Ecommerce growth, driven by digital marketing

Augusta Sportswear Brands knows how to play ball. The company is a leading designer and manufacturer of sports team apparel. Youth and adult sports leagues around the world wear their products while playing soccer, volleyball, baseball, basketball, football, tennis, and other sports. Augusta sells its products in a B2B format to resellers ("dealers") of team apparel, called "decorators." These firms add team names, numbers, and player names to the company's products via screen printing, embroidery, and other personalization processes.

Augusta has been engaged in B2B Ecommerce for some time, and today, online selling comprises over 50 percent of the company's sales. Augusta's customers clearly have a preference for buying this way, particularly for re-orders of products they have purchased previously.

Through their experience with Ecommerce, Augusta has learned digital marketing's value to increasing awareness and sales, and has successfully adopted many of the tactics of B2C online retailers.

"We have seen double digit growth from B2B Ecommerce, and we attribute this directly to our digital marketing activities," says Nathan Maxwell, Augusta's Senior Director of Digital Experience. "And we are seeing very high return on our marketing spend, with revenues from advertising efforts as high as ten times our spend."

To achieve these results, the company has implemented a comprehensive digital marketing program, adopting numerous B2C tactics, including:

- Paid search on Google.

- Email marketing.

- Social media, particularly using display advertising that retargets web site visitors in their Facebook newsfeeds.

- Video advertising, including integrating videos into Facebook with targeted calls to action encouraging viewers to click through to learn more and purchase.

- Leveraging Amazon marketing to drive attention to the company's listings on the marketplace, and also to increase overall brand awareness.

Maxwell cautions B2B marketers to take the long view on their digital advertising approach.

"You can't just look at the ad unit that drove the sale from a click," he says. "Recognize that the customer's path to purchase in B2B is long, as long as a few days, weeks, and sometimes months. And this means you have to be patient with results from your advertising. Understand that all of these digital marketing channels work together to drive brand awareness and sales. A balanced approach across multiple channels is important. Make sure you look at marketing from an omni-channel perspective and not just on a channel by channel level."

The lesson here is that if you look at marketing channels individually, you may focus disproportionately on those advertising methods that have a direct impact on your revenue, but overlook channels that have a more indirect benefit. Developing a robust measurement program—at both the aggregate and channel levels—is integral to any digital marketing operation.

Says Maxwell: "We are managing our budget on a linear attribution model, spreading our spend across a variety of channels, with an emphasis on email, paid search, and retargeting. Taking this approach helps us uncover some unrealized opportunities with some surprisingly high ROI levels."

Augusta Sportswear Brands will continue its Ecommerce growth by putting digital marketing at the center of its efforts.

Marketing Automation

As you can see from the tactics we have discussed so far, digital marketing takes a considerable amount time and resources to be effective. Luckily, many of the associated tasks can be automated using digital technologies. When set up and maintained correctly, marketing automation can not only make your marketing more efficient and easier to manage, but also more effective, and can boost overall the return from your efforts.

Marketing automation breaks downs into essentially three different functions: awareness development, lead nurturing, and customer loyalty. Let's briefly take a look at each of these areas.

Awareness Development: These are tasks related to growing your overall online presence, and thus focus around increasing brand awareness and authority. Some automated tasks that fall under this category typically include:

- Pushing content from the web site to social media platforms.

- Maintaining follower lists on social media platforms.

- Capturing customer information and scoring the prospective customer's value to the business.

- Email list segmentation.

Lead Nurturing: Once a prospective customer is in your database, you will want to continue to communicate with that person. This can be challenging, but automation makes one-to-one marketing far more achievable at greater scale. Tasks in this area can include:

- Sending relevant product information based on pages browsed on your web site.

- Sending abandoned shopping cart emails and other triggered emails based on web site actions (see the Email discussion above).

- Triggered email drip campaigns with relevant content, and targeted and timed promotional offers.

Customer Loyalty: Keeping your buyers engaged over the long-run is important to business sustainability. Growing a customer's lifetime value has a direct impact on revenues, and marketing automation can help support efforts to maintain and increase this value. Functions in this area include:

- Re-order reminders.

- Personalized promotions.

- Customer win-back campaigns for dormant buyers.

- Proactive product maintenance and service or support reminders.

- Loyalty program communications (e.g. triggered communications on rewards received based on purchase activities).

These lists are by no means exhaustive, and marketing software packages offer a variety of options to help streamline your efforts in these areas. Note that effective marketing automation deployments will almost always require integration to your existing systems, such as your Ecommerce platform, CRM (customer relationship management), and order management systems. There are a variety of commercial platforms to choose from. The leaders in enterprise marketing automation solutions for B2B, as of this writing, include offerings from Oracle, Adobe (which purchased Marketo in late 2018), Salesforce, and SAP.

CASE STUDY

MyBinding: Building a Healthy and Productive Marketing Mix for B2B Ecommerce

"There is massive opportunity for suppliers"

MyBinding has office paper handling and presentation covered. Offering more than 45,000 products for binding, laminating, handling, presentation, and shredding, this mid-market distributor provides a wide assortment of products to government, educational institutions, print shops, corporate marketing and HR departments, and small businesses. MyBinding completes the vast majority of its orders via its Ecommerce web site, and considers itself a digital-first organization. Digital marketing is a primary method the company uses to find new customers and keep them coming back.

"In digital marketing for B2B Ecommerce, it is important to have a balanced mix of efforts and traffic sources," says Jeff McRitchie, the company's Vice President of Ecommerce. "This includes paid search, search engine optimization, email, display advertising, and even social media." McRitchie recommends a test and learn approach to marketing, and setting aside budget to try advertising in new channels.

MyBinding has found particular success with SEO.

"There is massive opportunity for suppliers to rank highly in search engine results by leveraging content and their own brand names," he says.

The content that brands produce to provide service and support for other selling channels, such as the sales team, can be used to reinforce a company's authority in a specific category.

"Google and other search engines love this content and reward firms with high rankings that follow best practices to expose this data on their web sites. We have used this approach to gain top search engine rankings on terms such as 'binding machines' and 'laminators,'" notes McRitchie.

Understanding that the B2B buyer is not only motivated by product discounts or deals is also important when marketing in channels such as email.

"Remember that the B2B buyer, such as a procurement officer, is not spending their own money when making a purchase, like a consumer would be in a traditional Ecommerce purchase," McRitchie says. "We have found success in providing a perk that the buyer can use for themselves, such as a gift card to their favorite restaurant or coffee shop, as a part of the online purchase. Just offering a discount on product isn't always the most motivating factor for the buyer to choose your product."

Clever digital marketing approaches like these have helped MyBinding to become a leader in its category.

Measuring Your Efforts

Active and accurate measurement of your marketing efforts against a set of defined key performance indicators (KPIs) is critical for success. This needs to be examined in both the short and long-term. Short-term measurement helps you correct any major issues with your marketing program and capture opportunities as they arise. Long-term measurement helps you identify trends and evaluate your overarching strategy to determine what larger, strategic initiatives are needed to boost your business. For short-term measurement, I recommend focusing on monthly reporting, though it is a best practice to review metrics weekly in the first three to four months of a new digital marketing effort. There are a number of metrics that need to be measured over both of these time frames. Let's take a closer look at the most important KPIs to focus on.

- **Web site traffic:** How many people are coming to your site? What pages are they visiting?

- **Traffic source:** Where is your traffic coming from? Is it coming from search engines, social media web sites, industry web sites, vendor directories, marketplaces, or other sources? Monitoring this will help you identify areas where you may want to invest future marketing dollars.

- **Navigation path:** How are people using your web site? What pages are they landing on and where are they going afterwards?

- **Bounce rate:** The percentage of web site visitors who visit a single page and then navigate away from the site entirely. Measure this not only site-wide, but for each source of traffic to your site.

- **Exit rate:** Often confused with bounce rate, exit rate is the rate at which visitors leave your site from a page when they have visited more than one page.

- **Conversion rate:** The percentage of visitors who become buyers. This is one of the most important metrics to track. Measure this on a site-wide basis, and for each traffic source.

- **Average order value (AOV):** The average amount of money visitors spend on each order. This metric, combined with conversion rate, is like the pulse of your Ecommerce web site. Benchmarking this statistic and figuring out how to improve it is a key way to enhance your Ecommerce performance. It should be measured site-wide and also for each traffic source.

- **Shopping cart abandon rate:** The percentage of buyers who put something into their shopping cart, but do not finalize a purchase. This is an extremely important statistic to keep your eye on, as a jump in this figure could indicate a problem with your web site effectiveness.

Note that measurement of the effectiveness of digital marketing programs in today's highly fractured media environment has become increasingly difficult. With many types of advertising and other touch points that a customer may engage with during a modern buying journey, it is not accurate to attribute a purchase only to a single marketing channel (such as an email or paid search ad). For example, a typical customer may see you at a trade show, download a white paper from your web site, find you later through a Google search, see your brand show up on their LinkedIn newsfeed, see an offline ad about your product in a trade publication, and eventually respond to an email offer before finally making a purchase. On your end, they might have clicked something online (such as your Google ad and your email), and you can measure these things, but you may or may not be able to determine which other places they saw your brand or product. The result is confusion for the marketer; e.g. "where should I invest my marketing dollars if I can't measure the effectiveness of each touch point?" Software giant Adobe calls this a "billion dollar problem" because it is a very complex endeavor that is not easy to solve.[91]

When analyzing marketing channels based on performance, the data is often skewed towards channels that are directly attributed to having produced sales results. In the example I provided above, email would get the "credit" for the sale, as it was the marketing channel that generated the click to the web site that resulted in a purchase. But this is not the best way to understand the effectiveness of your overall marketing program. While a perfect solution still does not exist, a number of technology solutions have emerged to help better understand how each marketing channel contributes to the sale of a product. The industry's term for this is "multi-touch attribution," as it measures the influence of each marketing campaign on the ultimate purchase. These tools allow marketers to allocate weights to each advertising channel utilized, based on how much they believe each marketing effort plays into influencing customer purchase behavior. This is called "attribution modeling." Marketing automation tools, such as those listed above at the end of the prior section, and web analytics tools, including Google Analytics, have some capabilities to measure attribution. When a marketer can understand the effectiveness of each advertising channel, even if estimated, he or she can more intelligently allocate budget to the best performing channels and improve results.

---

91 https://theblog.adobe.com/marketing-attribution-billion-dollar-problem/

Even if you do not implement an attribution model, it is unwise to dismiss channels that seem to be underperforming based on direct click results. Instead, determine what metrics are important to that channel specifically and correlate it with other things you can measure—such as traffic, conversion rates, and average order value. For example, if your brand is active on Twitter, you might measure clicks to content on your site that you are tweeting about, but you might also measure other engagement such as retweets, replies, and mentions. Just because people are not clicking a specific link in a tweet (or whatever other marketing channel you are measuring) does not mean your presence on that channel lacks value in influencing customer behavior.

Putting It All Together

Generating and converting leads through digital marketing is tried-and-true in the B2C world, and it can exponentially add value to a B2B company. B2B marketers can learn from their B2C colleagues in this area, and expand and customize the tactics described above to their own industries.

In many ways, digital marketing is a perfect vehicle for B2B marketing, where one-to-one relationships have long been the foundation of business success. Digital marketing has the promise to be even more effective for B2B channels than it has traditionally been in the B2C realm. For example, audience segmentation is typically very different in B2C, where it is usually based on demographics, geography, lifestyle preferences, and other high-level demographic and psychographic factors. By contrast, B2B audiences are typically smaller, and detailed information is known about each B2B customer. Marketing can be segmented and targeted in ways that are truly one to one, and reflect the B2B marketer's traditional relationship approach.

One of the keys to tying together traditional and digital marketing involves integrating the Ecommerce system with the Customer Relationship Management (CRM) system to create a single view of the customer across all selling and marketing channels. Passing leads generated through digital marketing and the web site to the CRM system pays strong dividends. Leading B2B companies are using these digital methods to automatically create activities through the CRM system for the inside and outside sales teams, based on product and purchase interest demonstrated by leads gathered through digital channels. Using this approach, the customer's need is clear and consistently communicated, leading to better, more qualified leads and higher close rates for the sales team.

Successful manufacturers, distributors, and brands are taking advantage of the shift to digital. They are capturing new clients and opening new markets by putting their products and the company's value proposition front and center on the Internet. This includes utilizing tried and true digital marketing methods, including paid search, search engine optimization (SEO), social media marketing, display advertising and more, to grow revenue and deepen market share.

Key Chapter Takeaways

- Digital marketing must be leveraged to stay in front of where B2B buyers are now conducting research and making purchase decisions.

- The digital marketing channels used by B2C marketers for many years can be leveraged by B2B marketers.

- A robust digital marketing plan should be developed and executed to include a mix of the following marketing channels: Email, SEO, Paid Search,

Content Marketing, Social Media, Display and Retargeting, Affiliate Marketing, Loyalty Programs, and Marketplaces.

- Best practices in each of these marketing approaches are well-established and should be followed; each of these areas require knowledge and skills (e.g. retaining agencies or hiring experts to work internally).

- Marketing Automation should be strongly considered to enhance the relevancy and timing of communications with customers, create efficiencies, and reduce day-to-day workloads of front-line marketing staff.

- B2B marketers can leverage their heritage of one-to-one relationships and concentrated customer bases to make digital marketing even more effective than it has historically been in B2C marketing; these relationships can be further enhanced by integrating to the Customer Relationship Management system to form a true 360 degree view of the customer across all selling and interaction channels.

Technology as an Enabler: Building a Solid Foundation

9

S o far, I have mostly focused the content of this book on the human side of developing and implementing Ecommerce in a B2B setting. The reason for this is that, even though the technology component is essential to success, none of it matters if you do not get the human side right first by aligning it with your business objectives. After all, what good is investing thousands or millions of dollars in software if your people do not use it, or your customers fail to adopt it?

That said, technology is a key foundational item for any successful Ecommerce operation. Too often, I see businesses putting technology first before establishing clear business objectives and thinking about how it will impact their staff, customers, vendors, and partners. Failing to consider these factors will significantly limit your success in Ecommerce. However, once the foundational components for success are in place—leadership, objective definition, understanding customer needs, return on investment models, and organizational and partner alignment—it is time to put the right technology in place, centered on selecting an Ecommerce software platform.

Unfortunately, many companies do not conduct the necessary due diligence prior to selecting an Ecommerce platform. All too often, I see companies fail to put in the time and effort required to create a thorough list of requirements, objectives, and interdependencies for their Ecommerce system. In doing so, these companies drastically increase the likelihood they will choose the wrong platform, which prevents them from taking full advantage of the opportunity. I have lived this myself during my 20+ years in the Ecommerce industry. Rushing to a platform decision without taking the time to fully understand your current technology environment and documenting what you need the new system to accomplish can be disastrous. Putting the technology first almost put one company I was running out of business; it took three re-platforming efforts in two years before I learned my lesson. Luckily, I made this mistake early in my career, and learned from it!

Taking the plunge into Ecommerce for the first time is an extremely time-consuming process and requires considerable organizational effort across functional areas. It takes the organization away from running and growing the day-to-day business. Because so much is at stake, it is imperative to choose the right platform the first time; it has to be one you can live with for ten years or longer. The only way you can ensure this is done correctly is by extensively documenting your technical and business requirements, overall digital commerce objectives, and interconnected business and technical components. You will need to include information about features, workflows, pricing, contract support, flexibility, and integrations. We will discuss running a thorough Ecommerce platform selection process in more detail later in this chapter.

Your company likely does not have Ecommerce expertise in house, and almost certainly does not have Ecommerce platform selection experience. Many IT departments may have system selection skills and experience. However, Ecommerce solutions contain a very specific set of features and functionalities tied to front-end digital experiences and back-end processes. Seemingly subtle differences between platforms can be difficult to identify during a selection process, but can have a large impact during the systems implementation process and beyond. As a result of these factors, many companies outsource these responsibilities to consultants or agencies who are experts in the space. Yes, it costs money and will add some time to the process. However, the return on investment and risk reduction from conducting a thorough, expert-driven process the first time makes it worth the upfront cost.

How to Choose an Ecommerce Platform

The process of choosing an Ecommerce platform can seem overwhelming, particularly for B2B organizations that have little internal expertise or experience in Ecommerce. However, there is a well-documented process that I will share here that breaks platform selection down into manageable steps. And by taking advantage of experienced consultants through the process, you can also build Ecommerce knowledge and confidence within your organization as you go through these steps.

Trends are working in your favor. Twenty years ago, if a B2B company wanted to build an Ecommerce presence, they would need to develop the technology from the ground up, building it mostly in-house and usually spending tens of millions of dollars in the process. In contrast, today there are many platforms that offer a wide variety of functionalities, at a lower cost and with more implementation resources available than ever before.

The challenge in having a wide variety of options, however, is *that there are a wide variety of options.* Finding the best platform can be exhausting and confusing, particularly when persuasive vendor marketing and sales teams are constantly vying for your attention, speaking a language that is new to you, and often sugar-coating things. I have seen this confusion lead to paralysis and inaction; this isn't the path to success. Getting smart about the process is the only way to successfully develop and implement an Ecommerce technology, while also limiting risk of failure.

Choosing the right platform (as well as the systems integration partner to build it for you) is the most important decision you will make in regards to how smoothly implementation goes. Here is a clear process that I have developed over the course of conducting more than three dozen platform selections for B2B and B2C companies, and I highly recommend following it:

Let's look at each stage of this process in more detail.

Document Objectives

Before you even think about what technology platform will be best suited to your company, you have to define business objectives. Objectives should tie to your expected Return on Investment (ROI) model (see Chapter 3 for details), and can also include intangible benefits that you expect from Ecommerce. Objectives can include:

- Increased share of wallet from existing customers.

- Incremental revenue from new customers.

- Shift of sales to more efficient channels (particularly repeat orders).

- Higher gross margins obtained through online selling.

- Increased customer loyalty obtained by making buyers' jobs easier, as evidenced by increased lifetime value of each customer.

- Enhanced competitive advantage vs. non-Ecommerce enabled competitors.

- Improved organizational effectiveness, particularly in the sales and support functions.

- Overall enhancement of enterprise value.

Your business objectives need to be translated into technological requirements; that is, the technology platform you choose must be able to support the objectives. Too often companies seek to deploy technology for technology's sake, but this is backwards. Objectives are the foundation upon which technology should be constructed.

Fundamental to this effort is acquiring sufficient customer feedback that will provide you with a thorough understanding of their needs and expectations. By putting the customer first in this process, your requirements and ultimate system selection will be based on a foundation of meeting the customer's needs, making it more likely that you will gain adoption after you launch your new web site. See Chapter 3 for my tips on how to incorporate customer feedback into your Ecommerce planning effort.

There are details and subtleties of a sophisticated Ecommerce system that are learned only from the experience of working in Ecommerce and past systems selections. I recommend hiring a seasoned consultant or firm to assist you with this process. A consultant can help ensure that you are not overlooking any major functionalities and selecting a system that fits your business needs and those of your customers. At minimum, have someone in your organization who has some experience in Ecommerce lead this effort, and carefully research the important aspects of web site functionality prior to starting the process. I have included a high level framework you can use to get started later in this chapter.

It is often best to structure this process by starting internally first and then working outwards, including any audiences your web site may touch (e.g. the customer personas we discussed in Chapter 3). If you have been putting your customers' needs first, then this part of the process should be straight forward for you. You may have a good amount of data already collected. It will be easy to become distracted by all the bells and whistles as you go through this process. That is why it is critical to always keep your customers' needs in mind throughout the process.

I strongly recommend taking the following steps to understand both your customer and your business needs:

1. **Interview your sales and customer support teams:** Look for common areas where your customers are seeking to use a web site to both buy online and receive support via your site (such as re-ordering products, checking order status, looking up inventory availability, finding product and compatibility information, administering accounts, and other tasks). Seek out ways that the sales and support teams can be made more effective by using online tools.

2. **Interview your customers:** Identify a group of customers that you can talk with in person or by phone

(or both) to understand their expectations of your Ecommerce web site. Explore areas such as:

- What are their expected purchase patterns online?

- What are their expectations from a digital usability standpoint?

- Which products will they purchase online (e.g. what products do they regularly buy from you on a repeat order basis)? Are there any categories which they don't want to buy online, and if so, why not?

- Which other web sites do they use to research and buy similar products?

- What parts of their current offline workflows would they most likely want to move online? For example, obtaining order status, finding delivery information, researching product details prior to making a purchase, or paying invoices or open credit balances. Look for repetitive tasks that will be made easier by bringing them online.

- Do they need support for "punch out" (ERP-based) ordering?

- How do customers want to interact with you across device types (mobile, desktop, etc.)?

Ultimately, you want to discover which customer interactions will become easier via online channels, and focus on building these into your technology requirements. Making these actions easier will be *critical* for you to drive adoption of your new Ecommerce site. Be sure to talk with at least 20 customers and survey different types of customers across industry segments, including customers of different sizes.

3. **Form a customer advisory board:** This can emerge from the group you interviewed and will help you through the Ecommerce development process. The most successful B2B Ecommerce implementations I have seen have leveraged a group of customers that can be involved at every stage of the web site development process, providing feedback as you build. This team of customers can be called upon to review your web site creative designs, provide a test panel for usability of the site, and be used as a sounding board for features you are considering adding.

One company I recently worked with, a multi-billion dollar healthcare, pharmaceutical, and medical device firm, effectively utilized customer and sales team feedback at the start of their Ecommerce effort. When they began interviewing stakeholders, they unexpectedly found that they had large gaps in the data that they needed to be successful in Ecommerce. This company had thousands of product data sheets and user manuals that they realized were presenting different information across their diverse product lines. Not only did these materials need to be digitized, including ensuring all content was up-to-date with accurate drawings and specifications, but the firm also needed to ensure that pricing was consistent. The company needed to show customers the prices they expected to see, not only in the online shopping cart, but when their customers were browsing the product list pages. Management built an intensive data cleansing and normalization effort into their deployment process. Now that they are live with Ecommerce, their customers feel confident in ordering through the online system, as they are getting the product data they need and seeing the prices they expect. Within the first few days of launch, the firm had almost 700 customers registered to use the new Ecommerce site and a tremendous uptick in orders. Thanks to their diligence around product data, Ecommerce has since grown to comprise a considerable percentage of the company's overall sales. Without upfront stakeholder interviews, they may not have realized and filled their data gaps.

Define the Technology Environment and Deployment Approach

You will be purchasing and implementing an Ecommerce software package, but this solution is only one piece in a broader technology environment that most likely already exists in your company. There are a number of technical environment considerations that should be documented and incorporated into your Ecommerce platform selection process.

The graphic below illustrates the overall environment and functionalities that the Ecommerce system will live within. These elements are described in the following two sections.

System components and requirements that need to be considered can include (but aren't limited to):

1. **Enterprise Resource Planning (ERP) system:** Typically the "heart" of an organization from a systems perspective, the ERP handles functions such as accounting, inventory tracking, order processing, customer and product information, merchandise management and forecasting, and other key functions. ERP's are often the most robust systems in an organization, from a functionality standpoint, and are frequently found to be the system of record for order, customer, inventory, and product information. It is the

Web Site Shopping Features

- Navigation, Search, Checkout, Product Compare, Reviews, Merchandising, Promotions, International selling, Mulit-site, many other 'commodity' features

Product Information Management (PIM)

- Product & Pricing by Customer
- Custom Catalogs
- Data Hierarchies, Inheritance Rules
- Digital Asset Management
- Product descriptions, category assignments, taxonomy, other product level information

Content Management (CMS)

- Content workflows and permissions
- Educational, technical product data, training
- Integration of content and commerce

B2B Workflows

- Account set ups, approvals
- Group and User Administration
- Customer Self Service
- Roles and permissions
- Product catalog, pricing administration

Business Requirements Document

ERP

- Order & Customer Data
- Inventory information
- Accounting and Financial
- Other Functions
- Often the System of Record

Data & Integrations

- Complex integrations for pricing rules, account management, product catalogs, etc.
- ERP
- CRM
- MDM

Payment Methods

- Standard B2C (e.g. Credit cards and Paypal) PLUS POs, Payment on account, Payment Terms, Will Call, and other methods

Mobile Commerce & Sales Force Enablement

- Mobile site to enable sales force effectiveness – product data, promotions information, re-ordering
- Mobile App considerations

most common system with which Ecommerce systems are integrated. Examples of ERPs include suites from Epicor, Netsuite, Microsoft (e.g. Dynamics), Oracle, and SAP. You should expect this to be a primary point of tie in for your Ecommerce platform, and integration will likely be one of the larger cost components in your implementation process.

2. **Customer Relationship Management (CRM) system:** Often used by B2B organizations as the primary system for managing customer relationships, particularly by the sales and marketing organizations. CRM contains features such as lead management, marketing automation, and customer segmentation. Examples of CRM systems include solutions from Salesforce, Microsoft CRM, Sugar CRM, Netsuite, and others. Integration between Ecommerce solutions and the CRM can be extremely powerful, as understanding and acting on customer actions across all channels (online and offline) has been shown to improve overall customer loyalty and revenue per customer.

3. **Product Information Management (PIM) system:** Acts as the system of record for product information and manages various types of product data, such as attributes, marketing media assets (e.g. images and videos), product categorization, and product data feeds (information passed between systems). Robust PIM systems are used by B2B organizations to feed information into the Ecommerce system, supporting a foundation of robust product data which is critical for success. Commonly utilized PIM systems include Salsify, inRiver, Stibo Systems, Riversand, EnterWorks, Contentserv, Informatica, Agility Multichannel, SAP, and others.

4. **Content Management (CMS) systems:** The primary system that is often used to manage content across all selling channels, including the web and in support of offline marketing. Typical functions include content creation, editing, and publishing workflows (approvals through the content creation process), content

organization and taxonomy, and content scheduling for publishing. CMS systems are often used to power non-transactional B2B web sites. Common systems include Adobe Experience Manager, Sitecore, Episerver, Bloomreach, SAP, Oracle, Acquia, and IBM.

5. **Order Management/Warehouse Management (OMS/WMS) systems:** These systems manage orders from both online or offline channels. OMS/WMS functionalities can include order processing management, inventory management, order picking, packing, and shipping, and other fulfillment capabilities. Sometimes these functions are handled by the ERP system. However, if these systems don't talk to each other directly, they will most likely be an integration point for your Ecommerce platform.

Other systems that are also often in place include marketing automation, sales force automation, field force automation, customer service systems, email service providers (ESPs), project management systems, business intelligence and reporting, web analytics, and mobile-specific applications. Regardless of what systems your firm uses, know that some Ecommerce platforms will offer similar functionalities. A critical step in your systems implementation process will be to determine whether you will utilize your existing solutions for these functionalities or leverage the new Ecommerce platform. At a minimum, your chosen platform will need to integrate within your existing technology ecosystem.

A preliminary idea of how the Ecommerce system will integrate to these other systems described above should be established at this point. One key aspect of integration that needs to be considered is how data will flow across systems and throughout your organization. Create a data flow model that shows what type of information is stored, where it is stored, and how it moves through your company. This visual representation of how Ecommerce will interact with and pass data back and forth from these systems will provide a clear picture to platform vendors on what integrations they need to address during the implementation process. Following is an example of a data flow model from one of my clients.

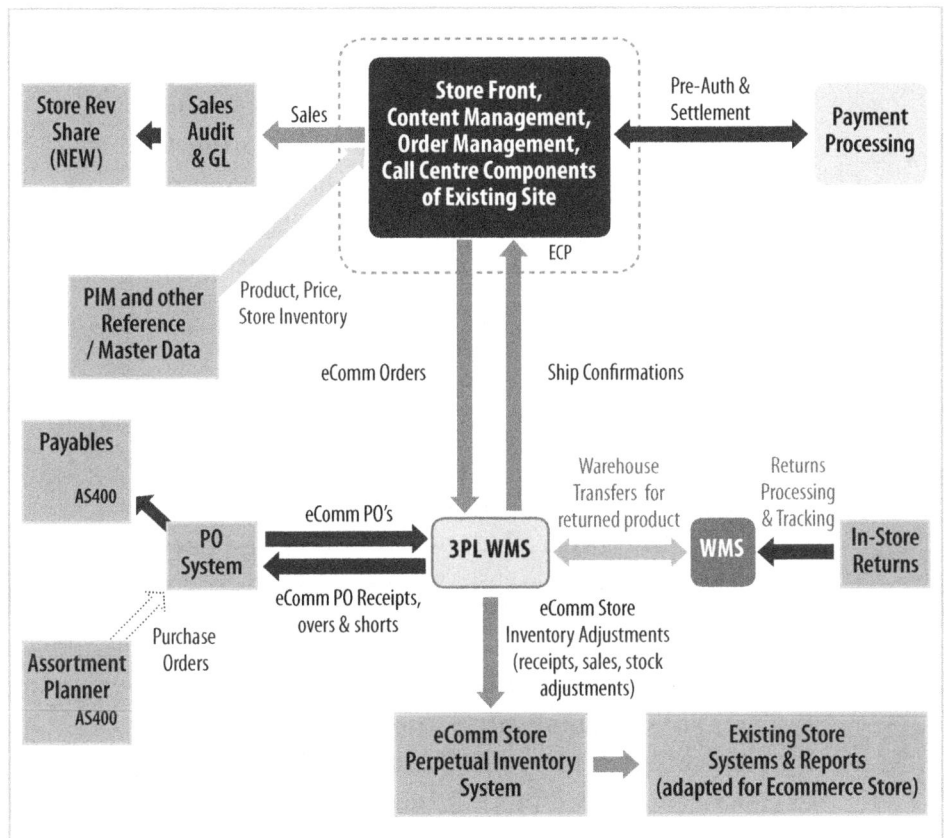

In addition to the systems environment, deployment options for your Ecommerce system should be considered at this stage. As you get deeper into the selection process, vendor capabilities can be assessed in each of these areas to gain a more complete understanding of the best option for your organization. Considerations for deployment include:

- **Web site hosting requirements:** Does your current web site hosting company support Ecommerce software packages? If so, which ones? Depending on the answers here, you may need to shop around for web site hosting companies to find one that matches the platform you choose. Alternatively, does the platform itself offer hosting? Cloud-based Software as a Service (SaaS) options have become very common and robust in recent years, and should be strongly considered. With a SaaS solution, the Ecommerce platform is hosted by the software provider itself, and has numerous advantages, typically including receiving upgrades and new features automatically. You may also look at hosting yourself, however this option should really be reserved for IT departments with experience and expertise in managing servers. Be honest about your company's capabilities here. Ultimately, at this stage of the selection process, you should have a general idea on your hosting preferences, but I recommend keeping an open mind as you move through the selection process.

- **Security compliance requirements:** Understand your level of PCI compliance needed, as this will impact your ability to accept credit cards (see the Glossary for a definition of PCI). Review and document other security features you need in order to ensure data security and comply with privacy laws (especially if you have customers in Europe, where data privacy requirements are stricter than those in the United States, as of this writing).

- **Development:** Ecommerce platforms have a variety of "openness," which dictates whether or not the software code can be changed by outside resources, such as your internal developers or implementation partner. This is an important consideration to understand early in the selection process, and your need for this will be shaped by the level of customization your business requires. Some software vendors will allow a tremendous amount of flexibility and openness of their software, so that customers may develop custom online experiences and functionalities. Others are more "closed," and only certain, more superficial front-end changes can be made. This limits what can be customized on the platform, but also generally provides for a lower cost, easier to maintain system. On average, closed software systems have fewer development resources available in the marketplace (often the software vendor is the sole party that can make changes), which sometimes translates into a higher cost for customization. Ecommerce platforms with an "open source" heritage or a modular framework, such as Magento or SAP, will generally provide more open structures and core code access. Platforms delivered within a more structured SaaS model, such as Netsuite, Shopify, or Salesforce B2B Commerce often provide less back-end core code access, but can be easier and faster to scale. Understanding which of the platforms allow for more or less flexibility, relative to your overall goals and requirements, can greatly help narrow the field down from a longer list of platform options.

One other important consideration at this stage is platform architecture. You will need to have a solid understanding of the conceptual structures in order to choose the platform that will best suit your needs. While there are a variety of approaches to how a platform accommodates Ecommerce functionalities, two main concepts to be aware of are "headless commerce" and multi-tenancy.

Headless commerce specifically refers to a platform structure where the back-end data management is separated, or de-coupled, from the front-end user interface. This can enable far greater flexibility in terms of how content and experiences are delivered. This is a popular architecture for firms that already have a solid, well-developed content management platform in place and are seeking to add complex Ecommerce functionality to their existing web site. Because content and transactional functionalities are managed separately with headless commerce, it is easier for firms to experiment with new forms of digital commerce, such as Internet of Things, voice search, and virtual reality (see Chapter 12 for more details).

Multi-tenancy describes software that can be used by many different users while sharing the same core back-end data management structure. This is commonly used for firms that manage multiple brands that often have no connection to each other. The biggest advantage of a multi-tenant platform is the cost savings from sharing resources and product data as well as centralized control over things like security and maintenance.

Document Requirements

The requirements documentation stage is the heart of the selection process, and the step that can (and probably should) consume the largest amount of time and resources, across the organization. During this process, a firm creates a list of functional and business requirements that the web site needs to support in order to meet your business goals. The list of requirements that result from this effort will be used to evaluate the match of various software solutions against organizational and customer needs. Thus, accurately creating a well-thought-out list of requirements, based on the organizational and customer input gathered in the first step, is critical to a successful Ecommerce platform selection.

A number of important areas need to be documented in detail during the requirements phase. Each requirements area should be aligned to the overall business goals as well as Ecommerce best practices, and describe what the web site should functionally support in order to meet objectives. Key functionalities to consider include:

Front-end web site experience

- **Site Navigation:** The way that site users find products by browsing.

- **On Site Search:** Critical for B2B web sites, particularly those with many products, the site search function allows web site users to conduct keyword searches and presents a list of relevant product or content based on the search query, along with filters for narrowing search results.

- **Mobile and Responsive Design:** Modern web sites MUST be mobile-optimized, and responsive web site design is a best practice approach that changes how a web site is presented based on the device through which it is accessed.

- **Web Merchandising:** Includes product upsells and cross sells, product associations, bundling and kitting, automated product recommendations, featured product display zones, and other functions.

- **User-Generated Content:** Includes product reviews, customer questions and answers(Q&As), and other content not created by the organization.

- **Store or Location Finder:** For companies with multiple brick and mortar locations, such as branches, offices, or stores. Includes information such as product availability by location and how to obtain product support/service.

- **Internationalization and Localization:** Support for different languages, currencies, shipping, and other international or location-based factors.

- **Gifting:** Providing gift cards, gift messaging, or gift wrapping services; less often utilized in B2B, but if you are looking to sell to consumers via the web, this could be an important set of features.

Marketing

- **Landing Pages:** Creation and management of landing pages, which can be leveraged for marketing purposes such as lead capture, promotional events, new product launches, and other uses.

- **Search Engine Optimization (SEO):** Capabilities of the platform to support best practices for SEO, including site maps, full web site crawlability, content types and presentation (e.g. title tags, header tags, etc.)

- **Social Media:** Incorporation of social login, social sharing of product information and purchases, customer-submitted product photos and articles via social media, and other functions.

- **Multi-channel Selling:** Includes support for printed catalogs, assigned sales rep contact information.

- **Multi-site Support:** Sometimes called "micro-sites," this is the ability to launch and manage multiple web sites from a single back-end interface.

Web site operations and content management

- **Product information and taxonomy:** Includes product information management—the way the Ecommerce system imports, organizes, and presents product information on product category pages as well as product detail pages; this type of requirement includes page layouts and functionalities based on best practices for every page type.

- **Inventory:** Display and management of product inventory, including messaging and rules around pre-ordering and allowing orders on backordered products.

- **Content Management:** Content types, display, editorial workflows, including static content such as PDFs, product how-to's and guides, and other brand-related content.

- **Online Customer Service Tools:** Including online chat and survey management.

- **System Tools:** Data import and export tools, security and compliance tools, and fraud prevention/management.

- **Ecommerce Reporting and Analytics:** Includes integration to web analytics software, financial reporting, and other business intelligence software tools.

Personalization and loyalty

- **Product Personalization and Configuration:**
  For products that require personalization, such as
  embroidery, logo application, or other personalized
  features or configurations desired by the buyer, such
  as a product "builder" or "finder" like an ink finder on
  a printer manufacturer's web site; for a good example,
  see Epson.com.

- **Personalization and Customer Segmentation:**
  Includes dynamic content and product presentation
  based on who is viewing a web page and customer
  group(s) the site visitor belongs to.

- **Customer Loyalty:** Includes integration with online
  and offline rewards programs, such as annual rebates.

Web site checkout

- **Shopping Cart and Checkout:** Following best
  practices for easy and fast checkout, and incorporating
  B2B requirements such as purchase approval
  workflows, customer-specific shipping options,
  customer pick up at branch or distribution center
  location, and multiple shipping addresses.

- **Payment Methods:** Including credit cards, alternative
  payment methods like Credit Key and Paypal, and
  traditional B2B buying methods such as purchase
  orders, purchase on account, request a quote, or
  configure-price-quote (CPQ) tools for building orders.

B2B workflows

- **Online Account Creation and Management:**
  Including new account request, assignment of roles
  and permissions within a customer's organization,
  address management, credit terms management,
  review of order history, and other areas.

- **B2B Workflow Management:** Matches customers'
  procurement or other purchasing workflows, which
  may include requesting approvals, saving and sharing
  shopping carts, and other related functions.

- **Quick Re-ordering:** Supported within customer
  accounts or via quick look up, allows customers
  to quickly re-order products they have previously
  purchased.

- **Support for Customer-specific Pricing and
  Customer-specific Product Catalogs:** Special pricing
  or product information based on a contractual
  relationship with a customer. This often requires
  integration to the ERP or other back-end systems
  to capture accurate customer-specific pricing
  information.

- **Subscription Management:** Also called auto-
  replenishment, allows users to "subscribe" to a supply
  of a consumable product that is delivered at regular
  time intervals, i.e. weekly, monthly, annually, etc.

- **Automated Customer Email Support:** Automated
  transactional emails such as order confirmations, order
  status; integration of email marketing support, such as
  a contact preference and integration to triggered email
  marketing programs.

Each of these functional areas can include subcategories and individual requirements that need to be considered, but this list provides a good starting point to creating your requirements. I have found the best way to organize these requirements is via a Microsoft Excel worksheet or a similar spreadsheet software. If done well, your requirements list should be hundreds of lines long.

As should be apparent from the list above, the Ecommerce solution will touch many aspects of the organization. As a result, the requirements gathering process should incorporate input from across your company, including representatives from marketing, sales, IT, finance, fulfillment, and operations, in addition to your existing digital or Ecommerce team. This goes beyond the members of your steering committee. It is essential to get front-line feedback from every department your Ecommerce operation will touch. I strongly advise against gathering requirements in a silo, where only your digital team or a single department comes up with the requirements list. This leads to a myopic set of needs and, ultimately, to a poor platform choice. Instead, I suggest selecting an executive-level sponsor to oversee the requirements gathering process. A thorough approach to this exercise will take at least two solid days of meetings and discussions, potentially with additional follow up clarification work with individual stakeholders from your requirements gathering team.

Ultimately, the right platform decision is only partially driven by the requirements, and there are many other factors, as I will highlight in the following section. However, a solid base of requirements gives you an objective way to evaluate the capabilities of various Ecommerce platform options.

CASE STUDY

Device Technologies: Looking Internally as a Place to Start

Launching on a small scale, and learning

As a market-leading distributor of medical technologies, Device Technologies has always listened to and acted on customer feedback. The company attributes its success to the innovative actions it has taken as a result of this customer-centric approach.

In 2016, when the company's customers were asking for digital methods to place orders, it knew it needed to act. However, management also recognized that implementing an Ecommerce solution in a large, complex B2B market all at once would be a challenge, given that the company was new to the world of digital commerce. This effort was not only going to be resource intensive, but take a considerable amount of time. Device Technologies had a complex environment of legacy systems, including enterprise resource planning (ERP) and customer relationship management (CRM) solutions already in place. While management saw the challenges, they also recognized that action was required to meet their customers' needs.

So, they found a way to crawl before they tried walking and later running!

"We decided not to try to tackle the big, hairy project all at once," says Darren Williams, the company's Chief Information Officer. "Instead, we looked to launch a proof of concept, something on a smaller scale that we could learn from." They looked to their internal employee store as a way to get started.

"We started by selling our skin care products in an employee-only online store, exclusively accessible to our 750 staff members. We learned quite a bit from this experience, and it brought Ecommerce competency to the organization in a low-risk manner," Williams notes.

This approach allowed Device Technologies to:

- Build and test the integrations to the ERP and other systems in a limited-pressure production environment.

- Create content needed to present products in an Ecommerce selling system.

- Establish processes and organizational competencies around product content creation for web use.

- Present this information to a forgiving audience (or, as Williams likes to say, a "mostly" forgiving audience).

- Gain confidence that Ecommerce was something the organization could and should execute.

The results have been strong. Internal sales from the company store tripled after the company launched the employee-only Ecommerce web site.

The next step is rolling out the solution to the company's customers. Armed with its learnings, process, and newfound confidence, Device Technologies is ready to take on Ecommerce on a much larger scale.

Find potential matches

The process of narrowing the field of possible Ecommerce platforms should start with getting all reasonable platform options on the table. I have provided a fairly extensive list and summary descriptions of viable Ecommerce platforms in a supplement to this book. Each platform has its own strengths and weakness. It is best to assemble a longer list of potential providers at the initial stage, and then cull that list down to your top five to seven choices for deeper evaluation. Look first for platforms that meet the most basic, top-level needs as outlined in your objectives and requirements documentation. These factors usually include:

- **Key, unique functional areas:** These can include B2B-specific requirements such as content and workflow needs, international needs, specific ways your products are fulfilled, online product configuration requirements, highly complex customer-specific pricing, and other factors.

- **Deployment model:** Do you require extensive customization or would an "out of the box" solution likely meet the vast majority of your requirements? The more customization you need, the more your chosen platform must support flexibility and access to core code. To that end, what tradeoffs are you willing to accept for flexibility in functionality and customization in exchange for speed of deployment and cost savings, as there are a wide range of options. Another consideration is headless commerce. If your firm maintains a well-optimized front end content management system, has the potential to incorporate web-based commerce applications for equipment that you produce, or is just looking for a "future-proof" option based on unknown business needs, headless commerce is a path you might consider.

- **Budget range:** Deployment and maintenance costs typically run well into the millions for enterprise-grade systems such as Websphere Commerce, Oracle, SAP, and Elastic Path while others can be manageable at lower costs (typically tens to hundreds of thousands of dollars to deploy, ranging quite a bit depending on your needs), such as Magento, Znode by Amla, NetSuite, GenAlpha, BigCommerce, Insite, Episever, Unilog, Shopify, Oro Commerce, and others.

- **Resource availability:** Platforms vary widely in their network of certified developers, including systems integrators. In general, the broader the number of technical resources available the more leverage you will have in negotiating development and support options. Additionally, having more resources at your disposal will potentially reduce risk.

- **Overall company stability:** You want your software partner to be around for a while, as implementing an Ecommerce platform is a significant and highly disruptive effort for your business. As a result, evaluating the overall stability and strategy of each platform provider should be considered early in the selection process. Acquisitions are also common in the Ecommerce platform sector, and this can be very distracting to a platform provider's customer focus and even market direction. The platform's likelihood of acquisition should be considered, as well as its funding situation (e.g. if the firm is venture capital funded, who is behind the platform, and how recent was the last infusion of capital). You certainly don't want to make a large investment in a platform, only for the company to later declare bankruptcy, leaving you without support options. Also consider the management's experience and ability to execute.

- **Target market:** The core target customer focus of the platform should be considered as well. How well does your company match against the typical current customer of the platform based on industry, company size, and their own target markets?

- **Roadmap:** The platform roadmap for features and capabilities should generally map to your own feature requirements and industry. This should be investigated further in the next step, but to narrow the field, find out if the platform is focused generally on developing features specifically for B2B firms, digital commerce, and your industry group.

- **Technology environment:** Any investments your organization has made in a particular software system or language should play a role in your decision to include or exclude a platform. Systems could include broad enterprise solutions such as SAP, Oracle, or IBM, or software programming languages such as .Net or php. Some Ecommerce platforms are designed to be deployed on top of specific systems a company may already have in place, such as Salesforce B2B Commerce on top of Salesforce.com CRM, or NetSuite's SuiteCommerce Advanced on top of the NetSuite ERP system. While this isn't usually the driving factor in making a platform decision, it can make it easier and faster to integrate and maintain an Ecommerce solution.

CASE STUDY

Bosch: Making the Case to Replatform off of an Internal Solution

 **BOSCH**
Invented for life

Commodity features versus differentiating experiences

Robert Bosch GmbH, or Bosch, is a $90 billion multinational tool and electronics engineering and manufacturing company, headquartered in Stuttgart, Germany. The company was founded by Robert Bosch in Stuttgart in 1886, and today is a global leader in its industry. The firm considers itself a technology company, and as such, has a long and proud history of internally building solutions. Thus, when Bosch made the move to Ecommerce in the early 2000s, the firm maintained this tradition, developing and deploying a homegrown Ecommerce platform. This worked for more than a decade, but eventually created challenges for the company.

"We were trying to keep up with commercial Ecommerce platforms, investing millions of dollars each year in new features and functionalities to enable Ecommerce purchasing," notes Sunny Mallavarapu, Bosch's Digital Transformational Project lead for the company's North America Power Tools Group. "We realized that we didn't want to continue to invest and re-invent features that were available out of the box with third-party solutions. Instead, we felt we needed to invest in things that were unique to Bosch and would help us differentiate in the market, not continue to spend on developing commodity web site features. Every region and country had their own systems, and this was untenable [with our original platform]. Information was not being shared across regions," says Mallavarapu.

After a detailed requirements gathering and platform selection process, the company replatformed to SAP's C/4 Hana solution (formerly known as SAP hybris).

"SAP's Ecommerce solution dovetailed well with our existing ERP, which is also from SAP. This provides solid support for our 60 countries. We can now sync product data across all of these regions, allowing for localized Ecommerce in a manner that is consistent with the Bosch brand. And we are no longer investing internal resources in re-creating features that don't give us competitive advantage," Mallavarapu notes.

Internally-developed Ecommerce solutions can make sense for some companies with very unique requirements. However, the Bosch example provides sage advice to companies new to the Ecommerce game: Don't reinvent where you don't have to.

Dive Deeper with a Request for Proposal (RFP) Process

Evaluating a long list of potential providers by the factors highlighted above will allow you to create a more manageable short list of five to seven providers who will be eligible to receive a Request for Proposal (RFP). I generally recommend an RFP process as a way to collect information from various platforms and provide an objective basis for evaluating and selecting finalist candidates. The RFP process should incorporate the requirements collected earlier, and also provide important context such as your overall business objectives, systems environment, deployment preferences, your internal technical, marketing, merchandising, and other personnel available to work with the platform provider, and ongoing maintenance and enhancement needs.

At this stage you should also consider the resources needed to conduct creative design, systems integration, and solution implementation. A web site launch needs to incorporate user experience design, including information flow and architecture, referred to in the industry as User Experience (UX) and Information Architecture (IA). Platform providers usually do not perform these functions themselves, meaning you will likely need to resource a third-party services firm. You can ask the platform provider to include recommendations on implementation partners in their RFP response. Note that you will mostly likely be working more closely with the implementation partner during the development and deployment phases than you will be with the software provider itself. Therefore, it is essential to also conduct a thorough review of any third parties you may need to complete the project. Another approach is to consult with an implementation partner first, hiring them to help you through the systems selection process based on their knowledge and experience with Ecommerce platforms. Keep in mind, though, that these firms are not always technology agnostic, meaning they may only recommend a solution that they implement and not explore other options.

Importantly, when looking at the overall project, don't just look at the upfront numbers. It is essential to capture total cost of ownership (TCO), including integration, development and creative work, software licenses, hosting, and other third-party software costs that may be incorporated into the solution. Request a quote that reflects at least a three year period, so you can estimate the long-term total budget needed to deploy and operate. I also recommend considering your own internal staff expenses for managing and developing the new platform, including costs of maintaining integrations with your legacy software systems.

Once the RFP is collected, I recommend evaluating and comparing your shortlist vendors on several factors, including:

- Thoroughness of response. A sloppy response at this stage does not bode well for the vendor's future work with you.

- Overall functional fit against the web site requirements, expressed as a percent score of out-of-the-box fit against requirements.

- Cost estimate fit against budget.

Your goal at this stage is to narrow down to three or four platforms that you can then review in an interview and product demonstration. This demo can be conducted either via a web screen share or in person, at your preference. Use the demo process to take a deep dive into any weaknesses identified in the RFP response, ease of use of the platform, and overall professionalism of the team and their approach.

The demo step should allow you to further narrow your field to two or three finalists. At the finalist step, I strongly recommend spending at least half to a full day with each vendor (either on site with them or have them come to you). When you are at the finalist step, price and functional match are likely to be less of a factor. At this stage, you should be evaluating:

- **Cultural fit:** Are these people you can work with for the next five to ten years (or more)? Be sure to also review the cultural fit of your implementation partner.

- **Flexibility of the platform:** Can the provider adjust to a changing landscape and shifting business objectives?

- **Functionality fit:** The platform's ability to support your unique functional requirements.

- **Current systems integration match:** Experience with integrating their solution with components of your current technology ecosystem. Choose an integration partner that has experience integrating the platform with systems you already have in place.

- **Industry expertise:** Knowledge of your field and your business model.

- **Product roadmap:** The platform feature roadmap and long-term fit potential.

- **Long-term budget:** Three year total cost of ownership, including internal resources.

At the end of the day, I have found the items listed above to be the true factors that drive Ecommerce platform selection among the finalists, and they typically outweigh things like pre-demo functionality scores and even implementation price.

Ultimately, there are risks in any platform decision. This is why, above many other factors, the flexibility, cultural fit, management, and business stability of the platform provider often become the most important influencers of the final decision. It is important to have a partner that will work with you when difficulties occur and change is needed to meet your business goals.

CASE STUDY

**Big Ass Fans: The Value of a
Thorough Ecommerce
Platform Selection Process**

*"Time spent upfront prevents wasted investments
down the road"*

Big Ass Fans knows how to stay cool. With wingspans ranging up to 24 feet, this commercial fan manufacturer's products circulate air throughout some of the world's largest and most trafficked venues, including sports arenas like Lucas Oil Stadium and Lambeau Field, dozens of major airports, huge manufacturing facilities, and hundreds of other venues. Next time you are in a high volume space, look up, and you are likely to see a Big Ass Fan. The name says it all. By moving more air using less energy, Big Ass Fans' products increase efficiency of air conditioning systems while increasing human comfort.

Realizing the benefits available to the company and its customers through Ecommerce, Big Ass Fans' management was seeking to launch B2B Ecommerce on their web site, bigassfans. com. It just wasn't sure which Ecommerce platform to select to support its business objectives of increasing sales, supporting the field sales team, and enabling customer self-service on the web.

"We were a bit overwhelmed by the options, but knew there was a good fit out there," says Dan Gdowski, the company's Director of Ecommerce. "We wanted to be sure the selected platform would not only support our business objectives, but would be flexible enough to adapt to future needs, while also having enough development resource options in the market for us to either outsource or develop ourselves."

To help them make an educated, informed decision, they brought in an expert consultant to help (full disclosure: the consultant was the author of this book!), and ran the process described in this chapter. By leveraging a thorough requirements gathering and platform assessment process, the company felt comfortable with the platform it ultimately selected, confident that it would support their immediate and longer term needs. Ultimately, Big Ass Fans selected the Magento Commerce platform by Adobe.

"We had several excellent platform options, but by following this process, subtle differences emerged that made Magento our clear choice," says Gdowski. "I encourage every company that is thinking about an Ecommerce implementation to take the time to conduct a thorough evaluation. Time spent upfront will save time and prevent wasted investments down the road."

Big Ass Fans is now poised to launch its new B2B Ecommerce site on a platform it believes can sustain it for at least the next decade. This is a good place to start the B2B Ecommerce journey.

The Ecommerce Platform Ecosystem

As I noted at the start of this chapter, the good—and bad—news about today's Ecommerce platform ecosystem is that there are a lot of choices. From global enterprise-level systems to open source software that can either be implemented by in-house or external developers, there are about as many flavors of platforms as there are of Baskin Robbins ice cream. In my many years in this industry, I have gotten to know many of these platforms very well. And thanks to the good work of industry analysts such as Paradigm B2B, Forrester, and Gartner, it has become easier to track and to get to know the players, their strengths and weaknesses.

Keep in mind that platforms' capabilities and available options shift over time, as market conditions change, platform providers are acquired, and new players emerge. I highly recommend reviewing the literature that market analyst firms produce prior to starting any platform selection process to ensure that you have the latest information. Also keep in mind that the research firms produce different analyses geared for different types and sizes of companies. For example, Forrester produces periodic reports on Ecommerce platforms in general, and they have also produced reports oriented towards mid-sized firms, though less frequently.

In order to get started and provide a general orientation, I have compiled a list of notable platforms in the marketplace as of this writing. This is not an exhaustive list, but these are some of the most commonly evaluated and utilized Ecommerce platforms in the market for B2B sellers. I have worked with most of these platforms, but please note that I am not endorsing any specific company or product. The platform that is right for you will depend on the factors outlined above. I encourage you to use this information as a starting point in your own research rather than a strategic recommendation. The platforms listed below are in alphabetical order, and are described in more detail in the supplemental addendum available for this book.

- Apptus
- Big Commerce
- Elastic Path
- Episerver
- GenAlpha

- Handshake (acquired by Shopify in 2019)
- Insite Software (acquired by Episerver in late 2019)
- Intershop
- Kibo Commerce
- Magento Commerce, an Adobe company
- Miva
- Netsuite Oracle
- Oracle Commerce
- Oro Commerce
- Salesforce B2B Commerce (formerly Cloudcraze)
- Sana
- SAP (formerly hybris)
- Shopify Plus
- Websphere Commerce (acquired from IBM by HCL in 2019)
- Unilog
- Znode, by Amla

How do you measure success?

With all the platform options available on the market today, it can be challenging to know which one is right. This is especially true given that the outcomes of your choices are not likely to be apparent for months, or even more than a year. Be prepared for a significant amount of effort to develop, launch, and upgrade an existing platform. Depending on the complexity of your implementation and, generally, the size of your firm, expect between six and 18 months from when you begin building your Ecommerce site to when you finish.

Constructing an Ecommerce operation is like building a house, especially when it comes to deploying technology. It is not uncommon to experience bumps in the road (uncover issues during construction) that extend the deployment timeline and often the budget. Here are my top tips for ensuring your technology implementation stays on track:

- Make sure you have a carefully drafted project plan, complete with timelines, dependencies, and clear-cut responsibilities for anyone involved in the effort.

- Maintain a high level of communication with your implementation partners; use them to help you meet your launch goal.

- Expect a lot of change along the way. Ecommerce platform development is a very complex and difficult process. *Do not expect it to go smoothly.* Keep this in mind throughout the project. Expect the scope to change, and with it, the cost. You will likely have to compromise on some things you want and things you may have to live without, at least at launch.

- Have tolerance for the process. Be realistic about your goal and when you will meet it. It is better to be conservative and give yourself some buffer time for when unexpected issues arise. Because they will. This is not just a piece of software, Ecommerce involves organizational development, and the technology is just one piece of the puzzle. A crucial piece, yes, but still just a piece.

- Take a long-term point of view. If you do this successfully, you will have a platform that you can live with for ten years or more. Because this process is highly disruptive, it should only be done when absolutely necessary. Launching a new Ecommerce platform takes your teams' focus off of their day jobs and can slow execution and business growth in other areas. This is why building the foundation properly is so important. Take the time to do it right and you will avoid many of the more common mistakes. The end result will be an Ecommerce system that will grow revenue, create efficiencies, and put your business on solid footing for a future of meeting and exceeding your customers' expectations.

Key Chapter Takeaways

- Performing the right kind and amount of due diligence before selecting an Ecommerce platform is key to a successful implementation.

- It is essential to put your customers' needs first in the selection process, thus allowing you to ensure they will be using the site and that your business will reap the revenue and efficiency rewards available to you through Ecommerce.

- Using a methodical process with detailed requirements documentation will help you prioritize features, objectively compare platforms, and realistically define your budget.

- Follow the requirements documentation phase with a thorough RFP process, to objectively vet providers against needed features, while also assessing qualitative factors such as cultural fit, market focus, strategic roadmap alignment, overall solution flexibility, resource availability, company stability, and other characteristics.

- While time consuming, going through this process upfront will ensure that the platform you choose will serve you for years to come. Changing platforms is timely and costly, so it is best to get it right the first time!

- Forming a customer advisory board can help you understand your customers' needs prior to implementation and create a roadmap for future features.

- When looking at the overall project, do not just look at the cost of the technology itself. It is essential to capture total cost of ownership, including integration, development and creative work, software licenses, hosting, and other third-party software costs that may be incorporated into the solution, as well as ongoing support costs such as annual licenses, development of enhancements, and internal staffing costs to support Ecommerce.

- Implementing a platform is not an overnight project. Take a long-term view of measuring the success of your Ecommerce platform implementation.

- A wide variety of Ecommerce platform solutions are available in the marketplace. As a starting point, take your time to research each to identify the best fit for a longer list of candidates. I provide an overview of a number of noteworthy platforms in a supplemental addendum that is available for this book.

Stealing Smart from B2C: Delivering a Great User Experience while also Accommodating B2B Needs

10

I have observed that B2B companies tend to have a nasty habit of putting up Ecommerce storefronts that are simple bolt-ons to or extensions of their existing Enterprise Resource Planning (ERP) systems. These firms often expect orders to come flowing in from Ecommerce without considering how their customers will actually use their site. When the orders don't come, or fall far below expectations, managers either blame their customers or decide that Ecommerce won't work for them.

They are almost always wrong on both counts.

When implementing an Ecommerce system, it is critical to focus on the user experience (UX), which includes web site navigation, on-site search, product page layouts, merchandising approaches and tools, product associations, the checkout process, and numerous other areas. If the UX is poorly implemented and does not follow consumer-like best practices, the resulting web site will make it difficult for visitors to find what they need and purchase it. How can you expect customers to actually use something that's not user-friendly?

B2B sellers are currently doing a very poor job of meeting the online user experience expectations of their buyers. A Digital Commerce 360 survey of B2B buyers conducted in late 2019 found that only 7% of corporate buyers rate the ecommerce sites they use as excellent. Major areas of deficiency that were cited include basic UX features such as lack of product images, inaccurate inventory, and lack of sufficient product content, among other areas.[92]

Ecommerce has been around since the late 1990s, when B2C pioneers such as Amazon.com, eBay, Dell, Footlocker, and others (including yours truly) first launched digital storefronts and began selling online. Since then, consumer-focused Ecommerce has become the driver of retail growth in the United States, with Amazon accounting for nearly 50 percent of all online commerce growth in recent years. The B2C sector is mature and highly competitive, with well-established best practices and technology platforms available to support retailers.

As a result of B2C's explosive growth over the past two decades, business buyers' expectations for an online experience have been set by their experiences as consumers (particularly as younger, digitally-native buyers enter the workforce). B2C Ecommerce is a fertile—and necessary—place to mine for ideas and successful approaches for the burgeoning B2B Ecommerce industry. The internet has empowered business buyers to discover new suppliers, breaking age-old norms and processes of product research and purchasing. B2B buyers have come to expect well-designed web sites, seamless and fast online ordering processes, relevant product recommendations, instant access to order status and shipping information, and more. The key to capturing the business of the new, digitally native buyer is deploying a B2B Ecommerce site that follows consumer-like best practices in user experience,

---

92 https://www.digitalcommerce360.com/2019/12/03/b2b-sellers-are-missing-the-mark-with-digital-buyers/

while also accommodating and enhancing traditional B2B workflows.

One of my favorite and most surprising examples of how B2C factors influence B2B behaviors comes from one of my clients, a mid-market manufacturer of dental equipment that has an Ecommerce site. As an experiment, they ran a Cyber Monday promotion on component parts for their equipment, and saw a sizable bump in Ecommerce sales. I found this strange: people generally shop for consumer items on Cyber Monday, such as apparel and electronics, but *dental offices shopping for drill bits? Really?* This is one example, and maybe an outlier, but it demonstrates that consumer-type behaviors are influencing business buying when transactions are conducted online.

While it has not been the case historically for B2B buyers to enjoy holiday promotions and deals, perhaps even this is changing. Apparently, for my client, dental supply buyers were feeling the urge to buy more equipment for their offices on Cyber Monday, saving their businesses some money in the process.

Despite changes in buyer expectations, though, B2B Ecommerce is still a new and maturing sector. While B2C has given us a roadmap of how to deliver a seamless online shopping experience, many companies overlook crucial best practices that B2C sellers have used to successfully drive growth. For many B2B companies, it can be easy to ignore some of the methods that have become a staple of B2C Ecommerce, especially the ones that have not been traditionally part of the B2B sales process. But B2B companies that don't pay attention to B2C user experience best practices will not succeed. Executives need to pay close attention to the lessons B2C has to offer in order to realize the significant returns on investment that Ecommerce promises.

With this said, there are some key differences between B2B and B2C user experiences. One essential difference, perhaps the most important one, is this: the central goal of a B2B site is to make the buyer's job easier. In B2B, it is less about enjoyment, browsing products, and immersion in a digital shopping experience, and much more about efficiency. Successful B2B user experiences take traditional purchasing and customer support workflows and make them more efficient, saving the buyer time and effort in the process. For B2B buyers, the effective online user experience is not about lifestyle and shopping for entertainment. Instead, B2B buyers are looking to obtain the speed and convenience of online shopping that many B2C web sites offer *so they can perform their work more effectively.*

There are many best practices that encourage this type of user behavior, developed over more than two decades of B2C Ecommerce experimentation. Stealing these tactics from B2C, while considering the B2B workflow needs of your customer, should be the focus area for your user experience approach.

DEFINING USER EXPERIENCE

User Experience (UX) refers to a person's emotions and attitudes about using a particular product, system or service. It includes the practical, experiential, affective, meaningful and valuable aspects of human–computer interaction and product ownership.[93]

User experience describes the way in which people interact with a product or service, such as a web site, and how well it allows them to achieve their goals for using it. In other words,

---

93 https://en.wikipedia.org/wiki/User_experience

good user experiences allow users to accomplish tasks easily, and often in a pleasurable way, whereas a poor user experience prevents or impedes users from accomplishing tasks, and can be frustrating. User experience for Ecommerce involves multiple major components and functionalities within the web site, many of which have well-established conventions from the B2C Ecommerce world. I highlight these in the following sections.

Web Site Navigation

Web site navigation remains the most common path visitors use to arrive at products, typically accounting for well over 50 percent of the way visitors find items they are looking for. Navigation incorporates the top-level page categories, which can be product groupings, reference information (such as support), company details, or other important content. Normally found at the top of web pages (or via an icon on mobile devices), menus often deliver subcategories through dropdowns when they are hovered over or tapped on a mobile device. Navigation also often includes filters and attributes, presented in order to narrow an assortment or content list to the most relevant selection for the user. Check out the examples of navigation elements in the following screen shots of Ergodyne's web site. Ergodyne is a forward-thinking mid-market manufacturer of safety products that has adopted many B2C best practices in its web site elements.

Unfortunately, many B2B sellers make site navigation too complex, fail to follow best practices, and fill the menu with jargon that web site users often do not understand. It is all too common for B2B Ecommerce sellers to use their organization's vernacular when trying to sell their products online, such as internally-used abbreviations. For buyers who have not worked at your company (i.e. most of them), this

Example of Top Level Web Site Navigation: Ergodyne.com

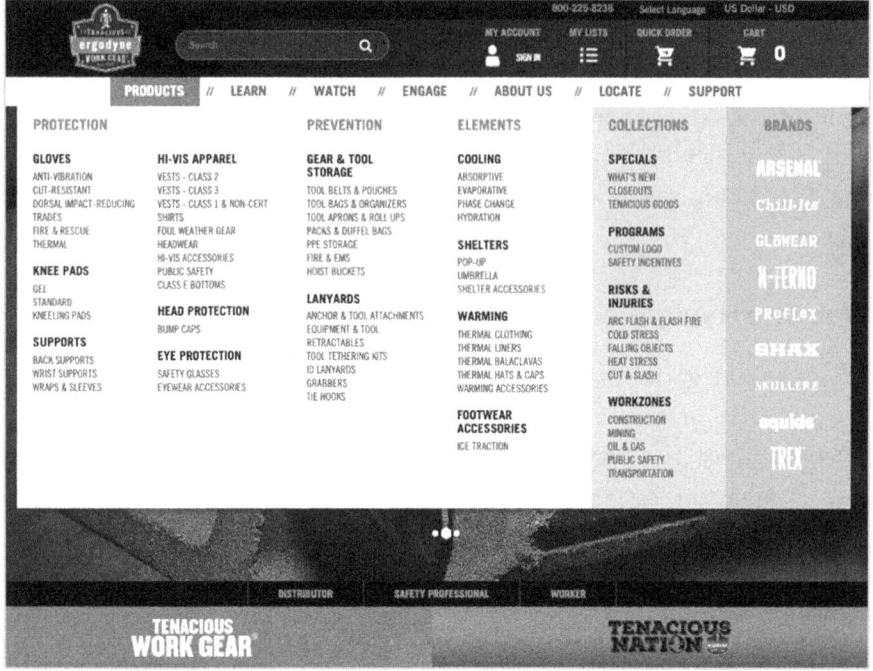

type of language can be confusing if not off-putting. It is best to understand what the major categories of product or information are that users are typically looking for, and then organize the site and navigation around these elements. For example, a firm that sells hardware accessories may try calling one product category "drill bits" instead of an internal technical term like "XF20 compatible incursion components." The key is to make your web site as easy to navigate as possible, using language and terms that customers understand and use on search engines.

With thousands of products available at many B2B sellers' web sites, it is also important to allow your customers to narrow a product assortment by key product attributes, such as

Example of Attribute Filters on a Product Category Page: Ergodyne.com

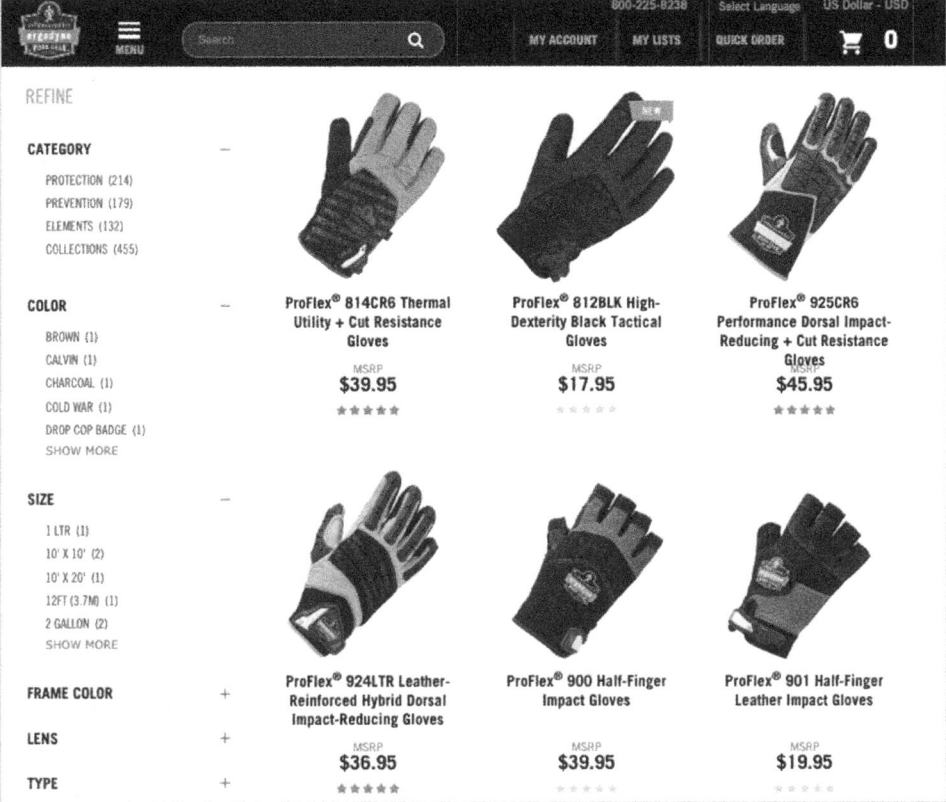

application, size, weight, color, price, compatibility, and other factors. Do not assume that by listing 2,000 products within a product category that your customers have the patience to go through the entire assortment until they find what they are looking for. Instead, leverage your Ecommerce platform and/or site search tools to allow your customer to narrow their selection of products to a manageable group so that they can compare and choose the best ones that fit their needs.

On-Site Search

Many B2B Ecommerce sellers have very large catalogs that feature thousands, and in some cases millions, of products. Successful web sites enable customers to quickly and easily find what they are looking for. Navigation is one component of this, as I highlighted above. However, as the assortment size grows, on-site search becomes even more important to the user experience.

Note that a well-optimized site search should convert site visitors to buyers at four to five times the web site average. Site visitors that use search are exhibiting a high degree of buying intent. A great site search experience is key to making the buyer's job easier, and therefore is a critical component of delivering a solid B2B Ecommerce experience.

Fortunately, B2C Ecommerce has taught us much about implementing a successful site search experience. The following best practices for site search yields considerable benefits to the seller as a result.

- Leveraging a capable, modern search software. This is your first and foremost priority. Having software that does not intuitively produce the results your site users want will lead to lost sales. The out-of-the-box site search solution included in Ecommerce platform software packages is often insufficient to support a best-in-class search experience. However, numerous search solutions exist in the marketplace, and many are quite affordable. Good examples of well-established site search solutions in the market as of this writing include products from Bloomreach, SLI Systems, Nextopia, Instant Search, SearchSpring, Algolia, Coveo, Lucidworks, and Celebros, among others.

- Include a search box on every single page, and make it visible to users.

- Make sure you allow users to narrow the search results by key attributes, such as price, weight, application, brand, product category and sub-category, etc.

- Ensure your search software presents suggested results as the user types the search query. These are suggestions presented via text and sometimes visually with product recommendations presented directly below the search box. Below is an example from the Ergodyne web site.

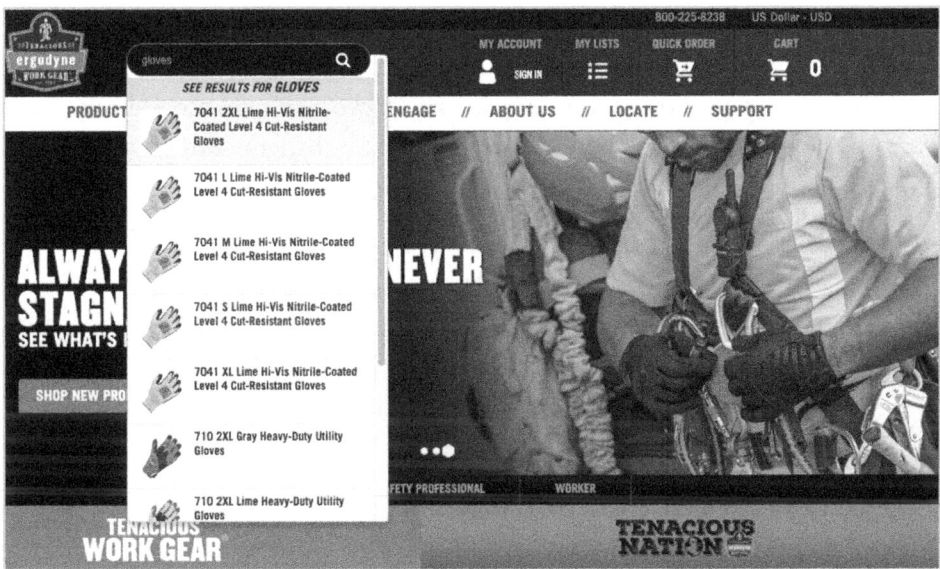

- Ensure you are merchandising search results. Your search experience must present users with the most relevant and compelling products in the search results, especially for the top searched terms on the web site. Be sure to regularly run reports on keywords being searched on your site to understand what your customers are looking for, and optimize the results presented for these terms. Also, users commonly mistype and misspell words when using search. Make sure you are redirecting these user errors to the correct results, and presenting suggestions on corrected spellings ("did you mean . . .").

- Allow for search on both product data as well as content, such as product manuals, how-to guides, software downloads, and customer support information. In the world of B2B, informative content is as important as products for many web site visitors, and your site search needs to allow them to find any type of information they are looking for. Doing this will allow customers to find answers to questions about how to use your products instead of them contacting your company directly for support.

- Regularly monitor search results from both desktop and mobile users. Analyze each result set separately (e.g. sometimes misspelled search terms on mobile devices are very different than those on desktop computers) and consider merchandising your search differently for each device.

- Be sure to properly categorize and tag each of your products, and build your search on a solid foundation of accurate data (more on this below).

CASE STUDY

**Cardinal Health: The Importance
of Great Site Search**

*Winning the battle of product findability with millions
of SKUs*

I discussed how healthcare giant Cardinal Health built an ROI
model for ecommerce in Chapter 3. Here I'd like to share with
you how the firm is using a user-centric approach to fuel its
Ecommerce operations.

An industry leading global healthcare products distributor,
Cardinal Health has been in the Ecommerce game for more than
a decade. The company has learned quite a few things along the
way. Ecommerce has evolved to become an integral part of the
firm's business, influencing sales across all channels. As a result,
improvements to the user experience being delivered to customers through the web can have an enormous business impact, both
in terms of revenue and profitability.

Cardinal Health's business success has been based in part on
providing a robust assortment of products to its healthcare customers, which include hospitals, healthcare systems, surgery centers, and labs. As of this writing, Cardinal Health's web sites offered a
vast assortment of more than 300,000 products. Enabling customers to quickly find products is critical to meeting customer needs
and making buyers' jobs easier, and this applies to the web even
more than other selling channels. World class site search enables
product findability, and Cardinal Health recognizes its importance.

"We started with understanding the customer buying journey," says Matt Wingham, the company's Director of Ecommerce
for its Medical Products and Services division. "When we surveyed

and interviewed our customers, they indicated that their number one need was to quickly find products on our web site."

Wingham also discovered that the way customers wanted to find product on the web site was primarily by using site search tools.

"Customers were looking for an on-site search experience like the one they receive on consumer web sites," he says. "This includes high degrees of relevance, tools to narrow search results by attributes, and display of key product information right on the search results page, such as great images and product details."

To deliver this experience, Cardinal realized it needed to enhance the foundation of data, create a more customer-friendly approach, and standardize the way they were describing product attributes.

"Previously, we had six different ways of describing a size attribute, such as 'sz,' 'size,' 'se,' and other terminology," says Wingham. "This didn't work in search, as it would just confuse the results and the customer would not know how to refine down to what they needed.

"To clean this up, we normalized product attributes and reduced the count from over 2,500 to just 350 attributes, using standard descriptions and categories for data. For example, Cardinal Health now has only one standard attribute for '"size."'

Accomplishing this was no small task.

"It took three dedicated people a total of four months to get this done," Wingham shared. "We started by defining what we wanted to achieve, the attributes and site experience our customers needed, and then filled in the data to meet this."

Today, web site search on Cardinal's site is used by over 75 percent of web site visitors and is contributing to the company's continued increase in Ecommerce sales.

"Customer engagement on our web site is growing every day, and our emphasis on site search is a key reason for this," says Wingham.

That's a clear endorsement for adopting the best of B2C web experience, particularly on-site search.

Product Data

Great web site search (as well as navigation) for Ecommerce starts with a solid foundation of product data. This is too often overlooked or underestimated by B2B firms in the process of launching an Ecommerce web site. Data must be comprehensive and standardized, so that products with similar characteristics and common attributes are easy to find based on searches that users execute and as site visitors narrow their search using attribute filters when browsing. Product data typically includes things like: product title, SKU number, regular price, sale price, benefits, product description, category, sub-category, and product attributes (e.g. size, weight, product uses, color, etc.).

For example, let's assume you are selling PVC pipe online (like one of my clients does). You will need to present pipe lengths as a way to narrow the assortment to what the buyer needs. In presenting the various lengths, this information must be standardized in the Ecommerce system so that prospective buyers can quickly and easily find and purchase the correct pipes. The unit of measure must be one single term (e.g. using the word "inches," and not alternative forms of this such as "in." or "inch"), and the data included in the database must follow a consistent numerical format (e.g. 1.0 versus 1.00 or 1).

This sounds simple and intuitive, but for sellers with many thousands of products, the task of preparing and cleaning data in preparation for a web site launch can be quite large. Luckily, automated tools and software can be used to ease this process. However, there is no way to fully avoid having human beings conduct this process. Depending on the state of your product data, you should expect to put a team of people on this task. It is important to have people that understand your products inside and out conduct this task, and the process should follow a well-organized, structured approach that enables the team to enter data based on a standardized set of fields. For companies that do not have solid product data already in place, this can be a substantial effort and should be started early in the Ecommerce deployment process. Outsourcing to firms such as Dakota Systems (www.daksys.com), can also be utilized for data standardization, product category design, and information architecture.

For example, one of my clients, a mid-market HVAC (heating, ventilation, air conditioning) manufacturer and distributor, assigned four people for a period of three months to create and enter product data into their new Ecommerce system, right at the start of the project. To be effective, they worked within a standardized set of fields and category structures (the information architecture, also referred to as taxonomy). Once the company launched their web site, Ecommerce rapidly grew from zero to over fifteen percent of total sales in a period of less than two years. The company attributes the foundation of data as a key element in their seamless and successful launch.

CASE STUDY

Tech Data: Web Site Experience as a Competitive Differentiator

Delivering the relevant information, more quickly

Tech Data is a master distributor of electronics and components, with more than $37 billion in revenues and operations across the globe. The company's 25,000 B2B customers include other distributors and resellers who use digital formats to purchase from Tech Data. As of this writing, electronic transactions represent over 70 percent of the company's volume, including Ecommerce, Electronic Data Interchange (EDI), and other formats. The company launched an Ecommerce web site in 1998 and views the web as a key competitive advantage and differentiator in the market, with digital user experience as the cornerstone.

"We realized the web was key to delivering the right information to the customer at the right time. Lots of pre-purchase research was being done via the web," says Pablo Zurzolo, the company's Vice President of Marketing for the Americas. "If we delivered this information better and faster than our competitors, we would have an advantage."

The company has several million products it offers on its web site, so getting customers quickly to products and information is critical. Following web site usability conventions proved key to achieving this.

"The products we sell are available elsewhere from competitors, and we see our online experience as an important part of our value proposition to keep customers coming back," Zurzolo says. "We want to make sure the experience is frictionless and breeds loyalty. Customers should feel connected to Tech Data when they visit our site, that we know them well, and we understand their needs."

In building this engaging digital experience, the company emphasizes:

- Familiarity in the overall user experience and interface design. The web site look and feel reflects what customers are used to using in their personal, consumer web shopping experiences.

- Providing rich product content, including video, and allowing Tech Data customers to leverage this information in their own sales efforts (most of Tech Data's customers are resellers, Tech Data acts as the master distributor).

- Providing easy-to-access order status information, including shipping and delivery status.

- Enabling workflows for buyers via the web, such as order routing and drop shipping support.

- Using web site search to quickly deliver the right product and information. According to the company, this helps to improve conversion rates across all selling channels.

"We looked to retail Ecommerce as we were building our digital capabilities, as retail web sites inform what our customers expect, particularly from a web site design and layout perspective" says Zurzolo. "And, from a B2B perspective, we aim to deliver work-flow efficiencies to our customers via the web, making their lives easier."

Tech Data's site is designed to make it simpler for buyers to do their jobs by accommodating common user experiences and workflows. For example, Tech Data helps their customers respond to new business opportunities that are often delivered by written bids. In order to support this process, Tech Data provides customer-specific letters of supply and special pricing agreements via its web site, facilitating bid response and fulfillment. This not only streamlines the bid process for Tech Data's customers, but also adds tremendous value by enabling them to get work done faster and thus ensuring repeat purchases.

The efforts have paid off. Tech Data reports its web site capabilities have supported increased conversion across all selling channels, in some cases doubling conversion rates versus prior levels. And they ended 2018 with an 11 percent growth in net sales, with more than half of that taking place online.[94]

Zurzolo notes that, "Customers are consistently using tech-data.com for research, then pitching options to their corporate end users and making fully informed purchase decisions, typically in less than three weeks. Our Ecommerce site has helped us to shorten the time to purchase by delivering the relevant information, more quickly."

Following Tech Data's example, a focus on delivering a great digital experience clearly yields results.

Web Merchandising, Product Recommendations, and Personalization

Web merchandising approaches are well-established in the B2C arena, and these practices can be leveraged in B2B. Ecommerce provides an opportunity for sellers to make buyers aware of products they might otherwise not know are offered, and to do so in a scalable fashion. Commonly utilized merchandising methods can be used by B2B merchants, including:

---

94 https://www.digitalcommerce360.com/2019/03/11/tech-data-grows-with-rising-demand-digital-transformation/

- **Product Cross and Upselling:** Ecommerce makes cross and upselling products during the shopping experience relatively easy. Complementary products can be displayed as recommendations on product pages, in the shopping cart, during the checkout process, alongside support information and educational content, and in other places throughout the online shopping process.

- **Product Bundling (a.k.a. Kitting):** Sellers can create product bundles or kits and present them to prospective buyers, highlighting how products can be used together. Sellers can leverage their deep product knowledge to inform these product associations, exposing more of the catalog to buyers.

- **Promotions:** In the B2C world, promotions are often used to encourage buyers to purchase more items in a single order. These tactics include free shipping over a certain dollar amount, free "bonus items" for larger purchases, and discounts on products purchased together. Your Ecommerce platform should support the ability to present promotions, utilize coupons (including customer-specific coupons), and show merchandised messages and features within key site sections, such as the home page, category pages, landing pages, in the shopping cart, and other areas of the site.

- **Product Sorting Order:** The order of products presented within product categories is important, as today's buyers tend to have short attention spans. If your web site visitors don't quickly see products that are relevant to them in your category pages, they will likely leave the site. Skilled web merchants will use the order of products to highlight items at the top of product list pages that are most likely to meet buyer needs, and they leverage data to make these decisions (more on this below).

- **Automated Product Recommendations:**
  Some Ecommerce software packages include a recommendation engine that suggests products to site visitors based on web site behavior, integrated with information such as customer purchase history. These solutions have existed for well over ten years in the B2C marketplace, and have demonstrated success in increasing web site effectiveness. Product recommendation software monitors site visitors' online activity, and presents products that the customer is most likely to buy, using algorithms that calculate probabilities of purchase of particular items. In addition to improving the rate at which web browsers become buyers, these solutions can free up (or eliminate the need for) web merchandising staff in some cases.

In the modern world of decreasing human attention spans, tactics that increase the relevancy of the online experience are critical. The tactics discussed above help sellers to quickly get the right product in front of customers at strategic moments in the buying journey. This is a component of personalization, which is the practice of creating truly one-to-one digital relationships between buyers and sellers. The vision of personalization is to present an online experience that is completely relevant and customized to the site visitor, across product and site content. Personalization has been pursued vigorously by B2C retailers in recent years, particularly as a means to compete against Amazon. Amazon itself is among the best at online personalization, quickly getting customers to the product they need, while working with an assortment that numbers over 550 million products. The good news is that these tools and methods can be adopted for B2B Ecommerce, provided the merchant takes the time to manage and structure data correctly.

In fact, I believe B2B Ecommerce holds the promise of delivering true personalization in online selling, going beyond what is possible in B2C Ecommerce. B2B sellers typically have a smaller universe of buyers, and also usually require a customer to be logged into a web site in order to make purchases. As a result, B2B sellers are able to specifically identify each web site visitor, and can truly customize their experience. Tactics can include:

- Recognizing the customer (and customer's company) by name on the web site.

- Presenting a personalized home page to the customer that includes recent orders and activity, relevant educational content, product features in their areas of interest, easy access to account administration and support, and relevant industry news and updates.

- Immediate recognition of the products the customer has purchased previously, and allowing easy re-ordering, upgrades, and cross-sells. Product compatibility information can be provided (e.g. "this component can be used with this piece of equipment you previously purchased"). Online ink finders for inkjet printers is a simple example of this (see Epson. com for an excellent implementation of this).

- Proactively recommending service or support, based on knowledge of the customers' product inventory (e.g. if a customer has a piece of equipment installed that was manufactured by the seller, proactively recommending service or parts based on machine age or usage).

- Relevant updates and product or service suggestions based on the customer's physical location, recent sales team discussions (based on integration to the seller's CRM system), account activity, prior purchases, or other factors.

Collectively, the merchandising and personalization tactics highlighted above can be leveraged by B2B sellers to expand their share of a customer's wallet and drive incremental sales. And because these product recommendations and merchandising methods are delivered online, they are always on and accessible to buyers, and do not require the intervention of a sales or support team member.

CASE STUDY

Crescent Electric:
Quickly Presenting the Right
Product Brings Larger Order Sizes

"We are seeing the fruits of listening to our customers"

Crescent Electric, the leading electrical distributor I highlighted in Chapter 7, is reaping the benefits of quickly delivering the most relevant products to its customers on the company's Ecommerce site.

"By listening to our customers, we learned that our most commonly re-ordered products were what they wanted to buy on the web site," says Craig Stilwell, Crescent's Director of Ecommerce Marketing and Development. "So we implemented an online feature to highlight these products for our customers when they arrive at our site, which has driven fantastic results."

The company calls this its "Previously Ordered" feature. This functionality highlights customer's frequently ordered products throughout the digital experience. Once a customer logs into Crescent's web site, this feature is automatically activated and they can quickly find and purchase their most commonly ordered products, saving them time.

Features include:

- Listing frequently ordered products first in category list pages on the web site.

- Marking products with a "previously ordered" flag, anywhere they appear on the web site.

- Allowing customers to easily create and access lists of products they order frequently, and to re-order from this list.

- Displaying frequently ordered products at the top of site search results when a customer executes a search on the web site.

- Integration of frequently ordered products into email communications with customers, with products listed first on landing pages when customers click through to the web site.

"Because we have thousands of products on our site, this makes it easier for customers to identify what they are likely looking for very quickly," say Stilwell. "And we are seeing the fruits of listening to our customers."

Crescent is realizing 26 percent higher order sizes and 15 percent higher conversion rates from customers that use the Previously Ordered feature. These results are impressive and a great example of how making a buyer's job easier pays off for B2B sellers.

Shopping Cart and Checkout

If you have ever used an Ecommerce site that had a long and cumbersome shopping cart and checkout process, you know how frustrating it can be. Modern online buyers have no patience for an inefficient or confusing checkout process. Streamlining here is critical, as it eliminates barriers to purchase. B2B merchants should follow the practices that have long been established in B2C (with some B2B-specific additions, such as those highlighted below). Online buyers have come to expect a number of standard features in the cart and checkout. In general, these include:

- **Persistent Shopping Cart:** Once an item is added to an online shopping cart, the Ecommerce system should indicate that items are in the cart, and present a persistent icon (often in the upper right corner of a web site), demonstrating the cart has products in it and allowing easy access to it for quick way to start the checkout process.

- **Minimized Checkout Steps:** Following the best practice set by Amazon with its one-click checkout, the shorter the online checkout process, the better.

- **Early Indication of Shipping Costs:** Shipping costs and timelines should be available throughout the customers' shopping experience (including before adding items to the shopping cart), but it is absolutely critical to display in the shopping cart, as well as throughout the checkout process. The number one reason that customers abandon their orders online is shipping costs, particularly surprise costs at the last step of checkout[95]

- **Clearly Identified Checkout Steps:** Each step of the checkout process must be clearly identified so users always know where they are in the process. This might include phases such as "Login," "Shipping/ Billing Address," "Payment Information," and "Order Review." Each step should clearly indicate where the buyer is throughout the process and allow them to easily navigate back and forth between steps.

- **Display Order Contents:** Shopping cart contents and order total should be clearly displayed throughout the entire checkout process. Easy editing of cart details should be enabled from within the cart itself (such as deleting items or increasing the desired amount of a specific item).

- **Auto-populate Customer Information:** Whenever possible, your system should take any information a user has previously entered and make it available to them to use in new orders. This includes stored addresses and payment methods, but can also include integrations to online maps, such as Google Maps for auto-population of address information. This is particularly useful in easing checkout on mobile

---

95   https://www.statista.com/statistics/379508/primary-reason-for-digital-shoppers-to-abandon-carts/

devices and can dramatically reduce friction during checkout.

- **Shopping Cart Storage:** Online buyers often use their shopping cart as a way to store products for comparison, evaluation, and future purchase. Sometimes these purchases happen online, while often the purchase is consummated through other selling channels. Regardless of where the order is completed, it is critical to store buyers' shopping carts for future reference by that buyer. There is no faster way to frustrate a customer then by erasing an order they have invested time in building on your web site. Some Ecommerce platforms even allow users to name, save, and share multiple shopping carts, as a way to further accommodate this buyer workflow.

The graphic image on the following page shows a shopping cart from the Grainger.com web site. Grainger is an industry-leading industrial products distributor, and a company that receives almost 60% of its total revenue from Ecommerce.[96] The company's shopping cart and checkout experience exhibits the best practices listed above, including minimized steps to complete an order, clearly labeled steps, display of cart contents throughout the process, and an indication of shipping costs, among other best practices.

In the world of B2B, there are several specific items that should be included in most Ecommerce experiences that deviate from B2C. These include:

- **Payment Methods:** It is critical to provide payment methods that your customers are accustomed to,

---

96   https://www.digitalcommerce360.com/2018/01/24/ecommerce-accounts-56-2017-revenue-grainger/

Grainger.com Shopping Cart

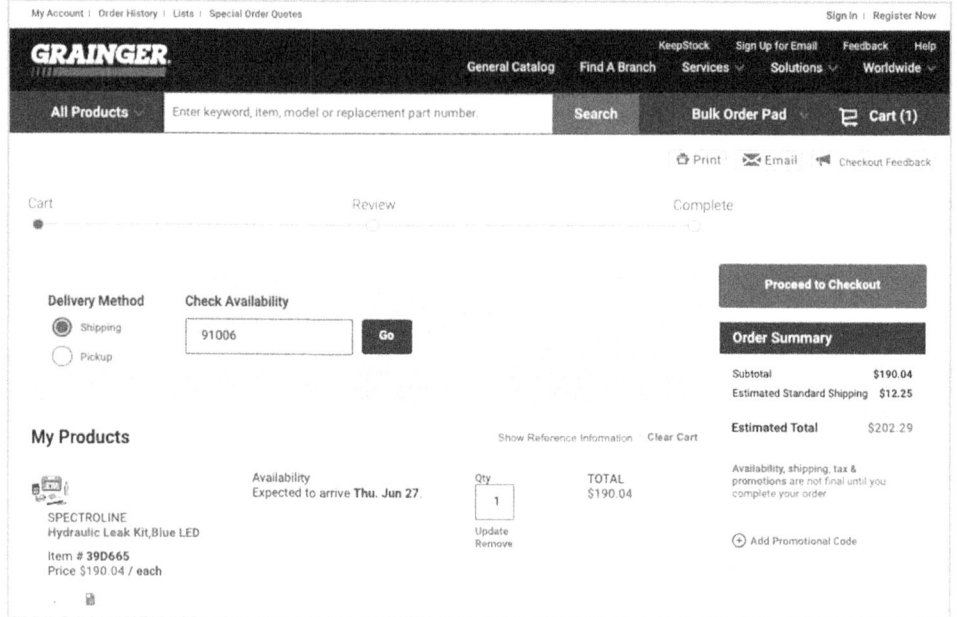

including payment on account, use of purchase orders (POs), credit card, and other methods such as Credit Key and Paypal (see the section on Payment Methods below for more).

- **Customer-specific Shipping Methods and Will-call Order Pick Up:** B2B customers often will ship orders on their own carrier accounts, and some B2B workflows call for pick up from seller locations. These methods need to be accounted for in the B2B checkout process.

- **Shopping Cart Sharing:** This is an essential feature for multi-step purchase approvals (e.g. procurement processes). In B2B purchasing, the ultimate user of the product is often the one that creates the online shopping cart, but may not have the authority to make a purchase. Likewise, the person making the purchase may not have the knowledge needed to choose the correct product. Purchase requests may need to be routed to a procurement department or manager for approval. Saved carts can accommodate this, and some B2B checkout flows allow users to push notifications to procurement teams in order to signal an order is ready for review.

- **Credit Limit Checks and Account Number Entry:** Purchase on account is a common form of B2B payment, as mentioned above. Credit accounts typically have credit limits associated with them. It is helpful to provide users with the ability to check these limits right from the checkout screens instead of having to visit a different site or make a phone call. This can reduce friction, making online purchases faster and easier to complete. Account numbers may also need to be entered for B2B purchases.

Quite simply, the less information a customer has to enter during the checkout process, especially on repeat purchases, the easier it is for them to use your site. And the easier it is to use your site the more likely you will rapidly gain customer adoption of Ecommerce. For B2B Ecommerce sellers to be successful, they must have a shopping cart and checkout process that meets the high standards that have been set in the consumer world. Carts and checkout flows must be easy to use. Period.

CASE STUDY

Regina Andrews Design:
B2B Ecommerce Is More than
Pretty Pictures

REGINA ANDREW
DETROIT

"Our main competitor is time—our customer's time"

Regina Andrews Design is a Detroit-based designer and manufacturer of high-end lighting products, selling to designers,
retailers, and other trade professionals. Founded in 1998, the
company has a long history of product innovation and a tremendous aesthetic sensibility. They also have a significant track record
in Ecommerce and have learned quite a few things along the
way, including the application of user experience best practices
to make the buyer's job easier. Regina Andrews Design's Ecommerce site goes beyond just looking nice; they've built functionalities into their site that their buyers find essential.

When the company first launched Ecommerce capabilities
for business buyers in 2008, it focused on design.

"We felt we needed to make our products look beautiful,"
says Jim Bonomo, the company's Chief Operating Officer. And
while the company achieved this goal, they forgot about the
practical aspects of web site usability.

"The site looked great, but we didn't have the content or
functionality our customers needed. From product specs to
assembly instructions and even product availability and order
tracking information—all of this was missing," admits Bonom.
This absence of data and practical capabilities impacted adoption of Ecommerce.

"We didn't see any growth from Ecommerce, and it took us a
while to realize site usability and lack of information were the cul-
prits," says Bonomo. Eventually, the company figured out these

factors were preventing online orders, and it made changes. They upgraded their Ecommerce system to Oracle NetSuite's Suite Commerce Advanced solution, which ties to their NetSuite ERP system and now provides real-time, customized pricing and product inventory for every customer. Content and product specs were added to the site to ensure customers could identify and purchase the correct product for their application.

The company's sales team also uses the web site to create and manage large orders on behalf of their customers, and suggests customers use the site for self-service on order tracking, which saves everyone time.

These Ecommerce capabilities have benefited Regina Andrews Design, particularly as their industry changes around them and the end user's channel preferences change. For example, an increasing number of interior designers are going directly to Regina Andrews Design's web site to purchase products, bypassing traditional resellers and distributors. Bonomo credits the site with being ready to accommodate these transactions, which otherwise might have been lost to competitors. As an additional benefit, these online transactions occur at higher gross margin than orders through other resale channels. This drops right to the bottom line profit of the company.

And it all stems from making their buyers' jobs easier and faster.

"I like to say our main competitor is time—the customer's time," quips Bonomo. "The companies that do the best job in saving time for the business buyer are the companies that will win the business."

And Regina Andrews Design is winning.

Payment Methods

Coupled with the speed of order processing, providing flexibility to B2B customers is essential, particularly when it comes to payment options. According to a recent survey of 400 Ecommerce executives by Intershop Communications, 47 percent of respondents cited flexible payment options—the ability to pay with credit cards, PayPal, and pay-over-time methods—as most critical to delivering the best user experience to their customers.[97] It may be surprising to see this on top of the list, but when you stop to think about it, it starts to make a lot of sense.

Traditional credit financing has been an integral part of business-to-business selling for hundreds of years. Manufacturers, brands, and distributors selling to other business owners have leveraged credit terms and flexible financing methods as a standard selling tool, and even a competitive differentiation point, since the time of the cotton gin. The U.S. Small Business Administration (SBA) reports that over 65 percent of firms use credit to make business purchases.[98] Flexible payment options presented online represent a huge area of revenue opportunity. The easier it is for customers to pay, the more likely they will be willing to buy. It's that simple.

New pay-over-time methods are being introduced to the B2B Ecommerce market. These services hold tremendous promise to transform and accelerate the adoption of this time-tested method of purchasing for businesses. What's more, credit card payment is still somewhat nascent in B2B Ecommerce. While payment by purchase order remains responsible

---

97   https://www.digitalcommerce360.com/2016/11/16/payment-options-and-inventory-top-b2b-e-commerce-concerns/
98   https://www.sba.gov/blogs/how-build-business-credit-your-start

for a majority of transactions via online channels in B2B, this is ripe for rapid change over the next few years.[99]

Traditionally, B2B purchases were completed through the good, old-fashioned purchase order. The purchasing process generally looked something like this:

1. Buyer at Company A fills out a printed purchase order.
2. Buyer circulates the purchase order to get internal approval for the purchase.
3. Buyer sends the purchase order to Company B.
4. Company B confirms the purchase order.
5. Company B fulfills order, sending Company A the products.
6. Company B invoices Company A.
7. Company A pays the invoice within the indicated timeframe.

This entire process took days, weeks, or even months, from start to finish, and this was even after the buyer had gone through their entire product consideration phase. Can you imagine using a web site that would take that long to fulfill an order? Today's B2B buyer expects the online purchase process to be as fast and easy as ordering tube socks on Amazon. In order to offer that type of experience, B2B sellers need to have the ability to offer a variety of payment options, some of which are much faster, and others that reflect the more traditional ways of completing B2B purchases.

Globally speaking across all Ecommerce channels, credit cards, debit cards and electronic payments like PayPal are the preferred payment methods for online shoppers, and are

---

99 https://www.pymnts.com/news/b2b-payments/2017/nacha-survey-accounts-receivable-check-ach/

increasingly expected by B2B buyers.[100] Many Ecommerce platforms have the technology built in to allow sellers to accept credit and debit cards, PayPal, and even ACH transfers, and it is often a matter of connecting the platform to an existing merchant or bank account. Some platforms offer the ability to sign up for a merchant account, while others simply act as an intermediary for an additional fee. Data security for credit cards needs to be a top priority, and you will want to ensure that your Ecommerce software provider and your credit card processor are PCI compliant (the industry standard for credit card data security). You should review the Ecommerce platform and payment card processor's data security protocols as a part of your platform due diligence.

While credit cards and electronic means of payment are a preferred method of buying online (particularly for smaller orders, by smaller business customers, and for one-off purchases), many companies still prefer using (or are required to use) the old-fashioned purchase order. Payment on terms is often required by business buyers, especially for large volume orders. As a result, credit purchase features are a requirement of the majority of B2B Ecommerce web site implementations. The good news is that an increasing number of Ecommerce platforms enable sellers to accept purchase orders from approved or qualified buyers.

New technologies are emerging that are evolving and modernizing B2B trade credit. These tools allow sellers to extend credit more easily to customers, without having to either accept credit cards or create further collection risks for the seller. On the B2C side, alternative payment methods such as Paypal Credit (formerly Bill Me Later) and Affirm allow consumers to make purchases and pay for their

---

100   https://www.statista.com/statistics/508988/preferred-payment-methods-of-online-shoppers-worldwide/

purchases over time (like a term loan). These solutions have evolved significantly, and today originate billions of dollars of consumer loans every year. The most prominent alternative payment method, PayPal, achieved a 63 percent market share for online retail purchases as of 2018.[101] The key to the success of these solutions is their ability to make instant credit available to consumers, thus expanding their buying power, all right from within the checkout experience, without the hassle of applying for a loan or credit card.

This same concept has been introduced into the B2B Ecommerce market by a company called Credit Key (full disclosure: I am on this company's Advisory Board). I truly believe this solution will transform the B2B payments marketplace. The B2B trade credit process is highly inefficient, requiring the completion of paper applications, manual application processing, days of waiting for approval, and other slow, manual processes. By providing instantly approved lines of credit to B2B buyers right from within the online checkout process (or in the call center or with sales reps in the field), this solution expands buyer's purchasing power, without the need for lengthy and cumbersome credit application processes. The solution charges both the seller and the customer when a purchase is made, similar to a credit card. The seller gets paid instantly, does not need to assume the credit risk or follow up to collect payment, and the customer is charged according to the terms of the credit line. Simple in concept, yet revolutionary, and meeting a customer need for a faster process.

B2C merchants recognized many years ago that offering multiple payment options during online checkout leads to incremental sales. Quite simply, buyers are seeking flexibility in payment options, and this expectation is translating to the

---

101   https://www.datanyze.com/market-share/payment-processing/paypal-market-share

B2B Ecommerce marketplace. The bottom line for payments is this: The more options you provide and the more flexible those options are, the more sales you will be able to close online.

The Importance of Good Design

B2C merchants have long known that good creative design can influence the effectiveness of an Ecommerce web site. According to marketing platform HubSpot, enacting proper web design and user experience best practices can dramatically improve online conversion rates.[102] There are many components of great B2C web design that are highly applicable to B2B. These design elements have been refined over the past 20 years and have been proven to work. Following are some critical best practices to follow:

- **Focus on your target audience:** Great design is not just about pretty pictures, but reflects the functional elements that ensure the target audience can DO what they need to with the web site. The target audience should be considered all the way through the design process as well, not just at the start.

- **Follow standard usability conventions:** For B2B Ecommerce, do not try to reinvent where and how people find things on your web site. Utilize standard methods for laying out navigation (e.g. using top "mega" navigations, drill down assortment refinements on the left navigation bar, etc.) and commonly accessed web site functions, such as site search, my account, order status, about us, and FAQs. These elements are all typically found either in the header or

---

102   https://blog.hubspot.com/marketing/design-ecommerce-conversions

in the footer section of the web site. Contemporary web site design trends follow the rule of simplicity: Keep it clean, focused, and engaging, with a limited number of competing elements on a page.

- **Provide clear calls to action:** You are looking to have web site users complete an action, such as adding an item to the shopping cart, signing up for your email list, or registering their interest in a certain product, on different pages on your web site. Making these "calls to action" very clear and compelling is a critical part of great web design. They should be placed in an appropriate place in the layout that makes intuitive sense to the user, and reflect the primary goal you have for each page on the site. In other words, if you are on a product detail page, the most important action a user can take from this page may be "Add to Cart." If you are presenting a marketing landing page, the call to action button may be "Learn More" or "Contact us" for lead collection purposes. Think about what the primary and secondary actions you want users to take on each page, and build your calls to action from there.

- **Use of engaging visual content:** Images and videos used on your web site should be of high quality. In the digital world, images speak louder than words. Invest in quality here and be sure to incorporate photos of your products being used by your customers, if applicable. B2C retailers learned long ago that images of people using products make the product relatable and can translate to increases in sales. Note that large image files can slow down a web site, taking a long time to load and hurting both your site's usability and your search engine rankings. Be sure that your web

team balances the quality of images against size; there is a happy medium. By way of example, above is an example of the imagery used on the web site home page of Thermon, a $300 million (annual revenue) producer of industrial heating applications.

- **Intuitive messaging:** Do not make the mistake of using industry jargon and complicated naming conventions that your customers or new users won't understand. Navigation options, such as category names and attributes, should be designed for the least common denominator user you expect on your site.

Keep language used in calls to action very simple and straightforward, e.g. "Buy Now," "Proceed to Checkout," "Click for Details," etc. Similarly, promotional language should be clear and direct, such as "Get Free Shipping on orders over $100."

These creative best practices really just scratch the surface. There is an entire discipline dedicated to web site design, with many nuances that experts can bring to life on your web site. I strongly recommend bringing in seasoned talent, such as a creative agency or systems integrator with a creative department, to assist you in the design process.

B2B-Specific User Experience Features

While the learnings from B2C Ecommerce can be extensively applied to B2B, there are a number of notable differences. The most important of these, in general, include:

- **Customer Specific Pricing:** The prices a B2B Ecommerce seller displays online to logged-in customers must be dynamic, and aligned with the prices that are being shared across all other channels— such as within contracts, by the sales team, and in print catalogs. All too often, companies only present a single price or basic set of prices to customers on the web, allowing pricing discounts and customer catalogs to be handled by the sales team or through the call center (see Chapter 5 on Sales Channel Alignment). This is a guaranteed way to miss the revenue and efficiency benefits that Ecommerce can bring to your organization. Your customers do not view your online and offline selling channels as two separate companies with different pricing, so you cannot present yourself this way. The good news is that many Ecommerce platforms allow you to provide account-specific pricing that dynamically adjusts based on user login. That means that pricing can be customized to each individual customer, but only upon login, while you can still present different prices to non-customers.

- **Custom Catalogs:** These are specific groups of products that are presented to a customer based on items that are most relevant to them, and can even be account-specific. This is usually a subset of the overall catalog, focusing on products applicable to particular customer segments or even specific configurations of products that work together for different applications. For example, a custom catalog could be a series of products that are used to operate a piece of equipment, such as an HVAC system, which might be designed either for commercial or residential environments. If the manufacturer sells to both commercial and residential installers, but each group has unique needs, custom catalogs can reflect each buyer's individual requirements.

- **Buyer Permissions, Roles, and Workflows:** In large organizations, the person researching products may not be the person buying the products, and neither of these people may be the end user of the product. Your customers may want different employees to see different types of products and information online based on their role within their company. For example, customers may require access to information for people in support functions, where those employees can request service, download product information and user manuals, and check order status. They may also want a different level of access for employees that are located in branch locations, e.g. to allow them to check order status and also place orders. The roles and types of access required can vary broadly in B2B organizations, and this is not usually found in a B2C setting. That means that your Ecommerce platform and user experience needs to account for all the different roles, responsibilities, and workflows that are present in your customers' organizations.

- **Sales Force Alignment and CRM Integration:** B2C platforms have taken advantage of mobile technology, such as what you find at the Apple store, where every associate has an iPad equipped with specific tools to help them serve customers. As we covered in previous chapters, empowering the sales force with real-time information and digital tools can dramatically improve their effectiveness with customers. For example, your web site could alert sales associates when their clients are viewing specific products online, giving the sales team an opportunity to be more responsive to the customers' needs and provide a more real-time and personalized experience.

CASE STUDY

**Softchoice: Making
B2B Workflows Easier Pays Off**

Digital process enhancement is the key to double digit Ecommerce penetration

Softchoice is a provider of technology products and services with significant operations and billions of dollars in revenue coming from customers across the United States and Canada. The company was founded in 1989 and has been a long-time believer in and implementer of Ecommerce.

"We started in Ecommerce before 'Ecommerce' was even a word," says Ron Hasslet, the company's Director of Ecommerce. "As early as the 1990s we were using modems and dedicated software to allow our customers to buy from us electronically." Through trial and error, and many years of experience selling online, the company learned the power of effectively accommodating B2B workflows via web channels. The firm's approach and capabilities have evolved considerably since the company's launch of Ecommerce two decades ago.

Hasslet notes, "We built our Ecommerce platform in house, and it has been a world of constant iteration and improvement. We learned early on that it was important to understand our customers' business processes, and then explore how the web could be used to help them become more efficient when these processes involved Softchoice."

Putting customers first in the process helped them understand how to build impactful experiences that would drive adoption of the web. For example, the company realized that simply enabling a buyer to put an item in a shopping cart and checkout via the web wasn't enough to meet customers' needs. Softchoice's customers typically required a detailed, multi-step approval processes for orders; the person requesting the product at a customer's organization (typically an IT manager) was not the same person who needed to actually buy it (typically a procurement officer). The entire process was also usually subject to approval of customers' accounting department (typically the accounts payable team).

Realizing this, Softchoice built multiple steps into the online buying process, allowing the requestor to create a shopping cart and pass it to the purchaser to process the transaction, as long as the total amount of the order is within the approval criteria of the customer's purchasing limits, which have been set by their accounting department. Electronic notifications via email and other means enabled rapid flow of information among those involved in the purchase, a process that previously was handled by fax, phone, and in person communication. Once the buying workflow was translated to a streamlined online experience, Softchoice's web site became an easier place for customers to make their purchases.

Over the years, Softchoice has implemented similar processes and usability enhancements via the web. Other examples include online asset management tools and integration of web shopping capabilities directly into customers' procurement systems (called "Punchout;" see glossary for definition). Going even further, considering the wide age ranges and varying web-sophistication of its buyers, the company created multiple views of its web site. Softchoice enables a table-based view of the customer dashboard, for example. This is the original layout of the company's web site, and is a comfortable format for long-time buyers who have been using the web system for many years. In contrast, the web site also supports a more standard and modern, Google-like view for contemporary users more recently entering the workforce.

These efforts have paid off. Today, Softchoice receives more than 25 percent of their revenue from Ecommerce, amounting to hundreds of millions of dollars in sales. The web is the firm's fastest growing channel and the company believes there is much more opportunity for continued growth.

"As we continue to accommodate our customers' processes via web channels, we expect continued and accelerated use of the web," Hasslet says.

That's a resounding endorsement for creating easy online B2B workflows, and an example that many B2B firms would be wise to follow.

Measuring Success

Online product selling provides enormous amounts of data that can be leveraged for merchandising purposes and as a way to measure the success of B2B Ecommerce efforts. This data can be used by skilled web merchants to improve product recommendations and merchandising delivered through the Ecommerce web site. Tools such as web analytics software allow merchants to see where web site users enter the web site, which pages and products are viewed, which merchandising banners and messages attract the most attention (via clicks and purchases), and what is ultimately purchased during user sessions. With careful analysis of web analytics and other business intelligence data, your merchants can improve the overall performance and effectiveness of the Ecommerce site.

In web merchandising and analytics reporting, key metrics should be measured, the most important of which include:

- **Conversion Rate:** The rate at which site visitors make a purchase (usually calculated as Ecommerce transactions divided by the number of site visits). It is typical in B2B industries to see conversion rates over 10 percent, as opposed to B2C industries, where the average is just under 3 percent.[103]

- **Average Order Value:** The average dollar value of orders completed on your Ecommerce web site (typically calculated as total Ecommerce revenue divided by the number of transactions). This metric varies dramatically by business and industry, but you can look at your offline metrics as a starting point for

---

103   https://www.smartinsights.com/ecommerce/ecommerce-analytics/ecommerce-conversion-rates/

understanding what you can aim for in Ecommerce transactions.

- **Bounce Rate:** The percentage of people who arrive at a page on your web site and leave immediately. In my experience in reviewing analytics with hundreds of companies, high-performance Ecommerce web sites generally have a bounce rate of 35 percent or lower.

- **Shopping Cart Abandonment and Checkout Completion Rate:** These metrics measure how many site visitors start a shopping cart and leave without completing a purchase (i.e. cart abandonment) and how many visitors place an order after starting a checkout (i.e. checkout completion). Taken together, these metrics reflect the effectiveness of your cart and checkout experience.

Numerous web analytics platforms exist on the market that can capably capture these metrics for you, the most common being Google Analytics. A free version of this software can be installed on your Ecommerce web site. Other commonly used web analytics packages are available from Adobe and IBM, among others. Your Ecommerce team should be skilled in the use of these packages in order for you to get the most out of these systems.

Stealing Smart from B2C: A Final Word

There are many things that B2B companies can learn from the world of B2C Ecommerce user experience. On the surface, it may seem like the two types of businesses have little in common, but the more we see the digital revolution touching every part of our lives, the more essential it is for B2B firms to understand the ecosystem, learn from it, and implement their Ecommerce web sites in ways that make it easier for their customers to do business with them. Many of the tactics I highlighted in this chapter are new concepts to B2B firms. As I discussed in Chapter 2, look outside of your organization, perhaps to the world of B2C Ecommerce, to find the skills necessary to engage in web merchandising, world class web design, analytics, and user experience optimization. The best way to steal smart is to hire talent from those you are looking to steal from!

DON'T FORGET MOBILE!

Unless you've been living under a rock for the past 10 years, it should be no surprise that Ecommerce activities have shifted away from the desktop world and towards the mobile world. In B2C retail, the number of mobile shopping carts created increased by 70 percent from 2017 to 2018 for the customers of one of the Ecommerce platforms I work with, Salesforce Commerce Cloud.[104] Mobile carts act as a wish list that connects online with offline and are a clear sign of shopping intent. You will benefit if you recognize this, and if you find a way to deliver conversion of those carts, regardless of selling channel (e.g. through your sales force, call center, in store, or perhaps online purchase later on desktop).

From a B2B perspective, it might seem unnecessary to consider how your site looks on mobile. After all, most of your customers are probably doing their work on a laptop, not a mobile device. However, if you think B2B buyers are not using mobile, you are not paying attention. According to Forrester Research, more than half of all B2B buyers use their mobile phones to research products.[105] If they're already going to your web site to do the research, why not make it easy for them to buy, too?

---

104   Salesforce Commerce Cloud presentation at Fashion Digital LA by Rob Garf, 2017
105   https://www.avalara.com/blog/2017/02/02/top-5-b2b-ecommerce-trends-2017/

This approach can be augmented by arming your sales team with mobile applications that deliver real-time inventory, pricing information, and other customized digital tools that help expedite the selling process. One of my clients, Kelly Paper, uses this exact approach to drive sales and deepen their customer relationships. Today, their mobile application is responsible for one-fourth of all transactions the company makes.

Key Chapter Takeaways

- B2C user experience best practices must be adopted by B2B sellers in order to be successful and meet the expectations of B2B buyers, which are informed by their experiences as consumer Ecommerce buyers.

- The goals of the B2B buyer diverge from the B2C buyer. B2B buyers shop online to make their jobs easier, whereas consumer buyers shop more frequently for enjoyment.

- B2B Ecommerce businesses should follow well-established user experience and web site design best practices from B2C, including site navigation, on site search, web merchandising, personalization, category list pages, product detail pages, shopping cart, checkout, payments, and other areas.

- B2B user experiences often require complexity that goes beyond typical B2C buying experiences, including unique features around customer-specific pricing, custom catalogs, checkout options, roles and permissions, and sales force enablement.

- Success of your Ecommerce web site can be measured with web analytics and business intelligence tools, using metrics such as conversion rate, average order value, and bounce rate, using industry benchmarks as a guidepost for your progress.

- Look outside of your organization, including to B2C Ecommerce, to hire talent for web merchandising, creative web design, user experience, and web analytics.

- Dramatic and measurable results are available to companies that follow these best practices, as evidenced by multiple real-world case studies included in this chapter.

Congratulations! You're Digital. Now What?

11

Being Digital: Rethinking the Process

So your company has committed to undergoing a digital transformation. You've read each chapter of this book and have set into motion the wheels of change within your organization. Congratulations! Now what? What does your organization look like once you have successfully completed a digital transformation? How do you know if you have taken the right steps? What does success look like, and what exactly does it mean to be digital? And how do you know when you are done?

The truth is that you will never be done.

As should be apparent from the many interdependent functions and varying areas of effort I have described throughout this book, truly "being digital" as an organization is about more than just buying and implementing an Ecommerce software package. It is about organizational change and breaking down silos. Being digital is about process change, as B2B organizations reimagine how to approach business from an overarching standpoint and across all functions. But it is also about putting digital first across the organization; digital has evolved to be the number one place that customers research and find products, interact with brands, and expect to receive support. This chapter explores what it means to be a digital-first organization, and how you can measure whether or not yours is succeeding.

It Starts at the Top

According to Deloitte's Global Human Capital Trends 2017 report, "only 5 percent of companies feel they have strong digital leaders."[106] Similarly, a 2016 MIT/Deloitte survey of managers and executives shows "90 percent expect their industries to be disrupted by digital technologies to a great or moderate extent, but only 44 percent believe their organizations are adequately prepared for these digital disruptions."[107] Change is upon us, but leadership is not yet prepared in many cases. This does not mean you have to be one of the unprepared!

Early in this book, I described the need for leadership to drive change. It is worth re-emphasizing this point here. Without leadership, change does not happen. Too many B2B organizations are just successful enough to avoid evolving, and this is dangerous to the very long-term viability of the enterprise. The digitally-transformed organization is characterized by leaders who are not afraid to confront the realities of shifting buyer behavior and outside changes in selling channels. These leaders have driven evolution in their organizations by pushing their peers and subordinates out of their comfort zones and by finding ways to cultivate new thinking and digital competencies within their companies.

The leadership at a digitally-transformed organization thinks differently. Characteristics of these leaders include:

---

106 https://www2.deloitte.com/content/dam/Deloitte/us/Documents/human-capital/hc-2017-global-human-capital-trends-us.pdf
107 https://www2.deloitte.com/us/en/pages/about-deloitte/articles/press-releases/mit-sloan-management-review-and-deloitte-digital-global-study-finds-workers-ready-to-leave-companies-not-keeping-pace-with-digital-change.html

- **Flexibility:** These leaders recognize that the new, digitally-centered world is rapidly changing, and they expect and embrace this change while instilling an organizational culture of flexibility to accommodate and adapt to new customer expectations and capabilities available in the marketplace. Process takes a back seat to customer centricity, and will be compromised for the sake of improving a customer's outcome.

- **Humility:** These leaders are unafraid to admit what they don't know and look both inside and outside their organization for resources to help them understand new trends.

- **Collaboration:** Successfully deploying Ecommerce requires cross-functional collaboration. The most capable executives recognize this and create alignment and accountability across the organization, driving a common understanding of the goals and benefits of the Ecommerce initiative.

- **Digital-mindedness:** These leaders don't look at digital as a task to be done, but rather how tasks get done across the organization. They encourage experimentation and collaboration, as well as a culture that seeks to be innovative.

- **Data-driven:** These leaders take emotion out of the decision-making equation, and rely on data to help them make decisions. That said, these leaders also do not get hamstrung by indecision; they are comfortable making decisions with only 80 percent of the data in place. Waiting for perfect information in a fast-changing digital world is not a viable approach to remain competitive. They test new things regularly without fear of failure, measure the results, and adjust the approach.

Note that I did not indicate that these leaders need to be technologists. Often, I see B2B organizations focused only on the technology surrounding Ecommerce and digital. While technology is important, it *should only exist* to support business objectives. Capable, smart executives learn about technology and surround themselves with enough IT leadership and technology expertise to enable decisions. The most successful B2B Ecommerce operations are not typically led by the IT team, but instead by executives with backgrounds mainly in business functions (such as marketing, Ecommerce, product, or sales). That said, modern IT executives are increasingly focused on executing strategic business objectives, so exceptions certainly exist.

It's not just about an Ecommerce-enabled Web Site

As I've said, being digital doesn't just mean launching an Ecommerce web site. There are many other aspects of becoming a digitally-focused organization. Digital touches every function within a company, including marketing, sales, finance, supply chain, warehouse, product development, IT, and more. Recognizing the impact of digital on an organization requires a shift in thinking. For a great model of this, I like to turn to Jeff Bezos, the founder and CEO of Amazon (and my personal Ecommerce hero). Bezos very famously said (and continues to say) that Amazon needs to remain a "Day 1" company, meaning that Amazon, as an organization, should behave as though it were its first day in business—every single day. He went on to outline the philosophy, saying:

The outside world can push you into Day 2 if you won't or can't embrace powerful trends quickly, if you fight them, you're probably fighting the future. Embrace them and you have a tailwind.[108]

We are at a point in technology and culture where B2B companies MUST become Day 1 companies, meaning they need to embrace change and innovation across all functions in order to survive and remain relevant to their customers. The time for siloed thinking and slow action has passed. Here is what becoming a Day 1 company entails:

- **Put the customer first:** Put aside your assumptions about your customers, what they need, and what you have provided them up to this point. Go out and talk to your customers face to face, through surveys, through your extended team, through focus groups, and in other ways to understand how they expect to interact with you digitally.

- **Break the process and re-innovate:** Literally remove your business processes and come at your customers'— and not your organization's—problems as though you were inventing the process from scratch.

- **Update your employee rewards structure:** Instead of rewarding people based on antiquated KPIs surrounding traditional profitability measures, restructure your rewards and put digital at the center of it. Develop and set new types of KPIs that provide different measurement methods. These new KPIs can be measured from a marketing or operations standpoint, and can help you examine areas such as

---

108   https://www.amazon.com/p/feature/z6o9g6sysxur57t

cost savings and customer satisfaction. For example,
reward the Ecommerce team for generating sales leads
that the sales force follows up on. For reference, I
included a list of recommended KPIs for the digitally
transformed organization earlier in Chapter 4.

- **Embrace democratization:** Thanks to technology
today, even entry-level employees can have a huge
impact on your business. The sooner you embrace this,
the sooner you will find ways for your employees to
innovate upwards through your organization instead
of slavishly following a top-down process. The new
generation of employees is digitally native. Embrace
this as a way to infuse digital thinking throughout
the entire organization at all levels, structure a way to
gather ideas from all levels, and keep an open mind!

- **Understand influence across channels:** The old adage
about not knowing which half of your advertising is
working has taken on new meaning with our fractured
media and marketing landscape. The number of
customer touch-points is now nearly infinite. It's
essential to understand how a tweet affects a Facebook
post, which affects a Buzzfeed article, which affects
a Time magazine article, which affects where your
customers see your advertising, and which may
ultimately end up in a sale. Develop an understanding
of how your organization can exist in and influence
this digital ecosystem.

- **Test your way to success:** Here is one of the coolest
things about digital: it is highly testable, and results
are, for the most part, measurable. You can segment
email lists and test subject lines; you can parse web
traffic and test landing pages; you can test multiple

versions of lead generation forms and content and see which perform best. If you don't have a testing mindset, you are likely not going to make the best business decisions. Testing without a fear of failure is at the core of Amazon's Day 1 culture. Collecting data and adjusting the approach based on this is key to a digitally-transformed organizational culture.

- **Don't look only for direct results:** In the world of direct response advertising (and the legacy of B2C Ecommerce advertising), marketers could put $X into a Google paid search campaign, and look for $Y in sales coming directly from the Ecommerce web site. While that formula is still true to some extent, it is no longer the whole story. As I covered in Chapter 8, not all marketing activities will directly result in a sale, and it may be challenging to see its impact on the bottom line (which is why you need to reward employees for digital-first thinking and behaviors).

- **Accept and embrace change:** The digital world changes dramatically and quickly. The faster you recognize and embrace this, the better off you will be. Employees at Day 1 companies look forward to change and the opportunities it can bring.

DO YOU HAVE DESKTOP ONLY DISORDER?

Too many B2B organizations only think about desktop devices (PCs or laptop computers) in their web site implementations, and forget about the mobile experience. I jokingly call this trend a "disease," which I have coined Desktop Only Disorder. Best practices for creating mobile-optimized web sites have existed for quite some time. And yet, many B2B companies still suffer from this affliction. According to an eMarketer survey, approximately

40 percent of small businesses do not have a mobile web site.[109] This is not excusable.

This lack of mobile-optimized web sites in B2B exists despite the fact that mobile use among B2B buyers is growing. For example, a Salesforce survey found that the majority of B2B buyers say their mobile device is "essential" to their work.[110] This is heavily supported by other findings, such as that 48 percent of all mobile users (B2B and B2C) begin product searches on search engines; the rest typically either use an app or go directly to the site they want.[111] And conversion rates for smartphones are much lower than traditional computers or tablets, which is probably not surprising when you consider that many companies still don't have a web site designed for mobile access![112]

A digitally transformed organization puts mobile first—not only in the user experience design, but also in the process of rewarding the team for truly looking first at the mobile experience in their marketing and merchandising activities. This means ensuring your web site administrators evaluate the mobile experience they are delivering as a part of their daily routine. I even joke with some of my clients that we should take away the web team's desktop computers and force them to do all of their work on their smartphones. The point should be clear here: mobile-first is a way of acting, not just a buzzword. And it is an ingrained behavior of truly digitally-transformed organizations.

---

109   https://www.emarketer.com/Article/Some-Small-Business-Websites-Still-Not-Mobile/1013824
110   https://www.emarketer.com/Article/Mobile-Usage-Among-B2B-Buyers-Expected-Grow/1015024
111   https://www.wiredseo.com/mobile-marketing-statistics-2017/
112   http://www.smartinsights.com/mobile-marketing/mobile-marketing-analytics/mobile-marketing-statistics/

What Does It Mean to be Digital?

Being digital means embracing technology and digital approaches as tools to become more efficient in every aspect of your business, as well as to better meet and exceed customer expectations. Digital companies seek to infuse every aspect of their business with digital technology. From purchases to customer communication and marketing (which we have discussed extensively in Chapter 8), to more overlooked aspects of digital transformation found in functions like internal communication, fulfillment, product development, finance . . . the list goes on. A digital-first company turns to digital solutions to solve problems and drive efficiency, sales, and profits.

Take internal communication, for example. Many firms that have been around for 25 years or more still operate in a very analog fashion. If there is a question, either internally or externally, they may send an email (arguably a digital technology that's least equipped to help us manage communications), but they are often just as likely to use the phone, host an in-person meeting, or even turn to paper (believe it or not, I've seen companies send employees company-wide *paper* memos to announce *digital* changes). None of these things are bad, of course, and in fact there are times and places for all of them. But all of these communication vehicles can be enhanced by digital, and not just by email. It takes a shift in organizational thinking and behavior, and when the customer is turning to digital first to accomplish a goal, why wouldn't the entire organization? Ultimately, a firm's assumptions, processes, and internal behaviors need to be assessed and re-configured for the digital age. Because today's reality is that digital colors everything, including many things beyond an organization's control.

Thus, a digital-first company acknowledges that digital is now a main channel for communication, and builds this into its processes and behaviors expected from employees. These companies use digital channels not as a full replacement for traditional channels, but as reinforcement for other communications methods. A great example of this is using web site data to inform a sales team's communications and interactions with customers. For example, when a customer registers an account on your web site, the sales and marketing team can then see not only what products that customer has purchased, but also what products the customer has viewed online, potentially signaling buying intent. Sales team members can take that information and craft a pitch tailored directly to the customer's needs and interests.

But use caution! There is a perception, particularly among people who are not as familiar with digital etiquette, that digital will fully replace all communication. Just as it is unrealistic to believe digital will replace sales teams (as we discussed in Chapter 5), it is also unrealistic to expect customers to want everything to be all digital all the time. In fact, part of the process of becoming a digital-first company is personalizing experiences to customers' needs and preferences, and that includes how, when, and through which channels you communicate with them. Case in point: I once received a sales call from a company whose whitepaper I had downloaded. I normally don't mind this, but the call came in less than 30 minutes after I downloaded the white paper! I hadn't even had a chance to fully read it, much less think about whether I wanted to have a relationship with the company. It is great that this company was leveraging the data they had collected on me via digital channels, but at the same time, they failed at finding the balance.

Putting digital first in an organization is not easy and takes considerable evolution in terms of both process and thought. One leading mid-market distributor in the health-care industry that I have worked with receives over 50 percent of its orders via Ecommerce. It got there by evolving over time, driving change from the top and installing an experienced digital team. Their digital journey started in 2000, when the company first launched a private, customer-only web site, a common practice in many wholesale industries. This was originally developed when they realized that their customers wanted to do business via the Internet. They did not want to force people to call or use their traditional print catalog if they did not want to.

This served them well over a number of years, but site performance began to lag over time. The key to improving the site's performance was found in listening to their customers to drive change throughout the organization, and this approach served them well throughout their digital transformation. By surveying their customers, the company found that a significant portion of their buyers actually used Google to start product searches. Because their site was login protected at the time, none of their products would show up in search results, while their competitors' products did. This was enough to convince the leadership to change their approach to Ecommerce, and open their site content to the public.

By putting the customer first, this firm was able to effect a digital transformation that now touches every part of the company. This also includes cross-pollinating members of the Ecommerce team within other parts of the company to help spread the "digital DNA" across the organization (e.g. in the marketing and product development teams). Now, when they bring new products to market, the company has digital know-how to fuel their online activities and complement their offline ones. And as a result, Ecommerce is the company's fastest growing sales channel, and today more than one third of its web site traffic originates from search engines.

CASE STUDY

State Electric: Standing out from the Crowd with Digital Experience, Service, and Content

"We didn't want to run with the pack"

State Electric Supply Company is one of the largest electrical products distributors in the United States. The company has a long history of putting digital at the forefront of its efforts to service customers. State Electric launched its first Ecommerce web site in the late 1990s and knows a thing or two about being digital as a result. The company has been through multiple iterations of its online commerce presence, with the most recent launching in 2018. With each new version of its site, the company learned from mistakes, incorporated customer feedback, and today recognizes the value of standing out from the competitive crowd with a differentiated online experience.

Dave Gravely, State Electric's VP Ecommerce and Strategy Sales, puts it this way: "Have you ever watched kids play soccer? They are all running around in a big clump, swarming around the ball. Doing the same thing. We knew this wasn't what we wanted for our Ecommerce site. We didn't want to run with the pack. We needed to stand out."

And they have.

With the latest version of its Ecommerce site, State Electric exemplifies what it means to "be digital." In developing the site, they incorporated feedback from internal and external users, to ensure the site met expectations for ease of use and utility. They interviewed and integrated requirements from the company's 100+ outside sales personnel to determine key functionalities that would enable front line sales team members to be more effective in their daily tasks. As a result of this approach, the Ecommerce team incorporated extensive content, including videos, to help sales teams and customers quickly find answers to application questions for the company's products. For example, if an electrical contractor is designing a sports facility such as a basketball court, information is available on the site on the components needed to provide adequate lighting ("footcandles") for nighttime use during team practice or a game.

"We want customers to come to our site first, before going to competitors or trying to solve something on their own. Our goal is to be the top place our customers go for support in their daily work activities," says Gravely. "This helps us be a true partner to our contractors, making them more effective in serving their customers. And this helps us stand out and earn their long term loyalty."

State Electric also backs up its digital approach with world class customer support. The company has long distinguished itself as a service first organization, and has historically differentiated with a company-wide mantra of "Service Makes State." In line with this approach, the company's digital organization deployed a team called the "Advanced Customer Service Team" or "ACT" that proactively follows up on any exception on orders it receives on its web site. Each order is reviewed for possible problems, and they will reach out to the customer if they suspect any issues. The company views this service level as a way to blend digital with its traditional high-touch service levels and to differentiate from online-only players such as Amazon.

The "being digital" approach is paying off for State Electric. Ecommerce sales are up by over 35 percent since the launch of their new site. So is web site traffic. As a direct result of extensive integration of content, traffic coming from the Google search engine is up by over 50 percent since the site went live. As of this writing, the company often ranks in the top 10 search results in Google for keywords such as "electrical supplies." The company was also awarded at "top five web site" honor in the electrical industry by Apruve, an industry solutions company.

Management has put digital at the forefront of State Electrics' growth plans, and the firm is reaping the benefits.

Digital Doesn't only Mean Virtual

When we envision a business as a digital-first organization, it is important to understand that digital does not only refer to the web site, mobile, or communications. It can also drive processes in other areas, such as fulfillment, support, finance, product development, and many other business units and functions. Rethinking your processes does not mean only looking at how your organization manages sales and marketing, but also how the backend and support processes have to change in order to accommodate digital-first approaches, including handling Ecommerce orders. B2B Ecommerce impacts multiple functions, each with its own set of buyer expectations, as highlighted below.

- **Fulfillment:** Many B2B companies are set up to support large bulk purchases using the traditional wholesale methodology; i.e. customer X orders 5,000 units of widget Y using a purchase order, which is then packaged in bulk and sent out for shipment, while an invoice is sent (sometimes digitally, but oftentimes not!) to the customer with payment terms. However, being a digital-first organization usually requires other types of orders, often smaller, that are paid for instantly, and packaged and shipped rapidly. The scale is often different, and there is therefore the need to evolve fulfillment to reflect different types of customer orders. It is possible that a B2B company may need to set up a parallel process or even a separate fulfillment unit just for digital orders, or perhaps outsource Ecommerce fulfillment altogether to a third party logistics company.

- **Order Transparency:** With smaller, faster orders often comes a higher expectation for transparency. Traditional shipping is a "black box," where an order is only trackable when there is a tracking number and it has left the warehouse. Today's customer, especially those who are digital natives, have different expectations. They want to know what phase of the process their order is in. Indeed, it is often something they need to know in order to properly perform their jobs. Systems now exist that can integrate the fulfillment process with digital technology and translate that to data related to a customer's order. Depending on your fulfillment set up, products and orders can be tracked with RFID (Radio-Frequency Identification) chips or other technology, informing your staff as well as customers of the exact order status.

- **Customer Service:** Service and support is another area where digital technology can solve many challenges efficiently and effectively. We have discussed various modes of digital communication with buyers, such as customer self-service using the web, in other chapters. What is most important to understand here is how those digital channels will require support units to change how they operate. Not only do newer digital technologies help to manage the volume of customer interfaces through automation, but they also change the skill set customer service representatives require. In the past, these positions have often been entry-level jobs filled by just about anyone with a pleasant phone demeanor. However, today's customers may communicate by phone, email, chat, social media, or other digital channels. Given the large amount of writing needed, it is essential to find people who can type coherent answers quickly with minimal errors. As part of this multi-channel communications environment, you will need to provide systems training to your support personnel.

- **New Customer Service Models:** Digital can also reorganize how customer service units work. Depending on the volume of inquiries, units may need to split agents into sub-units with channel-specific knowledge and skills. Alternatively, some companies have opted to develop "super agents," who are trained in all areas of the company's products, services, processes, and digital tools, who can then respond to any customer inquiry, through any digital communications channel, at any time.

- **Finance:** Another area that is highly impacted by digital transformation is finance. This makes sense, if you consider that finance is responsible for the smooth running of a business from a budgetary perspective. New revenue and cost models must be developed to account for Ecommerce operations. As we discussed in Chapter 4, I recommend a separate profit and loss (P&L) statement be developed for the Ecommerce function, and finance will be required to support this effort. Another key impact on finance is the new data that digital can provide. When a company puts digital at the heart of everything they do, they are also putting data right at the center of it. Digital transactions, digital communications, and digital processes all leave massive data trails. Finance can take advantage of this at a variety of levels within the business, including developing more accurate risk models, developing tighter compliance controls, and predicting surges in customer demand or after-sales service costs. Possibly more than any other function in an organization, it is finance that requires access to all the digital inputs and outputs a company creates.

There are many other business functions that should be considered when it comes to digital transformation. Some of these functions may undergo a digital transformation organically, as the company proceeds to develop its digital capabilities. For other functions, it will require a full-blown process change that is similar to the process used to develop and deploy an Ecommerce platform. It is essential to understand that digital does not stop with Ecommerce, but rather that it is integrated throughout the company at all levels and functions.

Ultimately, a truly successful digital-first organization embraces the web strategically to make the business more effective. They use digital communications and processes to free up time in order to pursue larger opportunities. They relegate many routine customer support functions to automation or online self-service, and the sales and marketing teams spend time focused on more strategic, higher level tasks that add more value to the organization. Sellers have less time than ever to capture a buyer's attention, and the more efficient and strategic your organization can be, the more successful your company will be. The brutal reality is that your organization needs to be able to meet the needs of modern buyers. With digital natives making up an increasing portion of the workforce, the demand for digital solutions is only going to grow. Being a digital-first organization is no longer an option, it is an imperative.

Key Chapter Takeaways

- Leadership is required to drive digital transformation, and this starts at the top of the organization.

- Digitally transformative leaders exhibit these common characteristics: Flexibility, Humility, Collaboration, Digital Mindedness, and Data-driven decision making.

- Digitally transformative leaders aren't necessarily technologists, but leverage technology as a foundational element to accommodate change and support business objectives.

- Digital transformation goes far beyond just having an Ecommerce web site. Amazon's Day 1 approach provides an excellent model for companies to emulate in order to evolve their organizations.

- Transformation incorporates putting the customer first, breaking down traditional silos, changing employee rewards structures, embracing democratization, understanding the impact of digital across all selling channels, developing a fear-free culture of testing, and being nimble and flexible in your approach.

- The digitally transformed organization has updated the way it does business across the majority of operating functions to incorporate digital and accommodate Ecommerce, including fulfillment, customer service, and finance, and has also evolved internal communications and processes to incorporate digital efficiencies.

Our
Digital Future

12

I have spent the bulk of this book talking about why B2B companies need to plan, start, and manage an Ecommerce operation. The clear and present challenge for many B2B firms is just getting the foundation in place. I have shared the specific steps needed to get started, the leadership imperative, what organizational changes are required, how to select an Ecommerce platform, ways to "be digital," and many other related topics. Once the fundamental items are in place, what is next? What does the future for B2B Ecommerce hold once the industry has matured and most companies are digitally transformed entities? Is it even worth thinking about the future when, frankly, too many B2B firms are still 10—even 15—years behind the rest of the Ecommerce world?

Well, yes.

Once a company has the digital foundation in place, very exciting things happen that transform the way it does business and connects with customers. Incremental revenue, increased profits, and organizational efficiencies accrue to the firm (as I highlighted in the ROI discussions in Chapter 3), and are really just the tip of the iceberg. The company you are running today will seem like an old rotary phone in comparison to the high-speed fiber optic Internet you will be once your business fully goes digital. It will change your perspective, your approach, and most importantly, your bottom line. By starting today, you will be future-proofing your business, and can then turn towards taking advantage of the exciting opportunities new waves of innovation can bring to your business.

There are several key technology trends that promise to have huge impacts on B2B Ecommerce and can be considered for adoption by companies that have established a solid foundation. Many of these technologies have been or are being pioneered by Amazon. But this does not mean their sole purpose is to make Jeff Bezos richer (though some most certainly will). These technologies are being deployed across a wide variety of industries, and your business can use them as well, once you have developed a strong digital foundation. Let's start with the promise of personalization.

Personalization

Internet analysts have written about the potential for personalization for the past 15 years or more, ever since a smart marketer figured out how to dynamically insert individual customers' names into mass marketing emails, dramatically increasing open and interaction rates. Every few years the technology improves and we enter a new age of personalization.

The web site WhatIs.com has a very succinct definition of personalization:

> *Commonly used to enhance customer service or e-commerce sales, personalization is sometimes referred to as one-to-one marketing, because the enterprise's web page is tailored to specifically target each individual buyer. Personalization is a means of meeting the customer's needs more effectively and efficiently, making interactions faster and easier and, consequently, increasing customer satisfaction and the likelihood of purchase and repeat visits.*[113]

---

113   https://searchsalesforce.techtarget.com/definition/personalization

The B2C retail sector has been working hard for almost a decade to find ways to deliver truly personalized content, messaging, product recommendations, and full shopping experiences via digital channels. This has set the stage for B2B adoption of these best practices.

Note that personalization is not isolated to Ecommerce. In fact, online personalization builds on the well-established personal relationships between buyer and seller that have existed in the B2B selling dynamic for decades and extends these relationships online. Business relationships will frequently begin in the physical world in a more traditional manner—at an industry event, by referral, or other means. Once a relationship is established, though, digital communication is used to reinforce it, but not replace it. Increasingly, relationships are also beginning via digital means (e.g. a search on Google leads a new buyer to your web site). Personalization helps sellers to understand buyer intent and connect virtually with these new customers and prospects via digital means. As a result, these relationships will often grow to incorporate offline channels as well, and digital can help inform the physical relationships by providing data around customer preferences and interests. Once your firm has embarked on the digital transformation journey, you will be able to create new one-to-one relationships through any channel. Moreover, many relationships will be fluid, taking place over a variety of channels simultaneously and seamlessly.

What does personalization mean for your business, practically speaking? How does it come to life on a B2B web site? Primarily, a well-presented, personalized experience anticipates the needs of each individual web site visitor, understands how and when they engage with you digitally, and presents relevant content and product information on each visit at the right time in the customers' research and purchase journey. Personalization recognizes and leverages multiple data points to deliver these relevant experiences, including the content the customer has engaged with in the past, the customer's past purchases, and both their online and offline behavior. In some cases, this can even mean predictive ordering. For example, if a customer uses a piece of your capital equipment, you likely understand the maintenance cycle of that equipment and can probably predict when that customer will need more supplies or replacement parts. Using this key insight that *only your business can have*, you will be able to offer just-in-time replenishment and/or preventative maintenance.

These aren't pie in the sky futuristic concepts; they are happening right now. And, unsurprisingly, Amazon is leading the charge. All the way back in 2014, Amazon filed a patent for "anticipatory package shipping," whereby they prepare packages to be shipped to a customer based on previous orders, and ship them proactively to the customer—before they are actually ordered by the customer. In one iteration, the package is sent and remains in transit until the delivery address is specified.[114] Another example is the Amazon Dash button, enabling consumers to order household staples like laundry detergent simply by pressing a button. This is already being deployed by Amazon in the B2B sector for office supply buyers, ensuring customers never run out of paper, tape, or dry erase markers.[115] And what happens if the customer doesn't want the products? They can easily send them back at no additional cost, or Amazon just allows the customer to keep the items after refunding the purchase.

---

114   https://techcrunch.com/2014/01/18/amazon-pre-ships/
115   https://www.amazon.com/Office-Dash-Buttons/b?ie=UTF8&node=14368042011

JUST KEEP IT!

Amazon operates at such a large scale that the cost to cover return shipping is often greater than the cost of reselling the item; in these cases Amazon often lets the customer keep the product while refunding its cost to the customer. Amazon is big enough that they can absorb the loss while retaining the customer. While you may not be able to achieve this scale of Ecommerce right off the bat, or even in a few years, this illustrates the massive scale opportunities that Ecommerce can achieve. Take a cue from Amazon and run the numbers—this might also work for your business!

The power of digital personalization also translates to offline channels. This includes enabling the sales team to use data derived from your Ecommerce web site when talking with customers directly. This information can lead to a better understanding of customer behaviors and buying intent, showcasing more relevant products at the right time, and quickly obtaining real-time information, such as product availability. The sales team will be able to strengthen their relationships by using digital. Best of all, personalized relationships empowered by digital means can be massively transformative. Why? Remember that the key to B2B success is making the buyer's job easier and faster. With digital personalization, all selling channels are more effectively delivering relevant information more quickly, which has the result of deepening relationships while delivering higher value for buyers.

CASE STUDY

Illumina: Next Generation Personalization—The Art of the Possible

"A game changer for both illumina and our customers"

Cited as "the smartest company on the planet" by MIT Business Review, illumina is the global leader in equipment and consumables for biotechnology research in the field of genomics. Visitors to the company's corporate headquarters in San Diego, California stand as the minority if they don't have the letters "P," "H," and "D" on their resume (in that order). Illumina's customer base and market reach is very broad, across consumer genomics, applied genomics, research, and clinical diagnostics.

As I highlighted earlier in Chapter 2, illumina's technology leadership comes to life throughout the company, from its groundbreaking products to how it digitally enables its customer relationships. The company has pioneered new approaches to personalization in the process and is creating new digital B2B best practices as a result. For illumina, nothing is off the table— the impossible is possible, and pushing the limits of technology is the standard of doing business. They are a $3 billion multinational firm with the spirit and culture of a startup.

Leveraging the Internet of Things (IoT) to personalize and deepen customer relationships is something that has come naturally to illumina as a result of this culture and the company's internet-enabled product offerings. Thousands of illumina's advanced gene sequencing systems are used by medical researchers across the globe. With this broad base of installations, management realized an opportunity to leverage these assets to expand its customers' use of its products and deepen affinity with the illumina brand.

The key was to connect these systems to a customer-specific online dashboard, called MyIllumina, as well as to illumina's customer relationship management (CRM) system. With this integration in place, the company could now deliver content and product utility that was timely, personalized, and extremely relevant. Illumina no longer needs to wait for its customers to state their needs; they can predictively deliver value, in real time, as the machines are being used on an individual customer basis. This helps improve the daily professional lives of multiple people's roles in a research lab.

Illumina's innovative use of IoT and online tools allows the company to proactively deliver highly relevant product information and application content to its customers. This capability also enables illumina to communicate routine notifications and updates that keep the customer informed and in control of their lab with all the details needed to get their jobs done. This includes proactively notifying customers of required equipment maintenance, orders, contract renewals, system availability, and other lab management information.

For example, a researcher can start a sequencing run (an experiment) on an instrument, go home for the weekend, and maintain full visibility of the run on their mobile device or via a web browser on a desktop or laptop computer. He or she can monitor the run and its progress while sitting on the sideline of their child's soccer match, and receive a notification when the experiment completes. On Monday morning, the same researcher can reorder new consumables (chemicals that are used in the equipment) for the next run. The researcher can also read the most recent illumina expert content about his or her area of research, all based on the profile preferences that the user has indicated. And illumina can recommend products based on the specific research the customer is conducting, making it easier and faster for the researcher to accomplish the goals of their research.

The company's Senior Director of Digital, Dave Grimm (or "Digital Dave" as he's known within illumina), notes, "This has been a game changer for both illumina and our customers. We are reinforcing customer relationships by gaining a full understanding of their use of our equipment. This makes their lives easier and reinforces our value to the customer."

Illumina strives to make the impossible possible. Pushing the boundaries comes naturally, and this approach has served them well in pursuing digital transformation that benefits their customers and grows affinity for the illumina brand.

Fulfillment and Automation

Fulfillment is often thought of as the least sexy part of Ecommerce. It is a necessary evil, and something that appears to allow for little competitive differentiation in the marketplace. However, upon closer examination, dramatic change is occurring in approaches to fulfillment, powered by technology. These innovations are driving efficiencies at large scales, increasing profits, and delivering superior customer experiences. It turns out that digitally-enhanced fulfillment technologies can in fact be a differentiator, and allow firms to effectively scale to meet new customer demands generated by B2B Ecommerce.

Perhaps the first Ecommerce firm to realize the value of innovation in fulfillment was Amazon (surprise, surprise!). Early on, Amazon realized the value of exceeding customer expectations and invested accordingly. Amazon's speed of delivery on its vast, nearly infinite selection of products is a key factor leading to its current Ecommerce market dominance.

One of my favorite case studies of recent years focuses on how Amazon is deploying robots in its warehouses.[116] These are not humanoid robots. They are small orange boxes on wheels called Kiva robots, and they look a little bit like Roombas (robotic vacuum cleaners). Amazon figured out

Kiva Robots at work in an Amazon Fulfillment Center

that it is far more efficient to bring warehouse shelves to its human workers, versus the conventional method of employing human workers to hunt for products among warehouse shelves (traditionally called the "picking process"). Amazon's robots know where each product is located, so when an order is processed, the robots go to the modified shelves, pick up the entire shelving unit, and then wheel it to a human, who then

116 https://www.youtube.com/watch?v=g6DIFpaoI6A

takes the product from the shelf and packs it. Then the robot returns the shelf or moves onto retrieving a different shelf for a different order, all while the human workers who are packing orders stay in the same spot. This process may sound unusual or backwards at first, but when you think about the scale of operations that Amazon achieves, it actually makes sense. According to Amazon, they have been able to pack 50 percent more product in each of its warehouses, and have reduced average order fulfillment time from 90 minutes to 15 minutes since deploying this system.

This is just one example of how complex fulfillment and automation tools are making warehouses operate practically in real-time. In fact, Amazon has launched a service called Prime Now in some parts of the country, where customers can purchase items and have them delivered within as little as two hours from the time of purchase. This service has quickly gained popularity with Amazon's customers. And in the spring of 2019, Amazon announced it was moving many orders to one-day shipping for Prime customers.

What does this mean for B2B? Well, as I have said throughout this book, what happens in B2C shapes customers' expectations in B2B. Even if you are selling big-ticket items—for example commercial HVAC systems for industrial complexes—being the fastest to deliver your product can earn you a solid, positive reputation in your industry and is a significant differentiator. The good news is that many warehousing and fulfillment services already exist, making fulfillment a prime candidate for outsourcing. Of course, building your own infrastructure is an option, but know that this can consume a hefty amount of time, energy, and capital to gain the efficiencies that Amazon and others in the B2C market have achieved.

Artificial Intelligence (AI)

Almost all of the trends and advancements mentioned above are possible because of the development of artificial intelligence (AI). If you are thinking self-aware robots taking the place of humans, though, you may be surprised (and reassured) to know that AI (at least in the context of this book) refers more to the complex computer algorithms that companies are now employing to operate their businesses more efficiently. To be sure, there are some things that humans have historically done that AI is now doing. For example, computers did not invent predictive analytics; they are just perfecting it.

When we talk about AI, we are really talking about computer software that can be given a goal and act somewhat autonomously to achieve that goal, acting like or emulating human intelligence. Sometimes this requires some problem solving, but it can also require object recognition, statistical computation, natural language processing, and other capabilities we traditionally think of being accomplished by a human.

The Merriam-Webster Dictionary defines AI as:

A branch of computer science dealing with the simulation of intelligent behavior in computers; the capability of a machine to imitate intelligent human behavior.

The amazing thing about AI is how much it really is needed. Consumers and businesses alike are generating more data than ever. It is estimated that the world's three billion internet users generate approximately 2.5 quintillion bytes of information per day.[117] Much of this new data comes from our growing number of smartphones and other internet-connected devices. This is only expected to continue to expand

---

117   http://www.iflscience.com/technology/how-much-data-does-the-world-generate-every-minute/

as we plug more elements of our daily lives into the internet using components such as smart thermostats, voice-activated digital assistants ("Alexa, what is the weather in San Jose?"), televisions, cars and other vehicles, appliances and other machinery, and a wide range of sensors that monitor environmental conditions. Businesses in a variety of industries are now adding internet-connected sensors to equipment, creating networks that we often refer to as the "Internet of Things" (IoT). These sensors can record a nearly infinite number of data types—from temperatures to traffic patterns, from water pressure in a pipe to the parts per million of a chemical in the air. The global business intelligence firm HIS Markit predicts that there will be more than 75 billion internet-connected devices and sensors by 2025, and the amount of data they will produce will be mind boggling. Without the use of AI, though, all of this data will be useless. Businesses of all types—but especially manufacturers with Ecommerce operations—need AI to make sense of the data, to develop automation programs that increase efficiencies, and to make smarter business decisions.

The subset of AI research that involves computers taking a data set and finding the best way to achieve a goal (such as optimizing a web site experience for engagement and selling) is called machine learning. In the world of Ecommerce, machine learning is playing a huge role in making businesses operate more efficiently. For example, an Ecommerce firm may use machine learning to analyze customer behavior with the goal of determining the best sequence for offering product information or even when to offer a discount on a product. What is so powerful about this is that companies can use these analytics to determine the best way to engage *each individual customer*, even while operating at massive scales. In other words, we can recognize that not every buyer operates in the same way or is at the same stage of the buying journey, and by using AI, sellers can personalize the shopping experience and interactions at the individual buyer level. Marketing to customers based strictly on defined customer segments and business rules is quickly becoming old-fashioned. Today, AI can serve timely content and offers to customers based on their personal buying history and other related data, at precisely the right time the customer needs it. And it can do this entirely without human direction.

Related to this is predictive analytics, which uses pattern recognition and statistical analysis to make predictions about future behaviors. Many industries are using predictive analytics, and Ecommerce is no exception. Using this approach, sellers can analyze their entire customer database and every purchase every customer has ever made, and can identify a variety of customer behaviors that can be encouraged or mitigated. For example, sellers might want to identify key times when a customer is likely to buy a certain product, or when a customer is going to cancel an account. In both instances, the seller can engage the customer appropriately and anticipate their purchase or take actions to prevent the buyer from taking their business elsewhere. Similarly, upselling products to existing customers is a common use for predictive analytics. For a basic example, think of Amazon's "Customers who bought X also bought Y" displays throughout the web site as an example.

Another use for predictive analytics is inventory management. AI solutions for inventory management can ensure items are restocked efficiently, taking multiple factors into account, including not only stock levels, but other internal and external data that may affect the efficient use of raw materials. For example, an AI solution may identify seasonal trends in customer orders and manage the volume accordingly. Or it could take into account weather conditions, which may affect delivery times.

Both machine learning and predictive analysis can be used to fine-tune digital marketing programs as well. This has been developed and deployed extensively in digital advertising, and can be applied to email marketing, social media, and other areas. AI can be used to deliver a personalized message to a customer at the right time, and on whatever device they may be using at that moment.

Probably the best-known instance of AI's use in digital marketing is Facebook's advertising engine. Using a combination of user-generated data such as interests, likes, user uploads, and third-party consumer data, Facebook empowers advertisers to select key audience segments and deliver customized, personalized advertising. For example, if a Facebook user has indicated that they like drinking Coca-Cola, an advertiser who sells Coke memorabilia can target users with relevant Facebook ads and content. The advertiser does not have to know or be connected to the user directly, they only have to know what the user likes and how much they want to spend to target the individual as a potential customer (and create the relevant advertising to be delivered to the target user). The AI that runs the back-end of Facebook's advertising platform does the rest, delivering up the ad at key times based on the user's own personal behavior and engagement with similar content. As of this time of writing, there aren't any advertising systems like Facebook's platform that are strictly for B2B (LinkedIn's advertising platform probably comes closest), but you can be sure that similar platforms are on the horizon.

Front-line customer service is another area where AI is being applied, particularly in the B2C arena. Using Natural Language Processing software, retailers are able to deploy "chat bots" on their web site to answer basic questions and engage with customers. You have probably seen these on a variety of retail web sites, where a small window pops up asking the

visitor, "How can I help you?" Using AI, companies can identify their customers' top questions, provide the system with a
set of appropriate responses, and allow the system take over
and address common questions from customers. If a question comes up that is outside of the AI's question library or
capabilities, the chat bot transfers the conversation to a live
human being in a support center. Chat bots can also be used
to improve the experience for existing customers by tying
into a seller's CRM system. This approach allows the system
to learn about the seller's current customer base, and more
fully address and predict customer questions.

Voice and Visual Search

Two technologies that rely on AI as a backbone to how they
function are voice and visual search. Both of these technologies allow users to search for products online using voice
commands or simply pointing a smartphone (or smartglasses)
camera at an object to identify it. With these technologies,
we are essentially teaching computers to hear and see in ways
similar to humans.

Voice search is probably one of the fastest growing platforms, and you have probably seen it in use in the many digital assistants available on the market today, such as Amazon
Echo, Google Home, and Apple's Siri. These systems essentially allow users to ask questions in plain language in order
to retrieve information or even order products. For example,
a customer might want to find the best price on a specific
product type or even a specific product. Instead of opening
a browser on their phone, laptop, or desktop computer, they
can simply ask their digital voice assistant. They might say,
"Find me the best price on X," or even "Find X." Their voice
assistant will then "say" what it has found and potentially
prompt the buyer to make a purchase. Alternatively, if it's

a product the buyer uses often, they might have connected their voice assistant to a commerce engine, such as Amazon, and simply say, "Buy 3 new units of X," or something similar. The voice assistant, with prior authorization and the buyer's credit card number or payment preference on file, places the order and it is automatically processed and shipped to the customer. As you can imagine, this saves the buyer a lot of time and they can quickly and easily complete their purchase while doing other things. While this technology is still some-what early in adoption in B2B, it is growing wildly in B2C settings. This means that it's likely a good idea to invest in optimizing online content for this technology today with the goal of leap-frogging your competition tomorrow.

Visual search does away with text altogether. It allows users to either point their phone camera and snap a photo or upload a picture of an object, which is then processed by a specialized search engine, returning relevant results based on the submitted image. Perhaps to no one's surprise, Google has been offering image-based search technology for a number of years and is continuously improving its ability to return relevant results. The implications for B2B sellers is massive. For example, if a customer needs to reorder a product from a merchant, they could simply use a specialized Ecommerce app, created and offered exclusively by the seller, to snap a picture of the desired product and have the item automati-cally placed into a shopping cart for easy re-order. The effi-ciencies gained by such a system at a large institution is likely worth millions, if not billions, of dollars. Of course, before this becomes a reality, it is essential to recognize the value of high-quality product images that are properly tagged and cat-egorized, thus making the search engine (or specialized app) much more accurate.

Virtual Reality (VR) and Augmented Reality (AR)

Virtual reality (VR) holds the promise to bring buyers closer to a physical experience when interacting via digital means. We can define VR as follows:

> *An artificial environment which is experienced through sensory stimuli (such as sights and sounds) provided by a computer and in which one's actions partially determine what happens in the environment; also: the technology used to create or access a virtual reality.*

VR has been experimented with by B2C retailers and brands as a way to bring consumers closer to an in-store product experience. For example, in 2017 Sephora, a leading retailer of cosmetics, launched a virtual reality-based mobile application that allows shoppers to test out different products virtually before they buy or go to a store. The tool is called the "Sephora Virtual Artist," and scans a customer's face, determines where the lips and eyes are located, and lets the customer try on different looks. If the customer likes the look, she can buy it on the spot. The app also offers "virtual tutorials" that show shoppers how to contour, apply highlighter, and create winged eyeliner. This technology meets the customer in the digital world and shifts consumer behavior patterns by enabling customers to make better and more informed decisions before they buy.

Augmented Reality (AR) is another technology that has landed a solid foothold in the B2B realm. Similar to VR, AR uses technology such as smartphones and smartglasses to overlay information onto what we see in the real world. In fact, it is estimated that the AR market will reach $100 billion by 2020.[118]

A common application that you may have seen are map overlays, such as in driving direction apps and games such as Pokemon Go (see the picture below).

The Sephora Virtual Artist

But these are not the only applications. Furniture companies are using Augmented Reality to help buyers see what pieces of furniture might look like in their homes or offices. Medical schools and hospitals are using AR to provide hands-on training and instruction. Tourism boards and private firms are creating "walkthroughs" enabling visitors to experience history in all new ways. Architects are using these systems to

---

118   https://www.inc.com/james-paine/10-real-use-cases-for-augmented-reality.html

Augmented Reality in Action: Pokemon Go

both design and showcase projects, providing a layer of interaction and data that has, before now, been impossible.

For manufacturers, machine maintenance is a huge
expense for both the manufacturer and its suppliers. When
production equipment breaks, it either needs to be sent out
for repair or the equipment maker needs to send a service
technician to the customer's location to take care of the
repair." And in some cases, the manufacturer might have staff
on hand capable of repairing the equipment. In any of these
scenarios, the machine is offline, incapable of production,
and potentially costing the business thousands and thousands
of dollars in lost productivity.

AR has the promise to dramatically reduce these costs
and cut downtime by enabling a digitally-enhanced service

environment. That is, workers can either use a smartphone or smartglasses to view a piece of equipment and instantly get repair instructions, video, and other relevant information. What's more, some systems that are currently in proof of concept as of this writing can digitally connect to a service technician who can see what the worker is seeing, and provide further instructions. For B2B firms that provide parts and service, this technology has the potential to be a real differentiator. For example, a B2B seller could connect its ERP system to an AR system, enabling its customers to both evaluate problems as well as purchase replacement parts right in the AR application.

The multi-billion dollar German global engineering firm Thyssenkrupp AG, for example, recently announced that it is providing sales representatives in its elevator division with a "special toolkit, including mixed-reality technology and Microsoft HoloLens™ smart glasses." This set of tools empowers salespeople to gather and digitize data about projects, such as taking crucial measurements in the field. The result, the firm claims, is the ability to deliver projects up to four times

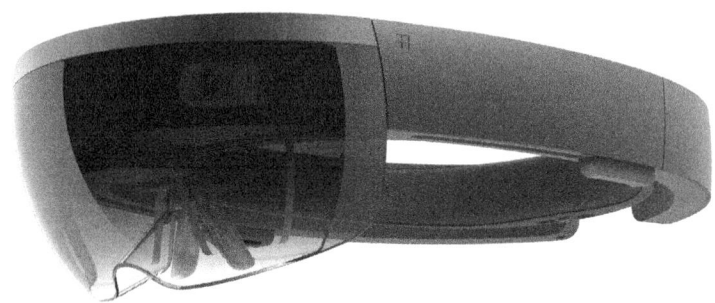

A Microsoft HoloLens headset (Used with permission from Microsoft Corporation)

faster using this technology.[119] Elsewhere, sports car manufacturer Porsche is deploying augmented reality in its quality assurance program, where technicians can take a photo of a part with a tablet or smartphone, and their system will match that photo to a file in a cloud-based database in order to compare dimensions and ensure it is the correct component.[120]

The Microsoft HoloLens in action in an auto manufacturing application

This is just the tip of the iceberg for VR and AR applications. While these are new trends, and adoption is still in its early stages, these technologies will continue to be developed and tested, and will likely have considerable utility in the B2B sector over time.

---

119   https://www.thyssenkrupp.com/en/newsroom/press-releases/press-release-142688.html?id=182402
120   https://www.slashgear.com/porsche-adopts-augmented-reality-for-quality-assurance-13447825/

CASE STUDY

**Bosch: Future-proofing
the B2B Customer Relationship**

"A whole new level of partnership with our customers"

B osch, the global tools, engineering, and electronics manufacturer I highlighted in Chapter 9, is continually pushing
the envelope on technology in order to deepen customer
relationships. Digital is at the center of how customers want
to interact with the company, and the future for Bosch is right
now. By putting the customer's needs at the center of how it
leverages technology, the company is winning.

A great example of this is the company's Bluehound system
for asset management. A large number of Bosch's customers are
construction companies. Many of these firms do not have effective or accurate ways of managing and tracking their physical
assets. This includes equipment and supplies used to complete
specific construction tasks, such as power tools, equipment (dig-
gers, skid steers, etc.), and palletted materials. Too often, construction firms do not know the location or utilization levels of these
assets. When tools and equipment aren't being put to work on a
construction site, their utilization (and value to the company) is
zero, even though labor is still being paid for. In fact, labor is one
of the largest cost components for construction firms, and with a
mismatch of labor to assets, productivity and profits drop.

Bosch's Bluehound system is a response to this need. The
solution embeds a tracking technology inside of Bosch's tools,
and it can even be added to non-Bosch tools and equipment
through a small, one-inch square device that attaches to the
asset. Bluehound uses Bluetooth technology to track the location
and use of tools in the field. The solution ties asset information

back to a cloud-based web portal and mobile app that allow construction companies to access location and utilization information. Assets can be reallocated in real time, for example to a different job site, to allow construction companies to maximize the use of each asset, and ensure it is used in its highest and best application. The system also provides productivity information on Bosch's tools, informing system administrators when maintenance is required and preventing equipment failure in the field.

The results have been impressive—both for Bosch and for its customers. "We are helping customers get jobs done more quickly and get more out of each asset, increasing their profitability as a result," says Eli Share, Bosch's Internet of Things and Mobile Lead for North America. "Additionally, our customers don't buy assets they don't need, because they now understand where their assets are located and how they are being used."

Return on investment from Bluehound is driven by reduced equipment downtime, which can be a substantial driver of cost and profit loss for construction firms. Inventory managers at Bosch's customers can see, in real time, when an asset becomes defective in the field. This allows these managers to more quickly respond, accelerating recovery times and allowing for more productive job sites. Tens of thousands of dollars are saved in the process.

This is also a capital efficient approach for Bosch's customers. Share says, "By only paying Bosch for the asset management system, which is delivered as a service, construction companies get the real value of the asset management system without a considerable capital outlay. They do not need to deploy an extensive technology infrastructure and wireless network required to track IoT enabled devices. We have done this for them."

This approach has enabled Bosch to deepen customer relationships. "In the past, we just sold product and provided support," says Share. "But now, by leveraging digital tools to solve customer challenges, we have a new level of partnership with our customers. This impacts how our customers think about us. We are not just a provider, but a true partner driving greater levels of business value. We have a stake in their success."

Bosch is future proofing its B2B customer relationships with leading-edge digital technologies.

Where to Go from Here

These are just a handful of examples of how technology will continue to impact Ecommerce and enable deeper buyer-seller relationships. For any B2B firm looking to develop an Ecommerce operation, using AI, personalization, Internet of Things, and other automation approaches may seem like something out of the future—a goal that is unattainable in the near term. While it is true that the foundational items discussed earlier in this book are important to achieve first, keeping an eye on these evolving technologies and adopting them at the appropriate time for your business is critical to meeting the rapidly evolving expectations of your buyers.

Keep in mind that none of the technologies and trends described in this chapter were realities as recently as five years ago. That's why establishing a solid foundation—right now—is a critical first step, which in turn makes deployment of these advanced tools more realistic for your business. As a digitized organization, you will have a seamless digital layer that allows your company to be far more customer-centric than it has ever been. You will have customer information at all touchpoints and create efficiencies that today may be hard to imagine. Maybe one day soon you will be the company that others are trying to catch up to!

Key Chapter Takeaways

- Advanced technologies are making their way into B2B sectors, though they should be pursued by manufacturers, brands, and distributors only after the foundation of a solid Ecommerce experience is in place.

- Digital personalization techniques and best practices have been pursued in the B2C sector for almost two decades; B2B merchants can learn from these practices to create highly relevant experiences for customers.

- B2B personalization can build on the deep personal relationships that exist in many B2B industries; working together with offline data, online personalization can further the effectiveness of B2B sellers by making it easier and faster than ever for customers to interact and buy from a company. Personalization can deepen competitive differentiation as a result.

- Internet of Things (IoT) can be used to more closely tie sellers to customers, and enhance the promise of personalization.

- Artificial Intelligence (AI) approaches can be used to present extremely relevant product information and content to B2B customers at the right point in the buying journey, enhancing online and offline conversion rates. AI can also be used to drive efficiency throughout the organization, including in inventory management.

- Virtual Reality (VR) and Augmented Reality (AR) can be leveraged by B2B sellers to recreate or enhance physical experiences and allow buyers to learn more about a company's products or obtain service in an immersive, interactive environment. B2C models, particularly out of highly personalized industries such as cosmetics, are setting the bar for use of VR in online selling, while AR has found a variety of applications in manufacturing and beyond.

- Next generation technologies become possible after the foundational elements of digital transformation and B2B Ecommerce are in place. Tackle these first, and you will be in a position to take advantage of the latest trends in digital technologies down the road. If you already have the fundamentals in place, pursuing personalization, AI, and other cutting edge tools can potentially provide you with competitive advantages in the marketplace.

Resources

Throughout the book, I mentioned a variety of resources readers might find helpful. Following is a collection of these resources, organized by topic.

Making the Business Case for B2B Ecommerce

On the Verge: B2B Digital Commerce is at an inflection point
https://www.accenture.com/t20180522T025432Z__w__/
us-en/_acnmedia/PDF-78/Accenture-Verge-B2B-Digital-
Commerce.pdf

Organizational Leadership and Business Transformation

Good to Great by Jim Collins
https://www.amazon.com/Good-Great-Some-Companies-
Others-ebook/dp/B0058DRUV6/

Amazon

Recommended Amazon Agency: www.enceiba.com (in the spirit of full disclosure, I am an owner of this company)

Sell on Amazon: https://services.amazon.com/

Seller Fulfilled Prime: https://services.amazon.com/services/
seller-fulfilled-prime.html

On-Site Search

Third Party Software Solutions (can be added to your Ecommerce web site):

- Algolia (www.algolia.com)

- Bloomreach (www.bloomreach.com)

- Celebros (www.celebros.com)

- Coveo (www.coveo.com)

- Nextopia (www.nextopia.com)

- Instant Search (www.instantsearchplus.com)

- Lucidworks (www.lucidworks.com)

- Search Spring (www.searchspring.com)

- SLI Systems (www.sli-systems.com)

Third-Party Fulfillment Resources

eFulfillment Service (www.efulfillmentservice.com)

FedEx Fulfillment (https://supplychain.fedex.com/fitsmallbusiness/)

Fulfillment By Amazon (https://services.amazon.com/fulfillment-by-amazon/benefits.htm)

Newgistics Pitney Bowes (www.newgistics.com)

Rakuten Super Logistics (www.rakutensl.com)

ShipBob (www.shipbob.com)

Shipwire (www.shipwire.com)

Digital Marketing

General Digital Marketing

Digital Marketing: Integrating Strategy and Tactics with Values, A Guidebook for Executives, Managers, and Students by Ira Kaufman and Chris Horton

https://www.amazon.com/Digital-Marketing-Integrating-Guidebook-Executives-ebook/dp/B00OM1I36G/ref=sr_1_9

Digital Marketing Strategy: An Integrated Approach to Online Marketing by Simon Kingsnorth

https://www.amazon.com/Digital-Marketing-Strategy-Integrated-Approach-ebook/dp/B01F3CDDK8/ref=sr_1_6

Contagious: Why Things Catch On by Jonah Berger

https://www.amazon.com/Contagious-Things-Catch-Jonah-Berger-ebook/dp/B008J4GQKW/ref=sr_1_16

SEO

The Art of SEO by Eric Enge, Stephan Spencer, and Jesse Stricchiola

https://www.amazon.com/Art-SEO-Mastering-Search-Optimization-ebook/dp/B0141LJ37Y/ref=sr_1_3

SEO Made Simple by Michael H. Fleischner

https://www.amazon.com/Seo-Made-Simple-4th-Strategies/dp/B00Q4ADIUO/ref=sr_1_5

Search Engine Optimization an Hour a Day by Jennifer Grappone and Gradiva Couzin

https://www.amazon.com/Search-Engine-Optimization-SEO-Hour-ebook/dp/B004PYDJ64/ref=sr_1_2

3 Months to Number 1: The 2019 "No-Nonsense" SEO Playbook for Getting Your Website Found on Google by Will Coombe

https://www.amazon.com/Months-No-1-No-Nonsense-Playbook-Getting-ebook/dp/B075HGN2L5/ref=sr_1_6

SEM

Introduction to Search Engine Marketing and AdWords: A Guide for Absolute Beginners by Todd Kelsey

https://www.amazon.com/Introduction-Search-Engine-Marketing-AdWords-ebook/dp/B072ZT1XRT/ref=sr_1_5

Ultimate Guide to Google AdWords: How to Access 100 Million People in 10 Minutes by Perry Marshall and Mike Rhodes

https://www.amazon.com/Ultimate-Guide-Google-AdWords-Million-ebook/dp/B074W6MRR7/ref=sr_1_3

Content Marketing

The Content Code: Six essential strategies to ignite your content, your marketing, and your business by Mark Schaefer

https://www.amazon.com/Content-Code-essential-strategies-marketing-ebook/dp/B00ULS1C26/ref=sr_1_19

Practical Content Strategy & Marketing: The Content Strategy Certification Course Student Guidebook by Julia McCoy and Mark Schaefer

https://www.amazon.com/Practical-Content-Strategy-Marketing-Certification-ebook/dp/B077SKLYNT/ref=sr_1_3

Marketing Platforms / Marketing Automation Solutions

Adobe Marketing Cloud: https://www.adobe.com/marketing-cloud.html#

Hubspot: http://hubspot.com

Keap (formerly Infusionsoft): https://keap.com/

Oracle Eloqua: https://www.oracle.com/marketingcloud/products/marketing-automation/

Salesforce Marketing Cloud: https://www.salesforce.com/products/marketing-cloud/overview/

User Experience/Interface

Don't Make Me Think, Revisited: A Common Sense Approach to Web Usability by Steve Krug

https://www.amazon.com/Dont-Make-Think-Revisited-Usability-ebook/dp/B00HJUBRPG/ref=sr_1_3

UX Strategy: How to Devise Innovative Digital Products that People Want by Jaime Levy

https://www.amazon.com/gp/product/B00XZF0J26

Glossary

A/B testing: Also called split testing, this is a web site optimization method that compares and evaluates the effectiveness of two different versions of a web page, design element, marketing message, or advertisement, and measures which version performs better against a stated goal, such as generating a sale on an Ecommerce web site. Usually, only a single variant is tested at a time, such as a different image or headline verbiage, but multiple variants can be tested as well (which is called *multi-variate testing*).

Affiliate marketing: An advertising channel wherein a product or service seller pays a third party (called an "affiliate" or "publisher") for referrals that convert into paying customers. The third party typically uses content to drive traffic to the seller's web site, which then tracks the traffic and conversion rates from that traffic. The seller pays the affiliate a commission on the sale or other action the web site visitor takes.

Amazon Prime: Amazon's highly successful loyalty program that provides subscribers with a variety of benefits, including free two-day shipping, free 2-hour delivery (where applicable), unlimited video streaming, limited music streaming, unlimited photo storage, and a host of other benefits.

Application Programming Interface (API): Software code that enables two different pieces of software to "talk to each other" and more easily exchange data, streamlining and simplifying the systems integration process. A good example of this is Customer Relationship Management (CRM) software sharing customer information with billing software or with Ecommerce software. Often APIs are used to automate routine tasks and streamline business processes.

Artificial Intelligence (AI): Artificial intelligence is the broad term used to define the field of computer science and applications where a device or software is able to "perceive" and "react" to its environment in order to achieve a pre-specified goal. AI provides instructions and frameworks to systems to learn how to perform a task, and then identifies the optimal way to accomplish the task. There are many applications for AI in the Ecommerce world, including (but not limited to) direct sales, marketing, product discovery and suggestion, and order fulfillment.

Audience segmentation: The process of dividing groups of people and/or customers into similar or homogenous subgroups with the goal of delivering a more personalized and relevant experience to each of the subgroups.

Average order value (AOV): The average dollar amount of purchases across all orders. To determine AOV, simply divide total revenue by number of orders in a given period.

Automation: The use of hardware, software, or machines to perform a task or process without human interaction.

Burn code: A snippet of computer code that prevents converted customers (those who have made a purchase) from seeing the same or similar advertisements again.

Channel conflict: The conflict that results when manufacturers or brands disintermediate their channel partners, such as distributors, retailers, dealers, and sales representatives, by selling their products directly to buyers through general marketing methods and/or over the Internet. Channel conflict can also extend to distributors and resellers that create private label version of their suppliers' products, disintermediating or replacing their traditional suppliers' products.

Checkout: When occurring online, this is the process of completing an E-commerce transaction. This usually includes gathering information about the buyer (name, address, phone number, email address, etc.), presenting shipping information and selecting a preferred shipping method, and gathering other details needed to complete the transaction, as well as processing the customer's payment.

Checkout funnel: An Ecommerce industry term referring to the steps between when a customer adds an item to the shopping cart and proceeds through the steps of the online checkout process, resulting in a completed order. Measuring funnel completion rate is a valuable way to determine the effectiveness of the online checkout process.

Click through rate (CTR): The ratio of users who click on a link or a digital advertisement to the number of people to whom the link or advertisement was shown.

Configure Price Quote (CPQ): Software that helps buyers determine a price quote for goods in environments with constantly shifting variables, such as stock levels, product configuration options, bundling with other products, and other variables. Commonly used in industries that require complex product configurations in order to provide a price to a buyer.

Content Management System (CMS): Software that manages all the content on the web site, including any text, images, videos, and other digital assets. Typically contains user workflows for content creation, approval, and publishing, among other processes.

Content marketing: A marketing discipline that involves creating content for a web site and social media with the goal of driving traffic—and ultimately conversions—to a web site and other sales channels, such as the sales force. Content can consist of blog posts, images, videos, social media posts, white papers, ebooks, webinars, and more. The goal of content marketing is typically to demonstrate thought leadership and authority, and to reinforce a company's position as a leader in their industry category.

Content workflow: The editorial process content needs to pass through before going live on a web site. Typically includes content creation, editing, approval, and publication scheduling.

Conversion rate: The ratio of people who perform a desired action on a web site, such as making a purchase online or filling out a lead form that is passed to the sales force, against the total web site traffic (sometimes defined as "sessions"). In the Ecommerce field, conversion rate is a standard and commonly utilized measure of the effectiveness of the web site in generating sales. Conversion rate is often calculated for each step in the sales funnel in order to identify weaker areas in the process. Conversions can be defined for a variety of actions, including signing up for an email list, filling out a lead form, or for online transactions.

Customer engagement: For Ecommerce, customer engagement typically refers to the effectiveness of the web site in maintaining a visitor's attention once the visitor arrives as the site. Engagement is typically measured via bounce rate (the percentage of customers that immediately leave upon reaching the web site), time on site (measured in minutes), and pages per visit (number of pages visited by site visitors, on average).

Customer relationship management (CRM): A software system that provides businesses with a means to track the activities, behaviors, and interests of prospective and current customers. Advanced CRM systems contain functions to divide customers into similar or homogeneous groups (see "Audience segmentation"), to execute highly targeted and personalized marketing and advertising programs, and to perform advanced customer analytics and reporting.

Desktop Only Disorder (DOD): The poor digital experience that results when a company designs its Ecommerce experience solely around a desktop or laptop web browser, and does not take into consideration the design and functionality needs of smartphone users.

Digital marketing: A general term referring to the marketing of products and services via digital channels. Can include web sites, online advertising, search engine marketing (such as pay-per-click marketing on Google), search engine optimization (SEO), social media marketing (such as advertising on Facebook, Instagram, LinkedIn, and other channels), display advertising, email marketing, and more.

Digital transformation: The process a business undergoes to incorporate digital technology into every aspect of the business operation.

Digitally-enabled sales team: When a sales team uses digital tools to enhance its capacity and capabilities to pursue and close sales.

Display advertising: Advertising that consists of text, images and/or video found on web sites. This often includes banner ads, side ads, pop-ups, and similar ad units. Good examples of display advertising are the marketing messages that appear in Facebook news feeds.

Ecommerce creative: Any form of creative related to selling a product online, including images, marketing and merchandising copy, banner advertisements, home page and landing page designs, and product and/or technical specifications.

Ecommerce merchandising (Web merchandising): Merchandising refers to any activity related to presenting a product for sale in an engaging and enticing way. Therefore, Ecommerce or web merchandising is related to activities required to effectively present a product for sale online. This includes presenting product imagery and detailed product information, but can also include technological aspects such as video, interactive digital media, and the use of other digital assets. Web merchandising also encompasses the marketing and merchandising messaging used to engage web site visitors, the creation of urgency-driving offers and promotions, and the manipulation of product presentation on the web site to present the most appealing products to potential buyers (such as the order in which products are presented on a category listing page).

Ecommerce platform: An Ecommerce platform is software that enables businesses to fully manage their online sales process. These solutions typically include functionality to manage the display of product images and information, the shopping cart and checkout process, customer account administration, web merchandising and promotional capabilities, web page creation and manipulation tools, and other functions needed to support and manage a transactional web site experience.

Electronic data interchange (EDI): A predecessor to B2B Ecommerce still in wide use today, this is a system for two businesses to communicate electronically with each other using a standardized format. Information is formatted and exchanged privately, and typically used for sending purchase orders and invoices. Although the technology was introduced in the 1970s, many businesses still operate and conduct transactions using this approach.

Email marketing: The practice of using email to guide prospective buyers through the sales funnel. Email marketing often includes newsletter communications, special and timely promotional offers, use of email list segmentation to speak to subgroups of customers with more relevant messages, triggered emails to communicate with potential customers based on actions taken on a company's web site, and other forms of direct marketing.

Frequency caps: A methodology for restricting the number of times a web site visitor is shown a specific advertisement, typically utilized in display advertising (see definition above). Often digital marketers will use this method to avoid overexposure to their brand and prevent reduced rates of engagement and response to advertisements.

Fulfillment: Activities related to physically delivering an order to a buyer, including picking and packing products in the order, shipping and package tracking, delivery, and return processing.

Headless commerce: Describes a type of Ecommerce architecture wherein the front-end user interfaces (the visual components of the web site experience) are decoupled or separated from the back-end elements. Each system component operates independently of the other, but the components are integrated to enable coordinated operation of the overall solution. This enables more flexibility and customization in terms of how content and Ecommerce experiences are delivered.

Landing page: A single, often stand-alone page on a web site, landing pages are useful for driving targeted traffic to a web page with messaging and/or offers designed specifically for that market segment or traffic source. For example, landing pages could be used to provide a specific offer or promotion to a defined portion of a company's customer base, without exposing the offer to the broader marketplace.

Lead generation: Marketing activities related to developing and securing potential buyers ("leads"). Companies with long sales cycles (e.g. a lengthy period of time, such as months or years, between the initial contact with a prospective customer and the time that the lead becomes a customer) often require a large pipeline of potential buyers. Many marketers expend a considerable amount of time, energy, and resources to acquire leads. Leads are often ranked in terms of where they are in the sales cycle, the size of opportunity, and likelihood the prospect will become a customer. This approach can help sales teams become more efficient with where time is spent, focusing more directly on potential buyers who are more likely to make purchases. Lead generation activities in B2B marketing often involve thought leadership and content marketing (see definition above).

Lifetime customer value (LCV, also commonly referred to as "Lifetime Value" or LTV): A metric used for calculating the revenue and net profit of an average customer over the course of their relationship with a business.

Marketplaces: Web sites that offer a platform for selling goods and services from a variety of merchants. Marketplaces may serve both vertical markets, focusing on merchants in specific niches (such as aerospace, chemicals, or medical equipment), or more general, horizontal markets, providing a platform for a wider variety of merchants across a spectrum of industries. Well-known Ecommerce marketplaces include Amazon, Alibaba, and Wholesalecentral.com.

Mobile application (also known as "mobile app"): Software designed to run on a mobile platform, including smartphones and tablets, taking advantage of the mobile devices' native functionalities. Also typically designed to be used in cases when the mobile device is not connected to a network (the device is "offline").

Mobile commerce: Purchases made using a mobile device, native mobile applications or mobile-optimized web sites.

Mobile-first approach: An approach to web site design and digital user experience that posits that a user's first encounter with a web site or brand is likely to be on a mobile device. Thus, all new initiatives are conceived and developed for a mobile device experience before other types of experiences (such as a desktop computer). Many web sites receive a large percentage of traffic from mobile devices (some as much as 60–70 percent of total traffic from mobile devices), and mobile penetration continues to increase across industry categories (B2B and B2C). As a result, many companies have adopted a mobile-first approach for developing their web site experiences.

Multi-tenant platform: An Ecommerce software platform infrastructure approach that supports multiple business users on the same instance of the core software code and allows for the creation of separate buyer experiences while still utilizing a single back-end. This is a common need for firms that manage multiple brands or product lines that are not related to each other. Many modern Ecommerce platform providers have adopted a multi-tenant approach to delivering software solutions to their customers, as it provides a way to maintain and upgrade software consistently across the customer base.

Navigation: A user interface element on a web site that contains links to all other parts of the web site, allowing users to more easily and quickly find information that is relevant to them. Typically used to present product categories and sub-categories to users, often through links provided at the top of the page and via attributes presented on the left-most column within product category listing pages and on-site search results pages."

Net present value: The difference between the present value of inbound cash flow versus the present value of outbound cash flow over a defined period of time. This is often used in capital investment budgeting to help analyze the profitability of a capital project (such as the implementation of an Ecommerce web site).

Omni-channel: A method of selling products and services across a wide variety of sales channels, with the goal of being available to the buyer regardless of time, place, or platform. In the B2B realm, omni-channel can refer to the customer's experience interacting with and buying from the web site, sales force, call center, resellers (such as distributors or retailers), and other physical and digital touch points.

Online sales portal: A central online location designed to provide specialized tools and information for facilitating purchases from a company or set of companies. B2B companies sometimes refer to Ecommerce web sites as "portals."

Organic search results: The web sites and pages listed when someone uses a search engine to find information relevant to specific keywords. These are the results that are presented "organically," i.e. not as advertisements or paid listings.

Payment Card Industry Data Security Standard (PCI DSS or "PCI"): The credit card industry standard for protecting customer credit card data. These standards require merchants, processors, and payment gateways to implement a number of technical and procedural controls to ensure credit card information is stored and communicated securely.

Personalization: The customization of a product, service, or experience catering to a specific group or segment of a merchant's buyers or prospective buyers, or to an individual customer or prospective customer.

Point of sale: The selling channel in which a transaction is completed. In terms of Ecommerce, this is typically the shopping cart and online checkout process. Offline purchases occur in stores, distribution branches, via the sales force, in the call center, and other locations.

Product data: Information related to a product's features and attributes. Can include (but is not limited to) product name, price, description, product dimensions, technical specifications, compatibility information, color options, and other information.

Product recommendations: A function of today's more advanced Ecommerce systems, this software allows firms to make automated, system-generated recommendations to buyers for items to purchase based on the buyer's previous purchases, product categories of interest, related products viewed, web site behavior, and other factors.

Punch out (integration with ERP systems): A method for a B2B buyer to make purchases from a seller's web site through the buyer's own procurement application or hosted ERP system.

Responsive design: An approach to web site usability and design that automatically optimizes the viewing experience across a wide variety of browsers and devices, including desktop computers, laptops, smartphones, and tablets.

Retargeting: A form of online advertising that targets potential buyers based on their previous online actions and visited web sites. Typically refers to visual and text advertisements delivered through web sites, such as social media and news sites, after a potential buyer leaves an Ecommerce site, with the intent of encouraging the visitor to return to the Ecommerce site with a promotional offer or other marketing message.

Return on ad spend (ROAS): A metric that measures the effectiveness of a digital advertising campaign. It is derived by calculating the gross revenue generated from a specific campaign against the cost of the campaign. By comparing return on ad spend across channels, marketers can gain an understanding of what is and is not working in their campaigns. ROAS is arrived at using the following simple formula: Revenue/Cost.

Return on investment (ROI): A measure of financial performance of an investment. In terms of Ecommerce, it is a measure of effectiveness of investments made in Ecommerce operations. This is arrived at using the following formula: (Gain from investment—Cost of investment)/Cost of investment. Often the resulting number is multiplied by 100 and expressed as a percentage.

Sales channel alignment: The process by which a business ensures all of its sales channels are operating in a uniform and consistent manner in terms of the data and information that is presented to buyers, including product information, pricing, customer contract terms and conditions, order history, and account information. By extension, alignment also refers to how each selling channel supports the other. For example, an aligned sales team is able to view and understand a customer's activity that takes place on the seller's web site.

Sales funnel: The phased process through which a buyer passes before making a purchase, with each step reflecting a stage in the buying journey. Typically the phases include Awareness, Consideration, Conversion, Loyalty, and Advocacy.

Salesforce enablement: A cross-functional practice designed to grow sales and sales force productivity using technology. An example of enablement includes mobile applications used by the sales team in the field to provide product information and availability to customers during sales meetings.

Search engine marketing (SEM)/Pay-per-click (PPC): Search engine marketing is a type of internet marketing where advertisers place ads in search engine results pages based on specific keywords that are bid upon by the advertiser. It is often called "Pay-per-click," as advertisers typically only pay for an advertisement when someone clicks on an ad. However, there are other models such as Cost Per Thousand (CPM), where advertisers pay for ad impressions regardless of whether customers click on the ads.

Search engine optimization (SEO/natural search, also called organic search): A form of internet marketing where a company seeks to increase targeted web site traffic by having their site listed in the organic (non-paid) search results page for specific keyword searches.

Share of wallet: The amount of sales a vendor receives from its customers, as compared to other vendors that supply its customers. Share of wallet can be used to estimate market share in some cases.

Shopping cart: Ecommerce software that enables web site visitors to "save" items for purchase when browsing a web site. Serves as the precursor to an online checkout process, during which a customer places an online order.

Site search: A function or extension of the software that manages a web site, site search enables web site visitors to search for products or other content exclusively on that web site using keywords or phrases such as product name, product category, SKU, and other relevant keywords. In B2B, site search is a critical feature, as it is commonly utilized by buyers who are attempting to quickly locate an item for purchase.

Social media optimization: The techniques and strategies of building online presences on social networks such as Facebook, Twitter, and LinkedIn. This includes ensuring that a company's social media profile has all relevant detail, but also can refer to the tactics of promoting brand awareness on social networks through content and engagement.

Sponsored product listing: A type of pay-per-click advertising that enables advertisers to promote specific products. These promotions may appear on a variety of web sites, marketplaces, and search engines. For example, this type of advertising is utilized by sellers on Amazon.com, appearing on product search results pages, product category pages, and other areas of the web site.

Targeted advertising: Advertising to specific market segments or individual customers and prospects using messaging, images, and other media to attract that particular market segment.

User experience (UX): Broadly speaking, user experience encompasses all aspects of the end-user's interaction with a company, its services, and its products. In web site design, UX refers to the experience of using a web site, specifically referring to how easy (or difficult) it is for the user to accomplish his or her desired task and the web sites' overall usability and design. User tasks can include finding information on products, making purchases, and other functions.

User interface (UI): In web site design, UI refers to the ways in which a user interacts with a web site. This often refers to the web site's navigation, page layouts, and design elements, but can also refer to more specific aspects of interface, such as a web site's shopping cart, online support system, or other point of interaction.

View-through conversion tracking: A type of conversion tracking that measures how many people see a particular ad, do not click, but make a purchase at some point in the future. This is helpful for marketers, as they may be advertising through a number of online outlets, and it is important to understand how online display advertising contributes to conversions even if the ads do not directly result in a sale based on a customer's click.